JUDGEMENT ON HATCHAM

JUDGEMENT ON HATCHAM

THE HISTORY OF A RELIGIOUS STRUGGLE

1877—1886

by

JOYCE COOMBS

THE FAITH PRESS
7 TUFTON STREET LONDON SW1

FIRST PUBLISHED IN 1969

© *Joyce Coombs, 1969*

PRINTED IN GREAT BRITAIN
in 10 point Times Roman type
BY THE FAITH PRESS LTD
LEIGHTON BUZZARD

SBN 7164 0125 8

CONTENTS

DRAMATIS PERSONAE

JOSEPH HARDCASTLE of Hatcham Park House, a rich evangelical land owner and benefactor.

ARCHDEACON KING who lived in Kender Street, New Cross, where a few Georgian houses still remain.

BENJAMIN FfINCH Vicar of Saint Paul's, Deptford, the mother church of Saint James, in 1845.

CANON MONEY Vicar of Saint John's, Deptford.

CANON MILLER Vicar of Saint Nicholas's, Deptford Green.

VICARS OF SAINT JAMES'S, HATCHAM

AUGUSTUS KERR BOZZI GRANVILLE	1845–1868
ARTHUR TOOTH	1868–1877
MALCOLM MacCOLL (priest-in-charge)	1877–1878
HENRY ASTON WALKER	1878–1886
S. A. SELWYN	1886–1891

BISHOPS OF ROCHESTER

THOMAS L. CLAUGHTON	1867–1877
ANTONY W. THOROLD	1877–1891
RANDALL T. DAVIDSON	1891–1895

BISHOPS OF LONDON

CHARLES J. BLOMFIELD	1828–1856
ARCHIBALD CAMPBELL TAIT	1856–1868
JOHN JACKSON	1869–1885

ARCHBISHOPS OF CANTERBURY

C. THOS. LONGLEY	1862–1868
ARCHIBALD CAMPBELL TAIT	1868–1882
EDWARD WHITE BENSON	1883–1896
FREDERICK TEMPLE	1896–1903
RANDALL T. DAVIDSON	1903–1928

CHURCHWARDENS OF SAINT JAMES'S, HATCHAM

PROTESTANTS	CATHOLICS
H. W. SANDERS	JOSEPH PLIMPTON
T. W. FRY	E. F. CROOM
E. COLLARD	R. A. WEBB
A. J. THORMAN	LLEWELLYN NASH
	D. P. WALTERS
	J. BRIDGES

CHARLES POWELL — Secretary of The Church of England Working Men's Society.

THOS. M'CLURE — Secretary of the Working Men's Protestant League.

A. H. MACKONOCHIE — Vicar of Saint Alban's, Holborn.

CHARLES LOWDER — Vicar of Saint Peter's, London Docks.

GEO. A. DENISON — Vicar of East Brent, Archdeacon of Taunton.

THOMAS BALGUY — The local magistrate.

SUPERINTENDENT GERNON — in charge of the Police.
INSPECTORS ROLFE and HAMBLIN

FRANCIS LE JEUNE — Counsel for The Church Association.

ANTHONY ASHLEY COOPER — 7th Earl of Shaftesbury, a Protestant reformer and anti-ritualist, closely connected with The Church Association.

CHARLES LINDLEY WOOD — 2nd Viscount Halifax, President of The English Church Union.

Messrs. SOLIAGUE, SIDE, DUMPHREYS, HOLLOWAY, HALLETT
supported
Messrs. HUDSON, GUNSTON and GARDNER, aggrieved parishioners.

CANON GEE, RICHARD CHAMBRES, BENJAMIN DALE and G. E. GARDINER, Bishop's nominees as Curates-in-charge of Saint James's.

CRAUFORD TAIT
RANDALL T. DAVIDSON } Archbishop Tait's Chaplains.

CURATES OF SAINT JAMES'S, HATCHAM

M. E. KIRKLAND
W. H. BROWNE
W. A. CROUCH
J. A. PEARSON
W. F. J. HANBURY

INCUMBENTS IMPRISONED UNDER THE ACT OF 1874

ARTHUR TOOTH

THOMAS PELHAM DALE	Rector of Saint Vedast's, London.
W. R. ENRAGHT	Vicar of Holy Trinity, Bordesley.
SYDNEY FAITHHORN GREEN	Vicar of Miles Platting, Lancs.
J. BELL COX	Vicar of Saint Margaret's, Liverpool.

PARISHIONERS AND WORSHIPPERS AT SAINT JAMES'S

ROBERT TOOTH	Patron of the living of Saint James's.
THOMAS LAYMAN	A barrister.
WALTER PLIMPTON	Chairman of the Hatcham Defence Committee, son of Joseph.
HORACE PLIMPTON	His uncle, a server at the church.
The Misses JANE VAUGHAN and AUGUSTA DUNCAN	} Parish visitors.
JOHN FULLER and JOHN FORBES	} Sidesmen.
OSMOND COLE	A Sunday school teacher.
H. W. HILL	Secretary of the E.C.U. and sacristan at Saint James's.
WILLIAM EVENDEN	A Protestant brawler.
JOHN ELLIOTT	A Protestant workman who damaged the confessional.

PART I

ARTHUR TOOTH

1868 – 1877

CONTENTS

TO ALL NEO-TRACTARIANS

INTRODUCTION

THIS is a late nineteenth century story of a prolonged and bitter religious controversy between men of opposite views in the South London parish of St. James's, Hatcham, when Arthur Tooth was vicar. The dispute was between Catholics, or Ritualists, on the one hand, and Protestants on the other; these are the terms that were used at the time and it seems best to retain them. The dispute continued under two other incumbents, Malcolm MacColl and Henry Aston Walker; and was resolved in the time of the third, S. A. Selwyn, by a complete reversal in 1886 of the former church policy. This revised tradition, typified at the time by the pews which Selwyn reinstated, continues to this day. Throughout, the battle was a fierce one. Conventional middle-class householders of impeccable propriety, whose families were often close neighbours and fellow worshippers, so far forgot themselves as to exchange blows and bandy insults about each other in public, as well as to resort to trickery and violence. Their behaviour caused large numbers of police to be stationed outside the church on Sunday after Sunday, and the congregation was once besieged inside the building, with thousands outside clamouring against its walls. Summonses in the local Magistrate's Court became a feature of parish life and differences were aired week by week in the local newspaper with considerable personal animosity. National papers from one end of the country to the other were copied by journals and weeklies as far away as New York, and all devoted columns of space to the notorious parish of Hatcham. There are over five hundred Press cuttings in Volume two of Plimpton's collection dating from January 19th to March 9th, 1877.

The issues involved were brought to a head by the Public Worship Regulation Act of 1874, introduced into Parliament by the Archbishop of Canterbury with support from the Conservative Government under Disraeli. This Act imposed a State interpretation of religious worship on the Church of England and set up a new court, doubtfully styled The Court of Arches. It was presided over by Lord Penzance, a former Divorce Court judge, to hear the suits of 'aggrieved parishioners' against offending clergymen who introduced ornaments and ritualism into the church. The penalties were monition, or suspension and inhibition from office. The plaintiffs could be any three rate-paying parishioners; these did not need to be worshippers at the particular church in question, or at any church at all.

Arthur Tooth was the first priest to be tried under the new Act, and he was condemned. He ignored the sentence of suspension and inhibition from office since he claimed that a Parliamentary court had no jurisdiction in ecclesiastical affairs. He was therefore put in prison as a 'contumacious clerk' for what amounted to contempt of court. Thus by his stand he set the pattern for other defendants to follow, and in turn Thomas Pelham Dale, Richard William Enraght, Sydney Faithhorn Green and James Bell Cox, all incumbents, were committed to prison for similar acts of defiance.

When Arthur Tooth challenged the Act, he was hailed as a 'Martyr for Conscience Sake,' and in two twentieth-century memorials he is styled 'Confessor of the Faith.' Without minimizing his stand for spiritual liberty it must be noted, however, that Tooth's most severe hardship was only three weeks in Horsemonger Gaol. Other priests who suffered protracted and painful proceedings approached martyrdom more nearly than Tooth did. Tooth's own successor at Hatcham, Henry Aston Walker, could not stand the strain of five years' relentless harassment and was driven to resign. Tooth's prison sentence looks minimal beside the twenty months Sydney Faithhorn Green spent in Lancaster Gaol.

But Tooth was the first to go to prison, and he broke the back of Lord Penzance's Court in doing so. He later appealed against the decision on the technical ground that the case had not been heard in the correct place, and won. After this he retired from Hatcham to live comfortably elsewhere and to carry on the educational and social work so dear to him. At Hatcham the struggle continued for nine more years. When Tooth died in 1931 ritualism had become common and respectable. Many of the issues that seemed to him of such burning significance, to-day seem unimportant and irrelevant.

The detailed history of Hatcham in the last century would have remained in oblivion had it not been for the industry of two laymen, Edmund Frederick Croom and Horace Plimpton. Croom was Tooth's churchwarden in his early years and preserved all the personal letters exchanged between the various parties from 1871 to 1886. Horace Plimpton, who was the unmarried brother of another churchwarden, Joseph Plimpton (whose son Walter also figures in this history), is supposed to have been employed in a Press agency. This would explain the opportunity he had to collect together eight volumes of Press cuttings, together with many other interesting posters and handbills. These books were eventually bequeathed to the English Church Union who handed them on to Pusey House following a change of premises. They were discovered in the cellar during a fortuitous visit. All quotations here are taken from material in these volumes unless otherwise indicated.

Unfortunately, the long search for the registers of Hatcham has not produced any result. Almost everything connected with the years of Tooth's and Walker's ministries seems to have been destroyed. A Services' register would have been an invaluable guide, as would a Baptism register, but neither has been found. The Services' Register of the early years in Granville's time ends with Tooth's Induction in 1868. A Baptism Register of All Saints', Hatcham, in 1869 includes a section of the parish of St. James's.

There are still legends. The first is that Tooth is buried at Walsingham, or that at any rate his heart is interred there. This is not so; his effigy covers a cenotaph. There is too an outdoor Crucifix at Walsingham known as the Hatcham Cross, but it appears to have no connection with Hatcham that can be traced and must simply be an attempt to perpetuate Tooth's memory. The Walsingham College authorities also own a maniple which is supposed to be one that Tooth was wearing when he was arrested. It may have belonged to Tooth but he was not wearing it at the time of his arrest. The chasuble presented to Walsingham is undoubtedly authentic since it was bequeathed to the old E.C.U. by Tooth himself in 1927. Finally, there are still nonagenarians in Hatcham who claim to remember St. James's Church when it was cloudy with incense. As this must have been before January 8th, 1877, we have to take their word for it.

The object of this history is to produce the facts, and then to draw some conclusions about the reasons for the growth of ritualism from the soil of Tractarianism. It also sets out to tell the tale of how insignificant Englishmen defended their different forms of religion with passion and enthusiasm, uninformed by tolerance, mercy, or compromise. The reasons why they did this remain obscure, though there are certain inescapable conclusions to be drawn from the facts as we have them, and as they are recorded here.

I

DEPTFORD DISSENTERS AND HATCHAM

FROM the time of the Restoration of the monarchy in 1660, Deptford, on the south bank of the Thames, became a refuge for ministers ejected from their cures following the collapse of Cromwell's Commonwealth. One of them, Henry Godman, was forced to relinquish his living at Radmill, Sussex, and he founded a Meeting House in the High Street, which was used by local families on Sundays. Nearby, a Quaker Meeting House, built in 1692, also became quite well known; while another deprived minister, a man called Hardcastle, settled a little farther away in what was then the deep countryside at Hatcham. He acquired a magnificent estate of rich farmland where he built a large mansion, Hatcham Park House. Its former site is roughly that of the present New Cross Railway Station, but the name, Hatcham Park Road, is its only link with to-day. Around it clustered the hamlet of Hatcham with its thatched cottages and orchards and market gardens, while the farms on the estate provided a livelihood for the rest of the agricultural community not otherwise employed.

In the next century John Wesley frequently preached at Deptford, sometimes in the open air, sometimes in a place called Turner's Hall, and found attentive audiences there. This must have been in his high church days, for in 1770 he was horrified at the strength of dissenting opinion, which may explain why he did not venture as far as Hatcham. He complained that he thought he had got into a den of lions because most of the leading men were mad for separation from the Church. When he was asked to hold his meetings at the same hour as the church service, he refused indignantly and said that if his hearers wanted something so reprehensible, he would never visit Deptford again.

'This struck deep,' he noted thankfully, 'and from that hour I heard no more about separating from the Church.' But as far as the Hardcastles were concerned, the separation had already taken place, for Joseph Hardcastle continued the Independent tradition of his ancestor as a fervid dissenter. He and his family ran their own Sunday Schools, Bible classes and Prayer Meetings, distributed tracts and visited the sick and poor. His home was a centre for well known evangelicals such as Henry Martyn, Thomas Clarkson, Granville Sharp and Charles Simeon. He was a co-founder of the Religious Tract Society and the Treasurer of the London Missionary Society. A saintly and pious man, he mistrusted the Established Church, although he permitted himself to conform at the parish church of St. Paul's, Depford, at Easter, where he would like to have ensured the appointment of a 'sound' man. By this he meant a man of firm evangelical principles, and he tried without success to buy the advowson for £2,000 through a Dr. Darke, offering £100 towards it. Hardcastle replaced the old building in Meeting House Lane with New Cross Chapel on the west side of Lewisham High Road where Georgian ribbon development began in 1805.

It is almost impossible to assess the enormous influence this family exercised on the surrounding district for four or five generations. After the mansion had been demolished a Mission Church was built there in 1869, and a Hardcastle descendant leased the land, and asked that the title, All Saints, might commemorate the members of the Clapham sect who used to gather at his grandfather's house. This partly explains the evangelical tradition so deeply entrenched in that part of Hatcham, which soon lost its pastures, lanes and woods, and by the middle of the century was indistinguishable from the rest of the metropolis to which it was joined.

By 1841 the 22,000 strong parish of St. Paul's, Deptford, was bulging with its poor and overcrowded population of which only one sixth were ratepayers. On one fine Sunday six hundred adults crammed into the pews with benches placed in between. There were more than the allotted sixteen in the christening pew, while an overflow service for the children was held in St. Nicholas's, Deptford Green. Mr. King, the Archdeacon, who lived in Kender Street, then a beautiful Georgian row, made up his mind to open a mission church in Hatcham with a view to starting a new parish with its own resident minister.

He made an application to the Ecclesiastical Commissioners explaining that urbanization was reaching Hatcham and that for him, too, the church was a mile away, and filled by residents from the far side. He added that a new church was desired by all parties, by which he meant rich and poor, and said 'there are not many dissenters this end of the parish, though they form the bulk of the population in the district from which we have been moved,' a legacy of the Deptford Independents.

Mr. Ffinch, the vicar of St. Paul's and a Deptford man himself, was not over-enthusiastic about losing even the less prosperous part of the parish. He regretted the loss of 'surplice fees' that would ensue, and since burials in the cemetery were frequent he said he would be doubly disappointed financially. In spite of this he took the chair at the first meeting of the Hatcham Building Committee in 1844, and agreed to forego a strip of his parish. About three thousand persons in 180 houses were then transferred to the new district in St. James's of which forty-five were 'cottages of the poor and the rest second class houses' (small terrace houses), 'composed of a mixed population of labourers, mechanics, engineers and others employed by the Brighton and Croydon Railway Companies.'

It is most unlikely that many heads of these households were ratepayers; and if they and their families attended St. James's Church later on they would certainly not have had a vote at the vestry meeting. On the other hand, along New Cross Road smart Victorian villas were going up fast. More followed in Shardiloes Road, Amersham Road, Laurie Grove, St. Donatt's Road and Church Road (to-day known simply as *St. James*), together with substantial houses in the main road. Families from them supported the Building Fund on paper, and promised to 'occupy' seats, that is, pay pew rents. In those days there were no offertories or collections, and pew rents provided the basic income for the incumbent. However, when it came to putting the money down, many of the newcomers conveniently forgot their obligations. Some may have been part of the overspill from industrialized Deptford and tinged with its prevailing influence of dissent. Others may have found life in a new and upcoming district more expensive than they had reckoned. And when Hatcham House was demolished and the city encroached on the market gardens of Hatcham another seven thousand people poured into the parish, following the line of the advancing railway as it was extended to Croydon. So the pastoral problem intensified the need for a new church, and Archdeacon King spent £50 on fitting up a loft with benches to hold two hundred people.

On a bright morning in 1845, the nurseryman, Cormack, rigged up a bell in an apple tree to call the people to worship, and they flocked in. Soon the loft was inadequate, so the minister, Augustus Granville, built a temporary church in the Old Kent Road at his own expense. He informed the Ecclesiastical Commissioners that it would stand in the centre of a poor population, and this must have been true because bread used to be distributed after the morning service every Sunday. Unfortunately, the ground lease fell in and this building had to be demolished, and other accommodation sought. The materials were used to build the schools whose foundation stone Lord Shaftesbury laid in 1851, and perhaps afterwards he regretted doing so. The Ecclesiastical Commissioners bought a site from Christ's Hospital at the end of the two converging avenues, Laurie Grove and St. James, where comfortable houses were being built. Some of these had three and four storeys and were let at £60 a year, the equivalent of a working man's wage.

This new red brick, spireless church in pseudo English-Gothic style, ought to have been built for £4,500, but rising costs brought this to £6,000, saddling the congregation with a debt which Augustus Granville took over. His brother, Walter, was the architect and probably did not receive a penny for his pains. For some reason in 1854 Deptford was taken into the diocese of London, so St. James's Church, as it was called, was consecrated by Bishop Blomfield to whom are owed so many new churches in the eighteen forties and fifties. After its consecration the district again became part of the Rochester diocese.

Every one on the Building Committee was thankful to see the church opened at last, although it was still unfinished. The capitals of the pillars were uncarved, and decorated for the occasion with bits of coloured tinsel which aroused no comment. The Communion table in the south transept was backed by a red dorsal and flanked by the partially inscribed tablets of the decalogue and creed. This was the only altar. All the glass in the windows was plain, an improvement on what there is to-day. Near the east end the organ, which was raised up and approached by a flight of steps, stood under the non-existent spire. There was no north transept, and the font was just inside the west entrance. One of the most generous benefactors had been Alexander Read, the first patron and Mrs. Augustus Granville's father. Later he made over his rights to his son-in-law. He probably lent the chalice, which was a piece of family plate, and provided a pewter paten. A brass plaque in the church commemorating him can still be seen. Rents of the pews could have added another two or three hundred pounds a year to the vicar's stipend of £150 had there been families willing to pay for them, which it seemed there were not.

By 1857, Augustus Kerr Bozzi Granville, the vicar of St. James's, was installed in the roomy vicarage with his family which they certainly needed since eleven children were born to them, all of whom were baptized by their father. He was not a good business man. Though he sank all his own money in the church, yet the debts increased and hung round his neck like a millstone. He was an old Cambridge blue and 'polished and well informed,' but not worldly wise financially. His father had been a distinguished Italian doctor who was well known for his books on medicine, travel and politics; he had assumed the name Granville when he took British nationality. Augustus was proud of his supposed descent from the Corsican side of the family of Napoleon Bonaparte, but on which side of what blanket he never disclosed. Sensitive, artistic and musical, he became weighed down by his large family, shortage of money, and the uncongenial work in the poor and expanding parish. He attempted to popularize the church through its music, and introduced a surpliced choir which sang anthems on Sunday evenings, but this was not much of a success for long. The hymn book he compiled was considered 'vapid' by some. Because of the decorations with flowers at festivals he was accused of high church practices, although he only ever wore a black gown and preaching bands for services and never a surplice. In 1877 he dissociated himself from his successor's policy of ritualistic practices and showed that he was distressed and grieved at what had happened in the parish. Granville, however, was not an evangelical, but a Prayer Book man who inculcated Prayer Book principles. On one occasion he invited the warden of St. Barnabas's House, Soho, a Tractarian charity, to preach. He used to observe the feast of King Charles the Martyr on January 30th. He also kept Ash Wednesday and most Red Letter Days, and held a 'full Service' on them as on Sundays; that is Morning Prayer, Litany and Holy Communion. All these were signs of a high churchman, and probably a 'dry' one too, as the early Tractarians were nicknamed.

In spite of all his efforts, response was poor and the church always in debt. By 1863 Granville was worn out and dispirited, and he obtained leave of absence on the grounds of ill-health. He sold the rights of patronage to a Captain Drake, and went into the family business of paper-making at a factory near Oxford, evidently a more lucrative type of life.

He left in charge a fiery evangelical curate, but by this time the congregation was very small. Most of the former members had already taken themselves off to the newly consecrated church of St. Stephen, Lewisham, which had already established a high church tradition. Those who were more inclined to evangelicalism went in the opposite direction to the temporary Mission Church of All Saints, Hatcham Park. When the permanent church was consecrated in 1871 many former St. James's members remained there until 1877, the time of the Tooth case, when these 'old stagers' conceived it their duty to return as aggrieved parishioners, a point to be remembered later.

Meanwhile the fabric of the church and the vicarage deteriorated. The windows in the clerestory rattled so badly that one day the service was inaudible; other windows were broken and fences destroyed. The police disregarded 'tenth-rate costers' on their way to Kent who tied up their horses on the vicarage lawn, since it was not their business to interfere. It was still Granville's vicarage. With his continued absence interlopers became bolder; hooligans broke into the house and tramps dossed down for the night. No one lived there and no one wanted to live there, was one comment.

In 1867 Bishop Thomas Claughton was enthroned as Bishop of Rochester and like a new broom he began to sweep clean. In the course of so doing he came to Hatcham and disapproved of what he saw, and Augustus Granville resigned shortly afterwards, having discharged the debt on the church for which he was personally liable.

He became domestic chaplain to the Earl of Ripon. In 1877, nine years after leaving Hatcham, he took charge of St. Oswald's, Durham, a church with a Tractarian tradition where the vicar, J. B. Dykes, had died in 1876 from overwork. It is possible that in his Hatcham days Granville nourished underlying sympathies with the Tractarians, although he later denied this. As a legacy for his successor at Hatcham, he left a pile of small domestic debts, a dilapidated vicarage, a half finished and deserted church with a congregation of 'moths, spiders, black beetles and kindred created objects . . . whose time for excommunication had now arrived.' It is not surprising that Captain Drake sold the advowson to a barrister, Robert Tooth, whose brother, Arthur, a man of independent means, was in charge of the Mission Church of St. Mary Magdalen in the parish of St. Nicholas, Chiswick.

II

BACKGROUND HISTORY, 1868

IN the autumn of 1868 society was changing in Church and State. While the middle class was becoming more affluent, achieving a moderate property status, the proletariat had reached the nadir of its existence. With the legalizing of Trade Unions soon to be achieved, the workers were soon to obtain a more secure position in society. This may partly explain the solidarity and success of the Church of England Working Men's Society at this time. The Act for universal education was as yet two years ahead. At the other end of the social scale, Queen Victoria had been a widow for seven years; her grandson George, the younger son of the Prince of Wales, was three years old, and thirty-two years later succeeded her on the throne as George V. Flogging was abolished in the army as a peace-time punishment. Disraeli was Prime Minister for the first time, but was ousted by Gladstone and his Liberal Government at the end of the year. The riots at the London churches had diminished although prosecutions against Puseyites continued. Two were in process at the time: W. J. E. Bennett of Frome, the former vicar of St. Paul's, Knightsbridge, indicted for 'false teaching'; and the vicar of St. Alban's, Holborn, Alexander Heriot Mackonochie, for 'illegal practices.'

Mackonochie and Tooth were friends and both belonged to the Society of the Holy Cross, suspected as being a hotbed of ritualism. It is certain that every move for and against Mackonochie was known by Tooth, since they were great friends; and on Sundays Mackonochie used to walk the six miles that separated Holborn from Hatcham. In 1868, Archbishop Longley died and was succeeded by the Bishop of London, Archibald Campbell Tait, a dry and legalistic Scot, who ought to have stuck to the Presbyterianism to which psychologically he was attuned. As Bishop of London in 1866 he made the ritualists one of the targets of his episcopal charge. 'They have taken upon themselves to alter the whole external celebration of the Lord's Supper, so as to make it scarcely indistinguishable from the Roman Mass. . . . If admonitions fail then at last a legal enactment must explain how that controlling influence . . . shall be made to bear on the discretion of individual clergymen.' Meanwhile the Royal Commission on Ritual had reported unanimously against the use of vestments, and Lord Shaftesbury was indefatigably drafting Bills which he hoped would bring the ritualists to heel by penal methods. So far he had been singularly unsuccessful, partly owing to the astuteness of Samuel Wilberforce, who managed to induce his brother bishops to refuse to be overinfluenced by the Protestant earl. This advice was followed until Tait introduced his own version of a similar Bill through the House of Lords. It is useless considering what the course of the English church history might have been had Samuel Wilberforce, Bishop of Oxford, been appointed in 1868, to London or York, as he himself hoped. Instead he followed his cousin, Charles Sumner, as Bishop of Winchester in 1869, and in the same year two other controversial figures were removed by death from the episcopal bench; the unyielding and solemn Phillpotts of Exeter whose refusal to license Gorham had rocked the ecclesiastical boat, and Renn Dickson Hampden of Hereford who had been the centre of a storm at his consecration in 1848 because of his supposed modernistic tendencies. When Frederick Temple, father of Archbishop William Temple, was raised to Exeter, another heresy hunt took place because of his contributions to *Essays and Reviews* in 1860. Atlay's appointment to the bishopric of Hereford made no such stir in the previous year.

In 1868 compulsory Church rates were abolished, to the relief of dissenters. Keble College was founded under the wardenship of E. S. Talbot, and set a seal of respectability on Tractarianism. Pusey published the second edition of his *Eirenicon*. The *Church Times*, at that time a voice of thunder, was five years old. The *Church Times* of the 1870s has been stigmatized by Roger Lloyd as 'violent and hysterical,' though S. C. Carpenter describes it as 'vigorous and well written.' *The Church Association* formed for 'the purpose of ascertaining the Law on any point involving Romanizing doctrine and ritualistic practices,' as well as paying the costs of plaintiffs, was three years old. It launched the violently Protestant weekly *The Rock* as the organ of the ultramilitant section of the party. This society was well supported in Parliament and by the upper classes. Its opposite number, *The English Church Union*, recently joined by the great Dr. Pusey, replaced its first President, Colin Lindsey, by the young and aristocratic Charles Lindley Wood, later Lord Halifax, though in so doing he severed his connection with the Court and his royal master. He remained in office for over fifty years, and died in 1934.

The Church of England was certainly not at peace within its borders, but all was quiet in Hatcham when its new twenty-eight year old vicar arrived. The Tooth family had made money in Australia from meat preserving and sugar baking. (The label on

Liebig's meat extract then carried the name 'R. Tooth.') Arthur Tooth himself was rich and independent. He had been educated at Tonbridge School and Trinity College, Cambridge, and had travelled widely, visiting such countries as Australia, Japan and China. There is little material about his early life and none at all about his introduction to religion and ritualism, or the reasons that led him to seek ordination. There are two stories about his life in Australia, one from a priest in an arduous and isolated out-back station, who had a good deal of help from a young layman whom he later discovered was Tooth. Another, which must have come from his own lips, described how he became separated from the rest of the party when out shooting in wild uninhabited country. He made his way back after considerable hardship by following the stars, having been given up for lost by his companions. He was an excellent shot and horseman, so he does not sound the physical weakling some of his critics would have us believe; but he looked a rather languid dilettante. The sympathetic *Camberwell and Peckham Times* describes him as young and slim with a thoughtful expression, marked self possession and 'great extemporaneous powers.' *The Irish Times* complained rather sourly that 'his voice is squeaky' and that 'there is little in his appearance to attract any one, for it is priestly rather than manly,' whatever that may mean; and 'he looks as though he had stepped out of a pre-Raphaelite painting.' The editor gives a *coup de grâce* with the comment that 'if the Christian teacher should look like a Roman Catholic priest then Mr. Tooth is to be congratulated on his exclusively sacerdotal appearance and manner,' a malicious remark intended to alienate the sympathies of Irish Protestant readers, to whom sacerdotalism implied priestcraft.

Another critic declared that he was a 'gigantic difficulty to his foes and a glory to his friends,' and added: 'he is an ascetic, devoted, earnest, honest man incapable of seeing two sides of a question, a favourite with all who knew him' and 'endowed less with a great power than with an enormous power of won't.' So it was in character for Tooth to stick by his principles and his friends at all cost.

Tooth was made deacon by Bishop Charles Sumner of Winchester in 1865. He served at St. Mary-the-Less, Lambeth, under Mr. Gregory, later Canon Gregory of St. Paul's Cathedral, the contemporary of Liddon. If he left St. Mary's, Lambeth because Mr. Gregory found him too 'advanced,' as F. G. Croom, the son of Tooth's churchwarden at Hatcham, suggests in a slim pamphlet, the friendship was never broken and continued in the Hatcham days. After being ordained priest by Archbishop Longley, Tooth spent a year at St. Michael's, Folkestone. He moved from there to the Mission Church at Chiswick, where he is said to have lived frugally himself while making generous gifts of food to those in need, even when it was intended for his own use. It is not clear whether his brother Robert, who was churchwarden of St. James's, Hatcham, in the early years, bought the living and nominated Arthur; or whether, since it must have been difficult to find any one to accept St. James's parish, Robert bought the living during his brother's incumbency to preserve the high church tradition introduced by him.

III

COMING EVENTS

THERE is a baptism register belonging to All Saints' Church, Hatcham Park, which includes what later became the north part of the parish of St. James's. It gives us a good cross section of the inhabitants, and cannot have been strikingly different from the adjacent area. It shows that in all the entries where the father's occupation puts him safely in the middle class, such as gentleman, architect, auctioneer, or merchant, the family was drawn from the solid villas along New Cross Road or Queen's Road, like Mr. Layman's Stanton Villa opposite St. John's Church, or Mr. Croom's Surrey Villa in Queen's Road, Peckham. Mr. Layman was barrister with offices in the Borough and Mr. Croom shared in a family 'milling' business. Behind the main road, however, and particularly on the north side, was a jungle of small terrace houses with four, five or six rooms and no amenities. From these houses came a large number of railwaymen and labourers and gardeners and mariners. There are a few skilled men who describe themselves as foreman, gunmaker, coppersmith, hay merchant, printer, engraver, police constable, bank clerk and tripe dresser. After that there is a variety of over twenty occupations: costermonger, horse-meat dealer, hardware factor, starch-maker, bricklayer, plasterer, plate-layer, painter, blacksmith, hosier, cook, waterproofer, milkman, coach builder, joiner, clothier's salesman, warehouseman, bookbinder and hair-dryer. This does not present a picture of the rising middle-class but of the hard pressed artisans and struggling workers. It is also interesting to note the number of deceased fathers recorded: there are no children born to single women, as there were in the parish of St. Paul's. Was this a way of being kind to an unlawful relict whose irresponsible partner was as good as dead so far as wordly assistance went? These were the sort of people to whom Tooth was to minister. He was inducted on September 18th, 1868, and began at once his policy of renewal. He took on a curate, J. W. Biscoe, followed by M. E. Kirkland who was extremely popular, for in 1884 the parishioners would have liked him to return as vicar. However, Kirkland could not stand the pace and resigned three years later on grounds of health, when the congregation made him a handsome gift of a set of vessels for sick communicants. Meanwhile the work of restoration in the vicarage and in the church went on apace. The altar was moved to the east end of the nave, and a new one installed in the side chapel. The now rotten red dorsal with the 'patched up and ragged surplices of an obscure shape' were discarded for ever. The choir of men and boys melted away so that a weekly practice was not obligatory, and the church was cleaned and decorated. Perhaps this is the moment when the capitals above the pillars were carved, and the heads added to the chancel arches. It is difficult to decide to whom they belong but they could be those of Queen Victoria, Augustus Granville, and the Bishops of London and Rochester.

The pews went and all sittings were now free. In any case they produced very little in the way of income, but Tooth was a follower of John Mason Neale's tradition and abominated them. As they were carted away on a van one witness said that the 'door closed on the mournful cortège of a defunct system.' Without pew rents the church was open to rich and poor on equal terms, and the ability to pay for a seat no longer ensured precedence. Tooth also abolished fees except for bridegrooms at weddings. He refused to take collections at churchings and baptisms, and this again won over parishioners to whom money was an ever-pressing problem.

The structural changes Tooth began took years to complete and were still not finished in 1875, by which time there was a Building Fund with a healthy annual income. An oak screen divided the nave from the chancel and from the Lady Chapel. Tooth painted the panels himself with mythical and symbolic figures and scenes representing the triumph of virtue over vice, harmless enough it would seem in spite of the treatment they afterwards received. A rood beam supported a large crucifix with stands for two more figures in the traditional style. Later on Tooth built a north transept for use as a baptistery and installed one of the continental-style confessionals which had an entrance through a door each side of the priest's seat. It looked very unanglican but was accepted with gratitude by the parishioners at the vestry meeting in 1874. During some of these improvements 'the gaudy decalogue, never finished for want of funds' managed to be buried in the church and Tooth must have acquiesced in this informal interment.

In Laurie Grove Tooth founded a convent, the Order of the Holy Paraclete. He rented three houses next to the church in the avenue of St. James (or Church Road), as an orphanage for twenty-four fatherless boys from the age of eight to fourteen who wanted a good education. Tooth's old vicar, Canon Gregory, was one of the patrons and the Earl of Glasgow another. It was a comfortable boarding or choir school run partly by the Sisters. Government Inspectors gave it an excellent report saying that the boys had first class equipment, books, furnishings, food and recreational facilities. They were taught music, and provided the choir and servers necessary for the services. With this revival of church life, the fame of the parish spread and a new congregation began to gather, some of them well-to-do non-parishioners to whom Tooth's policy and churchmanship appealed. After all churches like this were few and far between.

The services changed too, for Tooth introduced the hotly debated *Six Points*. These were regarded by evangelicals in much the same light as the Chartist Six Points were by Conservatives. They all concerned the service of Holy Communion and in particular the use of the eastward position, the mixed chalice, unleavened bread (wafers or pressed bread), candles as altar lights, eucharistic vestments, and incense. The battle had raged in the ecclesiastical courts of the Dean of the Arches over what was, and was not, legal in public worship. But the final appeal from this court was to the Judicial Committee of the Privy Council, which, though it might be the most dispassionate and unbiased court in the land, was a secular court with secular authority, and therefore anathema to many churchmen. Once again in this ding-dong battle of technical legalities or illegalities there were prizes for every one. The Privy Council Judgment of 1851 in favour of Robert Liddell, the vicar of St. Paul's, Knightsbridge, abrogated its own decision in 1871 when John Purchas of St. James's, Brighton, was arraigned.

About the position of ritualists at this time something further must be said. During the intervening twenty years there had been a gradual growth in the use of ritual. For example, Samuel Wilberforce, when Bishop of Winchester, took the eastward position following the Mackonochie Judgment in 1870; so did Canon Gregory and Canon Liddon at St. Paul's Cathedral. Even Pusey used the eastward position in Christ Church Cathedral, Oxford, after 1871. It was assumed among high churchmen that the far from ultra-montane interpretation they placed on the ornaments rubric preceding Morning Prayer had been accepted.

Tait, when Bishop of London, had consecrated the church of St. Alban the Martyr, Holborn, in 1863, where Mackonochie began at once ritual in accordance with five of the Six Points. In 1867 a non-parishioner, John Martin, charged him with illegal practices, and a relentless and malicious prosecution began which lasted sixteen years, only ending with Mackonochie's final deprivation and death on a Scottish moor in a snowstorm. The suit was undertaken and financed by *The Church Association* who sent paid informers from outside the parish to spy and report back. In 1870 Mackonochie was suspended by the Privy Council from officiating for a period of three months because he disobeyed their injunction by genuflecting during the Prayer of Consecration (the injunction in in 1867 had been against kneeling after the consecration). Mackonochie therefore substituted a genuflection. This was now declared illegal and Mackonochie substituted 'an inclination of the body.' This too was to be the subject of a later charge. Mackonochie's case and the Purchas case in Brighton were the first lawsuits since the riots at St. George-in-the-East, Stepney, from which parish the vicar, Bryan King, had retired broken in health. They therefore excited much interest.

Whereas to-day in such circumstances diocesan bishops are inclined to support the parish priest in his pastorate unless the conditions are exceptionable, a hundred years ago the diocesan bishop was a public enemy to priest and people of Tractarian parishes. Archbishop Tait was no exception to this. At Lambeth Palace in 1870 he argued unsympathetically and dictatorially with the representatives of the Church of England Working Men's Society led by Charles Powell. Nettled by their persistent championship of ritualism and infuriated when he found that the interview would be communicated to the Press, he stumped out of the room without the formality of a leave-taking. His treatment of Mackonochie was heartlessly prelatical, and though his final solution and death-bed message have been considered friendly moves, in fact they solved nothing since there was no equivalent plea to Mackonochie's prosecutors. Yet in his private life he was an affectionate and devoted husband and father who bore a crushing burden of personal grief. Five of his daughters died within the same number of weeks from scarlet fever. At the death-bed of his eldest child, the fourth to die, he burst into tears and she lovingly dabbed them away with her hot little fingers. In his dealings with ritualists not a flicker of this humanity ever ruffled the surface of his emotions. He believed it was his duty to act as an officer of the law and in so doing serve the Church of God.

Meanwhile opinion on ritual was shifting and hardening among parish priests who in a small way were becoming organized. They recognized and supported each other. The advanced and eclectic *Society of the Holy Cross* (S.S.C., which stood for 'Societas Sanctae Crucis') had over two hundred members, Arthur Tooth among them, for the purpose of the pursuit of holiness as priests and for mutual support and fellowship. There were also eight hundred priest members of the *Confraternity of the Blessed Sacrament* (C.B.S.). *The English Church Union* (E.C.U.) was strongly sup-

ported by several thousand priests and laymen, some of them
influential, and had branches all over the country. The E.C.U. had
launched a considerable defence fund for Mackonochie against
whom costs were awarded which eventually mounted to £5,000.

Most important of all, the use of ritual and ornaments began to
acquire a new significance, and became entangled with doctrinal
questions. In the year of the Knightsbridge Judgement these had
been no more than adjuncts of worship, albeit primitive and
aesthetic ones, which had fallen into disuse, and were sanctioned,
so it seemed, by rubrics in the Book of Common Prayer. By 1871
it became plain that the chasuble, or the number of candles, or the
position at the altar were not so important as the theology behind
them, which was inimical to Protestantism. To appeal to primitive
usage or the Prayer Book simply exacerbated the fury of the
prosecutors and plaintiffs, who imagined that they were being
treated by the defendants as second class Anglicans. On the other
hand once the ritualists realized that doctrine was being attacked
then a lawsuit became a matter of defending the faith rather than
scoring a point of academic or aesthetic interest. So the wheel
turned full circle with a miserable round of charges, counter-
charges and appeals. The eastward position, abandoned to-day by
many clergy, came to indicate the sacrifice of the Eucharist, which
was of course a cardinal, 'Romish' doctrine; so were the vestments
which were a sign, not essential but expressive, of the sacrificing
priesthood. 'Such things,' said Lord Shaftesbury as he wrestled with
the abortive Ecclesiastical Vestments Bill, 'are the marks of the
Romish Mass and the Romish priesthood, and must be eliminated.'
Instead they became a banner beneath which to fight and a battle
cry to rally supporters. The Second Report of the Royal Commission on Ritual would have been prepared to allow applica-
tions for suits against clergymen to be submitted to the bishop
in camera, an un-English procedure.

It was not therefore a propitious moment for ceremonial changes
in a parish. When Mackonochie finished his three months' suspension on February 26th, 1871, and celebrated the Eucharist in
chasuble and alb from the eastward position, it is certain that
Arthur Tooth was there.

By now the St. James's congregation had no illusion about
their own position. In the same summer a dissident parishioner
approached the Bishop of Rochester on the subject of 'practices'
at St. James's. The Bishop sent for Tooth who not only refused to
go, but published the correspondence in the Press; both unwise if
understandable responses, even assuming that a parish priest's

natural reaction to his bishop was a hostile one. Croom, as church-warden, and in the absence of his colleague, organized two memorials (or petitions) to the Bishop 'to pray your Lordship to allow the exercise of that undoubted discretionary power you possess to decline the invidious task of legal interference with those accessories to divine worship which most of them greatly prize and to allow the exercise of that Liberty in Religious Matters which have hitherto been left open questions.' One memorial was signed by 166 communicants, and the other by 896 parishioners. Croom expressed the vain hope that the 'petition will be acceded to by your Lordship and that the happy unity now existing between the congregation and vicar of their Church may not be broken through the interference of those who do not care to avail themselves of the many privileges we so greatly appreciate, and who can at another church in the parish (*presumably All Saints'*) obtain the services they are desirous of forcing upon an unwilling congregation.' Both memorials ask the Bishop to exercise his statutory power to 'protect the vicar and people from molestation in worshipping God according to the dictates of conscience and secure to them the exercise of Religious Liberty.'

Croom would probably have done better to leave well alone: what was sauce for the goose was sauce for the gander. The Bishop replied lengthily in his own hand, and turned the tables on the ritualists' desire for freedom to worship in accordance with the dictates of conscience.

St. James',
Hatcham.
July 4th, 1871.

To the Right Reverend and Bishop of Rochester.
May it please your Lordship,

I have in the absence of my colleague the honour of forwarding to you two Memorials which I have received; one signed by one hundred and sixty-six persons being communicants usually worshipping in the Church of St. James, Hatcham; the others signed by eight hundred and ninety-six parishioners and members of the congregations of St. James, Hatcham, the two being signed by a total number of one thousand and sixty-two persons.

The Memorialists, as your Lordship will perceive, desire us to pray your Lordship to exercise that undoubted discretionary power you possess to decline the invidious task of legal interference with those accessories to divine worship which most of them so greatly prize and to allow them the exercise of that Liberty in Religious matters which have hitherto been left open questions.

I beg respectfully to inform your Lordship that I most fully concur in the prayer of the memorials and would humbly express my earnest hope that you will prevent any interference with services that have been the means of great assistance to our spiritual welfare; Services that from personal knowledge of most of the congregation I know to be thoroughly appreciated, and the loss of which would be I feel convinced attended with great grief to the members of the congregation.

I trust your Lordship will forgive me in expressing my entire trust that the petition of so many persons will be acceded to by your Lordship and that the happy unity now existing between the congregation and the Vicar of this Church may not be broken; through the intereference of those who do not care to avail themselves of the many privileges we so greatly appreciate, and who can at another church in the same parish obtain the Services they are desirous of forcing upon an unwilling congregation.

With profound respect, I have the honour to be
Your Lordship's humble obedient Servant,

E. F. CROOM,
Churchwarden of St. James', Hatcham

The Bishop replied five weeks later.

Danbury Palace,
August 12th, 1871

Dear Mr. Churchwarden,

On my return to England after six weeks' absence I received the two memorials signed by 1062 Parishioners and Members of the Congregation of St. James' Church, Hatcham, which you forwarded to me on the 4th July last. Before I can appreciate the real weight of this memorial, I ought to know how many are Parishioners as distinct from attendants at the Church.

The request of the memorialists is that I will exercise my statutable power to protect the Vicar and People from molestation in worshipping and according to the Dictates of Conscience.

This implies that molestation is either intended or begun. I have not received any intimation that this is the case. I did indeed on the 25th May receive a letter describing practices used in St. James' Church; which I sent to Mr. Tooth, and asked him to come and see me, that we might calmly discuss the matter. He both declined that interview and sent his reasons for declining it to the Public Papers.

To do this in the present excited state of public feeling is, as I have already intimated to a gentleman who addressed me on this subject when I was abroad, neither more nor less than to challenge Prosecution. If such a Prosecution should ensue, I apprehend that the discretionary Power which you assume me to possess will depend on the mode in which the suit should be instituted. The memorialists ask us to protect them from molestation in worshipping and according to the dictates of conscience. Might not other Parishioners which you cling to, equally apply to me to protect *them?* I must also point out that under the phrase 'according to the dictates of Conscience' practices confessedly contrary to the Church's Law might be included, and the liberty claimed might be that for the sake of enjoying which Non-Conformists have separated themselves from the Established Church.

I cannot close this letter without expressing to you the very great pain which I feel at the concluding sentence in *your* letter, in which you imply that those who do not agree with you find what they want at another Church in the same Parish. Is Christ indeed divided thus? Ought we thus to look on our own things only and not every one of us with the same love and deep interest and holy sympathy, in the things of others? I am, Dear Mr. Churchwarden, with earnest prayer that Grace and Unity may be established and prevail in the Church at Hatcham, your faithful and aff. Chief Pastor, friend and Servant,

T. L. ROFFEN

But the appeal in the last paragraph was only addressed to one side and not to the other. However laudable the sentiments were, with Claughton's touching signature as Chief Pastor and friend, they should have been set before both parties to the faction. This was something that was never done by any bishop.

Arthur Tooth's intractability was in line with the solidarity of the Society of the Holy Cross which had presented a memorial to Convocation 'repudiating the authority of the Judicial Committee of the Privy Council in all things spiritual and ecclesiastical.' The Synod pledged itself to the mixed chalice, unleavened bread, lights and vestments and drew up a list of priests who would 'adhere to Catholic practices in the celebration of the Holy Eucharist . . . at all cost to themselves and in defiance of any decision of the Judicial Committee to the contrary.' The Master, A. H. Mackonochie, added, 'troubled times must come and our wisdom is to be ready.'

Meanwhile under the new vicar the parish of St. James's, Hatcham, was bursting with enthusiasm and spiritual vitality. It had come to life; it was also sound financially. There was not a house within its boundaries that was not aware of it in some way or another whether it agreed or disagreed with ritualism. A Kalendar for 1873 lists fourteen separate organizations and committees, besides the Orphanage, the Convent and the Schools. There were also evening classes for men and boys taken by one of the curates

C

at a charge of fourpence a week; a Building Fund, a Relief Fund for the Sick and Poor, a Coal and Clothing Club, a Blanket Club, and a Maternity Society which provided a 'bag' for confinements. It was the poor of the parish who formed the bulk of the congregation. There was also a branch of *The English Church Union* and *The Confraternity of the Blessed Sacrament*. The two Plimptons, father and son, along with Edmund Croom who became its first Warden, founded the Guild of All Souls. Arthur Tooth slightly re-ordered the objects, and the Guild Office was first said at St. James's as a regular practice and using the Litany of the Dead. The Guild revolutionized the treatment that well meaning but indifferent churchmen inflicted on their nearest and dearest between death and burial. The founders made the movement known by advertisement in the *Church Times* and by writing to sympathizers at first in adjacent parishes and then farther afield, until the Guild spread spontaneously among catholic parishes. To-day it has several thousand members and the patronage of at least one living.

Later that year 483 priests signed a petition to Archbishop Tait as President of Convocation praying that 'in view of the widespread and increasing use of Sacramental Confession, your Venerable House may consider the advisability of providing for the education, selection and licensing of duly qualified confessors in accordance with the provisions of Canon Law.'

It is surprising that it was supported by so many parish priests but the petition failed in its apparent purpose. Two months later the bishops declared 'The Church of England knows no such words as Sacramental Confession.' They considered that opening one's grief did not necessitate the enumeration of sins, let alone the ministry of Absolution. They conveniently disregarded the Ordinal. Protestants were appalled that this 'most hateful proposition . . . was received, discussed and deliberated on by the bishops' and, continued Lord Shaftesbury, 'Why did they not say at once "Away with this foul rag—the pollution of the red one of Babylon"?' Catholics for their part were dismayed by what they considered an untheological and unscriptural assertion.

In 1874 matters came to a head when Archbishop Tait introduced the Public Worship Regulation Bill into Parliament; it was passed and became law in 1875. No one had any illusions as to its purpose which, Disraeli made plain, was 'to put down ritualism.' Two fortuitous circumstances gave it an assured passage through the House of Lords and the Commons: the removal of Samuel Wilberforce, Bishop of Winchester, from the scene by death, and the defeat of Gladstone's Liberal government in 1875 with the consequent success of Disraeli's administration. The Convocations considered that they had not had sufficient time to discuss and digest the implications of the new proposed legislation. But the Archbishop refused their request for delay and pressed on with it, believing it to be for the good of the Church and eventual uniformity because 'what is legal would then become defined by law.' There were many who thought, like one Member of Parliament, Mr. Holt of the Church Association, that it could well go farther. He was one who would like to have constructed a more ruthless piece of machinery, and it was even suggested he would have revived the fires of Smithfield. Gladstone detested the Bill; though far from being a ritualist he was a devout high churchman and was prepared to see disestablishment follow if necessary. Lord Shaftesbury was jubilantly vocal in its favour. The Bishop of Lincoln, Christopher Wordsworth, resisted the Bill in a slightly casuistical way; and the new Bishop of Winchester, Harold Browne, farsighted, scholarly and eirenic, supported Tait, but pressed through one clause which gave a bishop the power of veto. It was this provision that eventually reduced the Act to a dead letter.

The purpose of the court was to try clerks charged by an archdeacon, both churchwardens, or three parishioners with illegal practices. The penalties were monitions, suspension and total deprivation of office. The Synod of the Society of the Holy Cross met in May 1875 when a paper was read on the subject of the new Act of Parliament. The meeting finally decided that if proceedings were taken out against any of their number the 'priest should respectfully inform the Bishop that he is unable to recognize his jurisdiction in so far as he is acting under the provisions of the said Act.' It was carried all but unanimously, with only one person not voting either way. This was probably Charles Lowder of St. Peter's, London Docks, who urged a pacific and personal approach to a bishop. Lowder himself could have made such an approach, but it is doubtful whether it would have worked with the less transigent of the brethren, of whom Arthur Tooth was one.

Meanwhile, in Hatcham St. James's Church celebrated its patronal festival with tremendous devotion and joy. On July 25th, 1875, as in previous years the church was full to overflowing, and the day ended with a party in the vicarage garden. It was an unbelievable contrast with the position eight years ago when the half built church was deserted and with no resident clergyman, a frowsy vicarage, and a general smack of washed-out, give-it-up indifference throughout the parish. The writer who left this account mistakenly laid the credit on the shoulders of the Bishop of

Rochester who, he said, reformed matters when the parish came under his episcopal sway; for now, 'there is a church with daily services, a parochial visitation second to none, schools crowded inconveniently, an orphanage, a sisterhood and all those fibres of mutual organization that the Anglican party seem to seize and tie up so effectively.' There was one cloud on the horizon. Father Stanton, assistant priest of St. Alban's, Holborn, who had preached before and was expected again, was inhibited from doing so by Bishop Claughton. There does not appear to have been any reply to Mr. Croom and Mr. Plimpton's written remonstrance which said it 'placed a stigma on the Vicar' and 'may tend to undermine his influence in the parish.' The churchwardens asked for the inhibition to be speedily withdrawn. They had already set up a Hatcham Defence Committee to preserve Catholic interests in the parish, believing that these casting shadows foretold more unhappy coming events than the loss of a popular preacher.

In August, the Church Association spies arrived and were detected at once by the churchwardens and many others. These were obviously visitors for they behaved in a different way from the St. James's worshippers. These non-parishioners, who were usually paid handsomely for their purpose, were a feature of prosecutions instigated by the Church Association. One hopes they were edified. They must have taken some pleasure in the music which was a feature of St. James's parish worship. On most Sunday evenings there was a choir and orchestra of over fifty strong which succeeded in producing works such as Handel's *Messiah*, Spohr's *Last Judgment*, Haydn's *Passion*, Schubert's *Mass in G* among others. At the end of the year there was a series of Advent Sunday evening concerts by ticket, evensong having been said in the afternoon. Surprisingly it was a scheme severely criticized in the least expected places. *The Camberwell and Peckham Times* pointed out that the tickets priced at four shillings for four evenings were a formality as they were not demanded from bona fide parishioners. This seemed reprehensible in his opinion for he accused the vicar of 'emulating our Roman brethren or the Metropolitan Tabernacle.' Even the *Church Times* decried it: 'This we believe to be wholly illegal, and we trust the scheme will be abandoned' wrote the editor, pompously. The spies, having obtained their evidence as first hand witnesses, went back to report to their legal advisers.

A letter arrived from the Bishop in Advent with news of proceedings to be taken in the Court of Arches by aggrieved parishioners against Arthur Tooth. It was a not unexpected blow. Hurriedly in the week before Christmas Mr. Croom and Mr. Plimpton called a meeting of the English Church Union supporters constituting the Hatcham Defence Committee. They promised to stand by their vicar, who, they were well aware, would not defend himself, and would refuse to acknowledge the authority of a secular court and a secular judge whose authority was derived from Parliament and the Prime Minister. They also organized a petition begging the Bishop not to allow the proceedings to go forward. But no one allowed fears and misgivings to mar the festival on Christmas Day (1875). The church was full; the music and ceremonial at its best. The devout and overflowing congregation rejoiced in the hitherto unsuspected richness of sacramental worship as a dazzling and delectable novelty. From the altar at the centre of this glory they returned to the drabness of Victorian respectability, whether of working class poverty or middle class smugness. After this things were never the same again, for the wheels of the law had begun to grind inexorably.

IV

THE ENCIRCLING GLOOM

THERE were three complainants to the Bishop: Mr. Hudson, Mr. Gardner and Mr. Gunston. They were Hatcham 'aggrieved' parishioners but never attended St. James's Church. One was often seen at a Wesleyan chapel, another left the parish before the case was heard and was living several miles away; and the third had not attended regularly for twenty years; he was now worshipping at All Saints' Church where he was churchwarden. They were all financed by the Church Association.

They brought eighteen charges against Tooth which were listed as follows: a procession with incense: vestments, biretta, red cassocks and surplices tied with a girdle, zuchettos (skull caps): lighted candles at celebration: incense at ditto: mixed chalice at ditto: eastward position at consecration: eastward position at Epistle and Gospel: genuflection and bowing at celebration: elevation: the sign of the cross at the absolution and benediction: the singing of the *Agnus Dei*: less than three communicants: the great bell of the church tolled at the consecration: torches carried by boys: biretta and skull caps (*sic*): images with gilt wings: large crucifix (*presumably on the beam across the church*): two altars in the south aisle.

Early in March Arthur Tooth received a notice of continued legal proceedings under the Public Worship Regulation Act. In reply he addressed a long letter to the Bishop which was ill-calculated to ameliorate the situation.

> The Vicarage, Hatcham,
> New Cross.

My Lord Bishop,

I have received notice from your lordship of legal proceedings under the Public Worship Regulation Act, for the use of vestments, lights, the eastward position, and other ritual observances at the celebration of the Holy Communion. I feel much indebted to your lordship for having kept closely to the point in question and for having refrained from the expression of any opinion likely to influence my line of action. When so many of our difficulties have arisen from the use of expediency instead of what is right, when opinion has over and over again been accepted for doctrine and sentiment for dogma, I feel most grateful to your lordship for having left me alone to meet the difficulty; the question is far too important to admit of personal influence. I most earnestly hope that nothing I may say may be taken as wanting in respect to your lordship's high office. I am required to state in writing within twenty-one days whether I am willing to submit to your lordship's decision without appeal. It is somewhat late to complain of any point in the Act, but submission without opportunity of appeal strikes one as a novel principle and the endorsement of every bishop's judgment as infallible is a theological triumph which the Church at home or abroad never meditated.

Your lordship addresses me under the Public Worship Regulation Act, an authority I know nothing of and cannot acknowledge, and I need not remind your lordship that it is an Act which has never been accepted by the Church, that it was hurriedly passed—unhappily by the influence of the bishops on a mixed Parliament of every possible religion or of no religion—and wholly in disregard of a resolution of the Lower House of the Convocation of Canterbury and of York. What the final result of this invocation of a non-Christian Parliament by the bishops in things spiritual may bring about has yet to be seen; but still you act and make use of the novel powers given you by the State to the prejudice of and against the will of the Church; it is not for me to reconcile the inconsistency of secular authority in question of Christian truth, and to say where in the bishops of the Church of England the temporal ends and the spiritual begins, it is enough for me that as my bishop you claim my obedience, you appeal to a principle I acknowledge most freely and by which I am bound.

My lord, I have known no doctrine of the Christian Church but that which was 'once delivered.' I have always held that the authority I possess came uninterruptedly from the Apostolic College, the discipline I have administered has been that of the Catholic Church; I have always believed too that the Church, apart from every external power, has her own inherent right to govern those committed to her care. I most freely admit the right of the bishop as her chief pastor to administer her laws; I have never been guilty of canonical disobedience, and I feel sure that on this matter I may speak for the whole party to which I have the honour to belong, that conscious disobedience to the laws of the Church is not wilfully practised. If Parliamentary legislation for the Church has developed as it has done—more than doubling itself in the last fifty years—it is no wonder that in seeking absolute power the State should at last claim complete control of her mysteries. Difficulties must arise from such intrusion, but are we to be censured as disobedient, and when suffering to be stigmatized and insulted from the judgment-seat as unwilling to obey any law at all, because, forsooth, we cannot reconcile manifest contradictions, and harmonize legal discrepancies which the judge himself allowed to exist? Are we to be blamed, I say, because we maintain Church law as our first obligation and rightful heritage, and claim at any cost a right to obey it? I am accused of offending against Church law. I will raise no legal technicalities, nor seek refuge in refinements; if I have offended I do not refuse to suffer. The question is whether the doctrine of the Real Presence is true or false. The State has imposed a considerable difficulty on your lordship. It requires you to accept the Bennett judgment, which declares the doctrine of the Real Presence to be tenable—on the other hand, to lend your aid to suppress it by the abolition of those accessories of Divine worship which express it. It is folly to separate ritual from doctrine; it is now frankly admitted that the use of vestments, lights, and eastward position, used all together or only in part—e.g., the eastward position used by some as the only ritual act—assert and maintain the truth of the doctrine. Fortunately, no standing room has been found for those who say they mean nothing. Catholics accept and Protestants reject ritual because it does mean something, and happily, those most intimately concerned in the controversy understand each other. You will remember that in reference to this controversy I appealed to your lordship to say that the Church still maintains the rule of primitive and Catholic antiquity (and lest in using the word primitive I should be thought to employ a term of no certain limit, let me repeat an extract from 2 and 3 Edw. VI, c.i., s. 7, which defines the term to mean 'the space of 500 years and more after Christ's Ascension') as the authority of final appeal and you did not deny it. It is to that court I appeal, and by it, if need be, I claim to be judged. If I have been in error, and mistaken my mission and teaching, your lordship, I feel sure, will do me the justice to tell me, on Church law how I am wrong, when it was that the Church of England discarded Catholic truth, when it was that with intention of condemning Catholic truth by law and by canon she suppressed and abrogated the use of primitive and Catholic ceremonial. I will not by any act of my own free myself from the responsibilities of my parish, and the many and varied interests which are dependent on me, but if your lordship can solemnly, in the sight of the Church and of its Great Head, vindicating the cause of right and wrong, pronounce me to be a breaker of the Church law and a heretic to the faith, for such grievous wrongs I am willing, without a legal process, to take the penalty of deprivation, provided your lordship will take the responsibility of pronouncing it. You would do this by the withdrawal of my licence were I a curate, and I will not claim the secular protection which the vested interest of my benefice affords me.

Your lordship most distinctly administering Church law, and not the Public Worship Regulation Act or undefended precedents, provided my obedience is not required to a new and strange authority, I am quite willing to concede many points of ritual and to forgo my lawful liberty in many matters of detail where no doctrine is involved; but on those which are primitive and Catholic, and which really do involve the expression of doctrine, it would be neither just to ourselves nor honest to our opponents to make any concession whatever; we can neither deny the doctrine nor withdraw the ritual. Whatever the gain or loss may be, I believe I am asserting a principle of the Christian Church in rendering obedience to the bishop when canonically called upon to do so.

I most sincerely trust that I have in some measure succeeded in asserting—first the duty of canonical obedience; and secondly, the moral responsibility of Episcopal judgments. The expression of opinion by a bishop may rightly claim attention, but opinion is wholly insufficient now; we require judgment according to the law of the Church, with authority and not opinion for its foundation; it would do more than anything else to allay the strife. The Church claims the reassertion of first principles; priest and layman claim from the bishop, as the head of our triple constitution of bishop, priest and layman, an official declaration that the Church is still the same—the same in faith, the same in discipline. The principle involved is grave beyond conception. The responsibility must now rest with you: the choice is still in your lordship's hands whether you will come forward to administer Church law independently of the State.

In reference to the papers I have received and the proposed proceedings under the Public Worship Regulation Act, it may be well to say that I am unable to admit its jurisdiction. I feel it would be inconsistent to plead before the judge. I do not propose to defend myself nor to obey when condemned. Believe me, my Lord Bishop, to be your faithful and obedient servant,

ARTHUR TOOTH

March 11th, 1876.

The middle passages of the letter give the clue to the whole situation and to all the resistance.

In his reply the Bishop was obviously unable to follow Tooth's argument, for he shifted his ground this time to the right of parishioners to have services in their parish church in conformity with the Book of Common Prayer. This cut no ice with Tooth who claimed that that was precisely what he was giving them, according to his interpretation of the Ornaments Rubric. The Bishop also showed that he believed himself to be a law-officer.

Danbury,
March 17th, 1876

Rev. Sir,

It was with great regret that I read the letter which you have addressed to me, and learn, if I understand you rightly, the course you intend to pursue.

You must bear in mind that it is not I, your lordship, who am calling upon you to render me canonical obedience, but certain of your parishioners who are insisting upon their right to have the Services in their parish church conducted in conformity with the Book of Common Prayer, which they allege you to have contravened in some particulars.

The inquiry I have had to make of you in the discharge of my duty is whether you are willing to submit to my directions in the matters complained of.

You ask to be judged according to the rule of primitive antiquity. I have before had occasion to express to you my conviction that the Church of England adheres in its principles to that rule. But I must call to your mind that it is the law of the Church and Realm, to which you have engaged to conform, that I am called upon to administer.

By that law the decision of any bishop must be guided. On that point there must be no misapprehension, and it remains for you to determine whether, so far as you are concerned, you desire that the case be submitted to the judicial determination of the diocesan, instead of its being committed to the court indicated in 'the Public Worship Regulation Act.'

Whether you are willing to submit to my direction in all the matters complained of rests with yourself.

You are aware that the question of the legality of certain of those matters is now under appeal. I may say that if this representation should come regularly before me by consent, my feeling would be to defer judgment in those particular points until determined in the appeal above referred to. I am Rev. Sir, yours faithfully,

T. L. ROFFEN

Rev. A. Tooth.

Tooth denied that the State had any claim over spirituality and again replied at length, reasserting his points.

The Vicarage, Hatcham.
New Cross.
March 22nd, 1876.

My Lord Bishop,

I believe I have gone to the very limit of what is right in defining the duty of canonical obedience. I have placed myself very unreservedly in your lordship's hands for trial and judgment according to the law and primitive use of the Christian Church. I have claimed my right to be judged by this the only rule of the Church; your lordship declines to accept the position, and refers me to the Public Worship Regulation Act.

The administration of law is the one great Church question of the day, and unless the old foundations and our mutual obligations are once more recognized, we must before long be involved in hopeless confusion. The bishops have resigned their right to their spiritual courts, and have abdicated their judicial functions. This breach of trust against the corporate life of the Church in England is one for which the bishops are responsible, and in which the inferior clergy have had no share; and now that the difficulty is beginning to make itself felt, it will not do for the bishops to attempt to transfer our canonical obedience to a new secular authority. We will not be a consenting party to an arrangement to which we never could have promised obedience; if it is true that the Church requires her priests to obey her laws, it is equally true that the church requires her bishops to administer her laws. There must be faithfulness from bishops and obedience from priests.

Your lordship very happily defines the real and secular nature of the proceedings which have been commenced against me. Your statement is clear and precise: 'It is not I, your bishop, who am calling you to render me canonical obedience, but certain of your parishioners.' It is true that these proceedings have your lordship's consent, but it must not be supposed for one moment that their real character is altered in consequence; they are still merely secular proceedings and have not acquired any ecclesiastical force, unless one is to believe that a bishop has super-Parliamentary power, and in passing State law through his hands can alter it and give it something it had not before, a spiritual force, conveying a new character to it. From the nature of the law the proceedings are but secular, and your lordship allows this to be the case. I am then relieved from a great risk, that of refusing canonical obedience; and when the cry of lawlessness and disobedience is raised against me, I trust it may be seen that it is not I who am unwilling to submit to lawful authority.

I cannot allow the validity of the grievance of certain of my parishioners. Some 1,450 of my parishioners and members of the congregation will shortly approach your lordship by a petition telling you that they are not distressed by the services and teaching of this church, they pray that no difficulty may be placed in my way to limit or hinder my work in my parish. On the other hand, it is I who have real ground of complaint against the three chosen champions of ecclesiastical order and Christian verity. One has left the parish before the fray has commenced, and has relieved himself already by his own act of clerical intolerance; another indiscreetly admitted to me the weakness of his claim to the protection of the Church, admitting that the good offices of the Evangelical clergyman of his own choice sometimes fail to edify him, and that he finds the exhortations of a Wesleyan minister more to the point. I really do not care to examine the morality of the cry 'aggrieved parishioners,' its worthiness has so often been disproved. It is true they have the legal advantage of me, and I will not dispute it.

I have to thank your lordship for asserting the principle that the Church still maintains her rule of primitive antiquity. All that we claim is the right to practise what we believe; our claim is both just and reasonable. I do not believe the State in requiring any engagement from me at ordination or institution did other than allow primitive antiquity. I believe it was quite honest; it made no qualification of a leading principle, it did not require me to accept any interpretation of its own of any Church doctrine.

Lastly, your lordship refers to your 'judicial determination.' You address me under the Public Worship Regulation Act, and exercise, too, a power not as my bishop, but as an officer under this unfortunate Act of Parliament; and if there were not sufficient reasons to render one cautious, there is your lordship's own allusion to 'the Law,' which I more than suspect refers to Privy Council judgments and precedents of ill omen. Under the circumstances it ought not to be a matter of surprise that I should have misgivings about accepting your lordship's invitation to submit to the Public Worship Regulation Act, even though I have the singular advantage of knowing the 'judicial determination' before my case is heard. It is not often that the defendant in criminal proceedings has thus early the mind of his judge before argument has been advanced and the case heard. Believe me, my Lord Bishop, to be your faithful and obedient servant.

ARTHUR TOOTH

This lengthy and verbose correspondence did not make much impression on the man-in-the-street but in academic and theological circles it was examined closely by scholars, some of them moderate men with no axe to grind. One of these was Edward White Benson, newly appointed as the first Bishop of Truro. He evidently believed that Tooth's willingness to submit to episcopal judgement if it could be divorced from the authority and legalism of Parliament was not meaningless. This scholarly and spiritually minded man, a liturgical expert, succeeded Tait as Archbishop of Canterbury in 1885, and when he was called upon to judge Bishop King in 1888 acted in his capacity as a Primate, almost exactly as

Tooth in 1877 wished Tait to behave. But on the whole Tooth's plea was largely misunderstood, and he was even accused of paying lip service to episcopacy, for he denied by his actions what in his words he professed to believe as pivotal to Anglican doctrine, so it was said then and is repeated sometimes to-day.

Mr. Croom and Mr. Plimpton had organized two considerable memorials or petitions from 1,454 worshippers of whom 1,335 were parishioners, and another from the churchwardens and sixty-two men. Men's signatures as householders were considered particularly valuable; women's were not considered worth the ink they were written in. However, they effected nothing. Their point was that proceedings should be stayed until after the verdict on Ridsdale, a case being heard against the vicar of St. Peter's Church, Folkestone; but the Bishop replied that he did not see how he could interpose under the circumstances. He could surely have exercised his veto. In another letter two days later he says he had forwarded the complaint of the three parishioners to the registrar, who had transmitted it to Mr. Tooth. 'After that,' the Bishop ended, 'I have no power to stop the proceedings under No. 6 of the rules orders as passed by Parliament.' Every one realized that Parliament was by no means a religiously homogeneous body in any case. The churchwardens, Mr. Croom and Mr. Plimpton, replied respectfully and firmly, pointing out that had the Bishop returned it (*the complaint*) 'with a "reason" attached that you would not allow proceedings to go on pending the Ridsdale case appeal, it would have effected the object that you say you wished . . . ' (but he never had wished it of course). They concluded by declaring hopefully: 'may we never be found faithless . . . in maintaining the right of the Church to be governed canonically and not by the secular power of the State only,' and concluded: 'The Church may have to suffer oppression at the hands of the State but we at least need not make ourselves consenting parties to it.' They had not an inkling then of what they had set their hands to; even if they had they would not have turned back. Tooth published the correspondence.

As soon as Easter was over the 'fire-brand', George Antony Denison, vicar of East Brent, Archdeacon of Taunton took a hand. He had fought the battle of the 'Real Presence' in the ecclesiastical court in Archbishop Sumner's time and won, not on doctrine but on an appeal through a technical point of law. In an open letter to the Bishop of Rochester, he declared, 'In 1856 I refused to surrender The Doctrine of THE REAL PRESENCE. In 1876 I refuse to compromise THE DOCTRINE by surrendering the Ritual.'

This was the nub of the whole dispute. Denison continued:

What do you mean by 'the law of the Church and Realm'?
Your language and your action supply the answer, leaving no
room for doubt. You mean the law of the Church as interpreted
by a Secular Court: A Court having no authority from, or sanction of, The Church; and not, only this, but constituted under an
Act, the P.W.R. Act, passed in violation of the principles of The
Church, and in opposition to the remonstrance of the Lower
House of the Province of Canterbury, representing the Priesthood
of the Province; and, it may be added here, in contravention to
the Constitution in Church and State.

You reject the power of the Church to interpret her own law;
and assign all such power to 'the Realm,' that is, as you understand 'the Realm,' to the Court Secular.

Mr. Tooth accepts also, on his part, 'the law of the Church
and Realm.'

But, adopting the same words, you and he mean by them
opposite things. For he rejects the authority to interpret upon which
you rely: he accepts the authority which you reject: that is to
say, the power of the Church not only to decree Rites and
Ceremonies—provided always that each local Church be subject
in such matter to the Church Catholic, as the Church of England
has bound herself to be—but, also, to interpret her own decrees
as need may arise; for *cujus est condere, ejusdem est interpretari*.

The interpretation of her own decrees by the Church in Synod
is the safe guise to true decision in matter of Worship by Courts.

In a word, your position in this matter, as Bishop and Father
in GOD, is the Secular position. Mr. Tooth's is the Religious
position.

As Priests we certainly have not 'engaged to conform' to 'the
law of the Church and Realm' so explained, limited, administered,
and enforced by a Bishop in obedience to a Secular Court.

The call therefore 'to obey the law,' in your sense of 'the law,'
is a call which cannot be hearkened to.

It is, moreover, to be noted here that your understanding of
what is meant by 'the law of the Church and Realm' carries you
beyond the Secular Court, and into Parliament. In other words,
your argument proves too much; showing thereby its unsoundness
throughout. It implies distinctly, if it does not in words affirm,
what here also is untrue, namely, that it is the proper business
of Parliament to pronounce *what* the decrees of the Church and
her interpretation of them in matters of Worship *are to be,* before
proceeding to make them and it to be the law of the land.

'Look,' Denison admonished the Bishop, 'at the Celebrations
of the Holy Eucharist and at the Communicants. Set both these
side by side with the manner and the sum of both twenty-five
years ago. Look at a thousand communicants in one Church in
one day. Look at the ritual these people love and *why* they love

it, "ritual" in details differing but in principle the same. THIS
THEN IS THE BATTLE.'

It was a real polemic and one sentence ran: When the Public
Worship Regulation Act became law, simple-hearted men among
us comforted ourselves with the prospect of the discretionary power
of the bishop in refusing to send cases for trial.

Denison was far from simple-hearted, and knew exactly what
was involved. So did W. S. Grueber, vicar of Hambridge, Somerset, a member of the Society of the Holy Cross, who had, like
Denison, already addressed an open letter to Lord Selborne on
Three Recent Decisions. By now every one was well versed in the
issues involved, and every one was taking sides.

The Hatcham Defence Committee sprang into action. It publicly thanked Archdeacon Denison in the Press for his letter.
Denison replied saying the only course for priests was to sit still
and take the consequences. The Defence Committee, whose secre-
taries were Joseph Plimpton's son, Walter, and John Turner, wrote
a long and erudite letter to the Bishop of Rochester. As a layman's
letter it was perhaps the most convincing and moving of all. One
of their points was that ritualism exemplified a renewed spirituality.
Another was the tricky business of contradictory judgments on
what, or was not, legal in worship. No wonder that the Liberation
Society whose motto was *Disestablish or Die* could command
vociferous support. It was only a matter of time before all secular
inhibitions came to be ignored by churchmen of this school. The
Bishop replied briefly and non-committally, and the Hatcham
Defence Committee produced another long letter mentioning the
supporters of the suit against Tooth, the Church Association. This
body was labelled by Bishop Magee of Peterborough as JOINT
STOCK COMPANY PERSECUTION UNLIMITED.

It again made the point that was by now well established: 'Surrender of the ritual would imply a surrender of the true faith in the
Real Presence of our ever Blessed Lord in the most Holy Sacrament instituted by Himself. That doctrine we cannot surrender. . . .
You ask us to forbear one another in love. The Catholic party has
not attacked anybody. . . . We most cordially wish . . . that forbearance, and not persecution, had been extended to the Catholic
party in the Church of England. . . . ' This argument had some
force. Had the policy of concession and retreat constantly urged
upon the Catholics been presented to the other side, as a live-and-
let-live doctrine, some compromise might have been reached. But
every move was by the law, within the law and of the law: and
the law was Lord Penzance's voice.

V

HUDSON AND OTHERS v. TOOTH

THE case of Hudson and others v. Tooth came up before Lord Penzance at Lambeth Palace on July 13th, 1876. Arthur Tooth had been served with notice as the defendant but, in accordance with his statement and the decision of the Society of the Holy Cross, did not appear. The Sundays quoted against him in evidence were the previous December 19th and January 9th. There was a description of the service and of a Mr. Tooth in the procession 'who wore an alb, girdle, maniple, stole, amice and chasuble and had a biretta on his head.' (This last was an imposing affair rather like those worn in the Eastern Church though narrower and with ribbing.) Then followed the eighteen charges including 'having lighted candles held by persons in cassocks and surplices, and wearing belts; and placing images near the Communion table.' These were probably the gilded winged angels on the top of the riddell posts. Several witnesses, all spies of the Church Association, were called; one was a parishioner but of course not a worshipper. Lord Penzance reserved judgment. A week later his Lordship issued a warning or 'monition,' that the practices must cease and that since no faculties had been obtained 'for certain structures' (the crucifix and the second altar), they must be removed. Costs were of course awarded against the defendant. Lord Penzance then went on to hear another case instigated by the Church Association (they had seventeen in process at the time); Serjeant and others v. the Revd. Thomas Pelham Dale of St. Vedast's, Foster Lane, also a member of the Society of the Holy Cross. Lord Penzance again issued a monition and awarded costs against the defendant. Dale eventually was imprisoned in Holloway Gaol in 1880 under the same statute and for the same offence *de contumace capiendo*.

The Patronal Festival passed and autumn set in. Tooth had no illusions about the next step, which would be suspension. He also fully expected the inhibition of his curate, W. H. Browne; the deacon, W. A. Crouch, held no licence apparently. The problem was to decide who would take the services for he would allow no one whom he had not himself appointed. He explained to the churchwardens and Defence Committee that whatever writ of suspension arrived from one of Lord Penzance's 'myrmidons,' he would ignore it; and continue, as he claimed he was, the rightful canonically instituted incumbent of the parish, and he must have

INTERIOR OF ST. JAMES'S CHURCH, HATCHAM
DURING THE VICARIATE OF FATHER TOOTH,
1868–1878

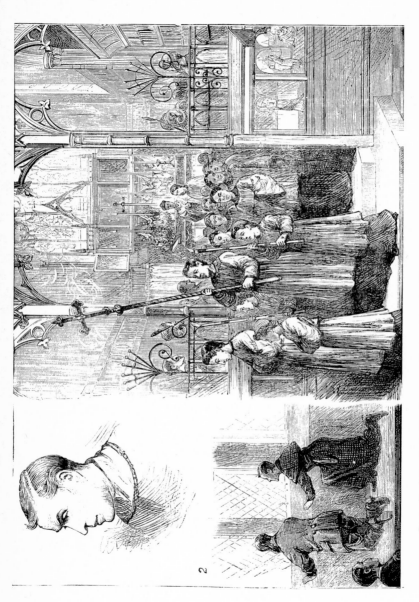

2

1. Portrait of Revd. A. Tooth.   2. Besieged in the Vestry.   3. The Procession from the Altar.
THE RITUALISTIC SERVICES AT HATCHAM — OUR ARTIST'S NOTES DURING LAST SUNDAY'S PROCEEDINGS
Reproduced from "The Graphic", January 13/77.

been aware of the penalty for such disobedience to a High Court order. This decision was fully supported by the church-wardens, the Hatcham Defence Committee and a considerable body of working men in the Church of England Working Men's Society, which A. H. Mackonochie had founded. He had a large branch in his parish, and the headquarters were in Baldwin's Gardens. The Society inaugurated branches all over the country in industrial areas where there were Catholic parishes and they were a con-siderable influence in the affairs at Hatcham. Charles Powell, the secretary, pledged his support of Tooth, and a photograph of his noble and determined face is among Croom's collected papers. He was a fine speaker and leader, and to-day would no doubt have been a Trades Union leader, if not in Parliament. When the size of the Society made it effective, the Church Association hastily formed a Society for Protestant men. It was derided by the C.E.W.M.S. because its members were obviously not workers and had superior offices in the Haymarket, whereas they had a room in Baldwin's Gardens. In the Royal Commission evidence of 1883 on Ecclesiastical Courts questions and answers showed that men were induced to join the Working Men's Protestant League on promise of payments for evidence given in the courts against ritualists, and for more than reasonable expenses in travelling to give such evidence.

Tooth was summoned to appear again before Lord Penzance's court on Saturday, December 2nd, 1876. 'Of course,' said the *Church Times*, 'the vicar of St. James's, Hatcham, will disregard this unconstitutional proceeding.' Every one connected with the church of St. James thought the same and realized that this was the critical moment. The next day many of the Hatcham residents went up to Lambeth to hear the case. They sat at the back of the court which was held in the Library of Lambeth Palace, the same one as to-day. Lord Penzance took his seat and would have been surprised had Tooth been there. However, in accordance with the accepted systems of British justice, the Apparitor, Mr. Kirkman, called Tooth's name three times, to the wry amusement of the St. James's spectators. In order that there should be no charge of partiality against him, Lord Penzance then adjourned the court for half an hour though he could hardly have expected it to make any difference to Tooth's appearance or non-appearance. When he returned the proceedings were brief. Affidavits were produced to show that the respondent had done nothing at all about his so-called ritualistic malpractices, nor had any of the offending orna-ments been removed. 'There is,' said Lord Penzance, 'no reason

D

why the hand of the Court should be stayed,' and he pronounced sentence of suspension from performing the divine service in the church for three months. The inhibition would continue unless Tooth consented to conform to the orders of the court. After this the court rose and the St. James's people returned home with the news. The vicar and churchwardens must have met and agreed on their tactics the following day, which was also Advent Sunday. In fact, judging from the printed notice that was ready at a few hours' notice, it seems that it must have been carefully prepared in advance.

VI

FRIENDS AND FOES

THE news of the inhibition reported informally to Tooth by his friends on the Saturday was published in the Monday newspapers, but he himself had not yet been notified officially. However, it was expected that a messenger from the court might arrive at any moment and nail the notice of the inhibition on the church door, and that the Bishop or one of his chaplains would then insist on taking the next Sunday's services in Tooth's place. Speculation in the parish on Tooth's prospects of imprisonment rose to fever pitch for it was useless for Tooth to accept the sentence of suspension and do nothing more. This is what had happened at St. Vedast's, Foster Lane, with the result that the church was no longer served by Pelham Dale, but by the Bishop and his staff, and eventually it had to be closed and was sequestered. The comment of the *Church Times* was that the law had triumphed and had thus 'suppressed an important centre of Catholic worship when patron, priest and congregation are all united . . . the case is clearly one for resistance unto the end. Nothing can be more silly than for clergy merely to get themselves suspended.' So the case of St. James's was crucial.

Every one was ready at the church on Sunday and it was full to the doors; even *The Times* sent a reporter. The service was exactly the same as it would have been before the legal proceedings. *The Times* reported rather sententiously, 'There was not the slightest change in the mode of conducting the service.' It noted that the 'officiating priest wore a rich vestment of a purple colour, similar to that used in the Roman Church during Advent. . . . Of the service itself it is only necessary to add that it was in all respects the same as the Roman Catholic Mass,' a phrase which infuriated the Defence Committee when they read it.

The St. Vedast's situation was never going to be repeated at Hatcham. Arthur Tooth made this clear in his statement, after the singing of the Creed. As he mounted the pulpit the silence in the church was such that 'you could have heard a pin drop.' Invoking the Holy Trinity he began the declaration:

> I, Arthur Tooth, Priest of the Church of England, Vicar of this Parish, desire in the present distess to make profession, in the face of God and of my People, of my willing obedience to all lawful authority, as binding every Christian by the Word of God and the Law of His Church.

He made three points. First he protested against the exercise of secular authority in matters spiritual. Secondly he called on his people to suffer for truth's sake and not to recognize the ministry of any priest other than his or one acting for him and under his authority. Thirdly he said that as he had not been inhibited by any lawful or canonical authority he declared that 'ministrations other than my own are schismatical and an invasion and a robbery of the rights of the Church of England.' He went on to preach a sermon on the text: 'My kingdom is not of this world. If my kingdom were of this world, then would my servants fight.' He made his own position abundantly clear, and he carried his hearers with him as he ended with the words: 'And now, Lord, behold their threatenings and grant unto thy servants that with all boldness they may speak thy Word.' As the congregation left, copies of the vicar's declaration were handed to them.

The Hatcham Defence Committee called a meeting in the schools following Evensong. All the leaders were there, and Croom as vicar's warden and chairman placed a limit of ten minutes on speeches. He said that if they accepted the vicar's declaration, which they obviously all did, it could mean the break-up of the congregation. They would have to withdraw from the services, give up communicating there and cease to support the church financially for a time. They must refuse to concede to alien and schismatical ministrations which would be to do evil in the hope that good may come. He was also convinced, and convinced his hearers, that victory would eventually be theirs if they did what was right in the sight of God and what was right meant obeying Tooth's injunction. They all had tremendous faith in the outcome. The next speaker, Thomas Waters, set the meeting on fire with enthusiasm when he declared, 'The Vicar is guarding an outpost . . . (*loud cheers*) NO surrender. May God defend the right' (*louder cheering*). There were many other speakers; the patron, Robert Tooth, was one and he said that all the Catholic party wanted was toleration. 'They let other people alone, and why should not they, the Ritualists, be let alone?' (*Hear, hear*).

Thomas Layman, who was one of the most acutely litigious members of the congregation, made a longish speech. A solicitor living in the Borough, and a worshipper at St. Alban's, Holborn, he communicated at St. James's and had been a supporter from the early days, and he was Arthur Tooth's legal adviser. He drafted the three resolutions that were passed and sent to Bishop Claughton of Rochester, and to which Claughton replied: 'In the extreme course you are adopting you will not have the support and sympathy of God-fearing men in his church and nation.' The sad thing is that he really believed this. The Defence Committee stated that the meeting supported the vicar in his persecution and upheld his public statement; they accepted him as their vicar in spite of court orders; they refused to receive any ministrations of an intruder and would withhold their support. They expressed great indignation at the terms of the report of the Sunday services in *The Times*. They also decided to lay certain plans which remained confidential until a crisis arose.

The *Church Times* printed a three column leader on the subject, printing one that 'the people are absolutely unanimous in their approval' of Tooth, and it gave the resolutions in full. It also made the point that the case of St. James's 'is a very strong one because the vicar, churchwardens and congregation are of one mind. . . . The peace and comfort . . . have been wantonly disturbed by three complainants who are absolutely outsiders.' The writer was certainly mistaken when he said 'Bishop of Rochester . . . perceives with regret the result of his ill-advised and unfatherly conduct,' but was nearer the mark when he wrote, 'no smooth words of the bishop will cause the laity of the church to depart from the line they have determined on.' The question has arisen as to whether it is better for an incumbent to adopt Mr. Tooth's line, or for him to submit under protest. In this latter case a congregation is kept together, but so far as the general public are concerned, the protest would stand for nothing, and the accused priest would be regarded as having given in as soon as he found that he would have to suffer something for acting upon his convictions. The result would naturally be that people would think private taste and fancy were all that could be pleaded in defence of 'ritual,' and that this being so, there was no great hardship in its being put down. In effect each instance of firm resistance will drive a very long nail into the coffin of the Public Worship Regulation Act, of Lord Penzance's court, and of the Church Association. The opposite view was exultantly expressed by *The Rock*: 'on Sunday Mr. Tooth may appear once more in the vestments etc., in which he takes such dear delight. *But it will be the last time.*'

The local newspaper, *The Camberwell and Peckham Times*, not unfriendly and extremely knowledgeable, spoke of the Tooth affair as an 'ugly crisis,' and wondered whether an actual assault of a physical nature would take place either on the Bishop or his representative. 'Or will the whole congregation . . . get up in a body and leave the officiant to conduct the service all to himself? . . . One of the above courses must be adopted and never since the Reformation has such a deadlock come to pass . . . '

So it was not surprising that on the second Sunday in Advent the church was nearly full by ten o'clock and forms had to be placed in every available foot of space. At half past ten a substantial number of neighbouring priests accompanied the curate, W. H. Browne, into the church for said Mattins. Meanwhile, the church-wardens and sidesmen were strategically placed round the church and blocked each end of the nave to bar any intruder. They obviously recognized their friends; Mr. Kirkland, the former curate, and assistant priests from St. Peter's, London Docks, and St. Alban's, Holborn. But there were local ministers too; a Congregational deacon from Peckham, a dissenting minister from Deptford, an old Camberwell clergyman, once a supporter of St. James's but now a papist; and others too, all drawn by curiosity and the desire for novelty. When the elaborate procession entered at eleven o'clock it took aback many of the old-fashioned church-folk present and one clergyman rose and walked out.' It was a time of suspense.

The vicar, who was also the celebrant, preached from the text, 'His banner over me was love.' He was obviously far from well, probably suffering from a type of influenza, but he kept going until he reached the words, 'present struggle is a wrong which had been done to the love of God.' At this moment there was a thunderous banging on the west door; the churchwardens, perhaps rather tactlessly, had locked it when the church became uncomfortably full. Every one in the congregation believed that the Bishop or his chaplain had arrived. Tooth stopped his sermon at once and outwardly, at any rate, was the least disturbed person in the building. Meanwhile, the churchwardens, Croom and Plimpton, with several men behind, unlocked the door and cautiously edged it open. It was only a posse of sightseeing late-comers, demanding entrance. It was not easy (or legal) to keep them out and the congregation was aware of, and from the pulpit Tooth observed, a 'desperate pushing on the part of some portly persons . . . but eventually the inside party got the best of it and closed the door.' Tooth finished his sermon in precisely the same tone of voice as he had been using before the hubbub. The service ended with the hymn 'Faith of our Fathers' lustily shouted by the singers and the Hatcham flock felt it had scored. There had been no emissary of the Bishop and the service was as it always had been. All the same a great many outsiders were puzzled and curious. The evening service was quiet with the church again full to the doors, and it ended with the singing of the *Dies Irae* and its grimly appropriate opening verse, prophecy of things to come.

Two important meetings were held the next week. The first one was called by the English Church Union at which Croom proposed and Layman seconded a resolution for a special meeting, and withdrew it in favour of another resolution to support Tooth's action and policy. It was a large and enthusiastic meeting, and Charles Powell was there. The resolution was carried unanimously; there has been dissentient voices against a leading member's (Dr. Phillimore) more cautious resolution beforehand. One of the points made was that St. James's Church had been built with high church money for a high church congregation. Augustus Granville wrote to the newspapers denying this; but the answer was that the movement had advanced since his time. It was now over thirty years since the days of the mission room and the bell in the apple tree, over twenty since the consecration of the church, and nearly ten since Granville resigned.

The second meeting, called by Charles Powell, was of the Council of the Church of England Working Men's Society. It pledged its support of Tooth who received messages to similar effect from fifty-four other branches apart from others formed later. They decided that those who lived within reach of Hatcham should attend the church and support the churchwardens in their plans. The Church of England Working Men's Society was a lively and passionately dedicated movement but anathema to some of the bishops. It is a pity that its counterpart does not exist to-day. A committee at the new branch of Hopton, Mirfield, for example, consisted of a book-keeper, a printer, a warehouseman, a cloth finisher, a painter and a plumber.

Punch had a comment on *The Tooth that Won't Come Out*, with a rather stiff cartoon; and *John Bull* reported the meeting of the English Church Union, noting that 'long continued cheers greeted Mr. Tooth's name whenever it was mentioned.' Newspapers all over England and Scotland and as far away as Canada printed accounts of the inhibition. It was easy to make puns on a name like Tooth: *How to remove an incurable Tooth: Punch it out* (from *Punch*), and *Sunday amusement at Hatcham: Drawing a Tooth*. But it was not so amusing when on the next Saturday the notice of inhibition was presented by officers of Lord Penzance's court to Tooth at the vicarage. The same man returned on the Sunday (Advent III) and pinned to the church door at ten o'clock a large sheet in a 'law-clerk's hand.' He then stayed for the service during which the document vanished in spite of the presence of a police sergeant and a constable. The church was again packed to the doors, and this time Alexander Mackonochie himself was there, as well as

Charles Lowder. Tooth preached on the text, 'More than a prophet'; and the only point relevant to the situation was that he denied that the word 'defiance' could be applied to him; he only understood the word 'duty.' A large crowd gathered outside the church after the service and lined the road and paths to watch the vicar and visiting clergy leave the church. 'They were shown marks of respect in most cases, but not in all.' One old gentleman harangued the crowd on what he would do if it were his church. 'But,' wrote *The Camberwell and Peckham Times's* reporter, 'the inner man reminded the disputants that the tocsin of the soul (did he mean *soul*) must surely be heard in their respective homes and after half-past one the road was pretty well deserted.' In fact, the affair was a gift to the Press at a time when there was a dearth of real news, and very few people were unaware of the issues by now. *John Bull* was not quite certain yet which side to take and summarized the opinions of its contemporaries including the correspondence columns. *The Rock*, the *Church Times*, *The Church Review*, *The Non-Conformist*, *The Standard* and *The Kentish Mercury* expatiated at length on the subject.

The fourth Sunday in Advent was Christmas Eve, not the most propitious season for an ecclesiastical encounter between bishop and people. News of the next step arrived at Hatcham on Saturday when the bishop's secretary delivered a notice of inhibition on Tooth at the vicarage. The Bishop intimated that he had appointed and licensed Canon Gee, a proctor in Convocation, and vicar of Abbot's Langley, then in the diocese of Rochester, to take services during the period of Tooth's inhibition; to act in fact as curate-in-charge. The Defence Committee had laid their plans with military efficiency. After eight o'clock celebration there was a speedy return to the church and by 10 o'clock it was full with an immense congregation. From the west door Croom and Plimpton watched the carriage turn into St. James and draw up at the foot of the steps opposite the Orphanage. Canon Gee and the Bishop's secretary emerged and mounted the steps to the west door, where the implacable and stony-faced reception committee was ranged behind Tooth, who was vested in cassock, surplice, and purple stole. Gee bowed to Tooth, and Tooth returned the courtesy. Reading from a paper, he stated that he had come with the licence of the Bishop to take the service at St. James's Church. The secretary handed the Bishop's licence to Tooth who glanced at it briefly and passed it on to Croom. Tooth spoke first and reading from a prepared statement quoted the relevant section of the Public Worship Regulation Act, saying,

'I have received notice that the Reverend Richard Gee, D.D., has been appointed to take the service of this church. I beg to be informed whether you are the clergyman referred to, and whether you have come to take the services.'

Slightly disconcerted Canon Gee assented with a nod, adding in reply 'You have been inhibited by the Judge of the Arches Court from taking services, and the Bishop has sent me to take them.' Without a pause Tooth continued,

'Lord Penzance's Court is a civil court to which I have never sworn canonical obedience. I do not wish to show disrespect to a brother priest but I must forbid you to enter this church or to take any services within the boundaries of this parish.'

Turning to Croom and Plimpton who flanked him he asked,

'Gentlemen are you prepared to assist me as the duly appointed vicar of this church to prevent the intrusion into it of any clergyman not recognized by me and acting under the direction of an unauthorized civil court?'

In turn each bearded and grimly determined churchwarden spoke up: I am, sir.

And from Robert Tooth and Charles Powell and the solid group of thirty or forty men behind them came an audible murmur of agreement. Obviously surprised Canon Gee answered incredulously, 'Do you really mean this?'

'Most certainly,' they replied in unison. Croom added 'If you insist on intruding here, the whole congregation will immediately leave the church and we shall use all means in our power to expel you from the church placed under our guardianship.' With considerable dignity, Canon Gee said, 'In that case I retire under protest,' and he did so along with the Bishop's secretary, returning in the hansom cab which had brought him.

'And those who were present,' said one local inhabitant, 'will never forget the scene.'

Tooth then turned round and passing between the ranks of his bodyguard re-entered the church as though nothing untoward had happened. This time there were thirty brother clerics present to support him including Mackonochie and Lowder, but they were not by any means all members of the Society of the Holy Cross.

Tooth did not mention the incident at the west door in his sermon on 'No man can serve two masters,' except in an oblique reference to obeying spiritual rather than temporal powers. His previous Sunday's printed declaration, conspicuously displayed on the walls, now included an addendum. This called on his congregation to accept no other ministrations than his own, or of a priest appointed by him, for *all* other ministrations, he declared, would be 'an invention and a robbery of the rights of the Church of England.' The service ended as it invariably did at this time with the singing of the hymn 'Faith of our Fathers.' Outside the church were unsympathetic crowds of curious onlookers and there was nearly a riot, for some of the opposition were vehemently denouncing the service they had not attended and did not wish to share in: and they were 'much hustled and pushed down the road' by the departing worshippers. The rest of the day was quiet. W. H. Browne's licence as curate had been withdrawn by the Bishop along with Tooth's. W. Crouch, a deacon, held no licence and was for some reason rumoured, incorrectly, to belong to the newly formed religious community for men, the Society of St. John the Evangelist. This action by episcopal authority, though regretted, was recognized. It left Tooth without assistance for early celebrations and other sacramental ministrations, since it reduced Browne to the equivalent of a lay assistant.

Somehow the preparations for Christmas Day were completed; the vases filled with flowers, the frontals changed, the rich vestments set out. In spite of apprehensions that the Bishop would arrive to take the services himself the united congregation rejoiced as one in the ever new remembrance of the Saviour's birth. They did not know that it was the highlight of the ministry of Arthur Tooth at Hatcham.

VII

TUMULT AND SHOUTING

IN the following week, all the newspapers came down on one side or the other. *John Bull,* afraid of alienating any one, had not yet jumped off the fence; eventually it decided to support Tooth. Every one wanted to know what the next step would be. *The Times* threatened police action, but a local paper derided its voice and called it the 'Thunderer of Blackfriars,' asking 'why should this happen?' *The Weekly Dispatch* declared that Canon Gee 'beat a mild and not undignified retreat and Mr. Tooth celebrated his triumph by indulging in practices of a Romish character more pronounced than ever.' (This was adding fuel to the flames as Tooth had done nothing new.) When *The Yarmouth Chronicle* said, 'Tooth's own friends lament his extravagances' to whom did it refer? Canon Gregory? Dean Hook? G. H. Wilkinson? Certainly not Mackonochie or Lowder or Denison. *The Scotsman* made the point that Tooth and his churchmanship were extremely popular in the parish and that a victory for intolerance could drive some of her members out of the church into the arms of her foes. *The Solicitor's Journal* pointed out the legal position, which could land Tooth in prison for contempt of court. Charles Wood wrote to the *Church Times* and appealed to the 'united episcopate,' and *The Standard,* generally inimical to ritualism and considered the voice of officialdom, protested against ritualism being considered as the 'natural sequence of the old High Church revival of forty years ago.' *The Daily Telegraph* thought it 'desirable to protect English-women from this unwholesome influence,' and hoped that the arm of the law would 'disturb the vestry slumbers of that very pretty proto-martyr, Mr. Tooth.' For it was rumoured widely and falsely that Tooth now slept in the vestry to preserve the church from entry. Mr. Hill of Hatcham sent about a dozen identical letters to different journals quoting an Act by which the ministrations of Canon Gee would be *ultra vires* since they infringed a clause of the Pluralities Act. This was a very clever move, for it showed that ecclesiastical authority was not legally infallible.

The next Sunday, the last in the old year, and the first after Christmas, no one was quite sure what to expect. The police were ready. The church was full a good half hour before Mattins (said), which preceded the Sung Eucharist at eleven o'clock. Tooth was still suffering from a cold and had difficulty in speaking, and only

preached briefly. At first all was reverent, but in the Creed someone shouted 'No Popery,' probably at the Incarnatus, and then kept
up a peculiar cough, but 'he was speedily quieted'—by Charles
Powell's assistants no doubt. Later on four men shouted offensive
epithets, drowned when the organ and congregation struck up
(appropriately enough) *Adeste Fideles*; a free fight had begun at
the west end of the church. By this time hundreds of people were
standing on their seats, 'some calling out for order and others
crying shame,' and of course, adding to the general confusion. The
police had no power to eject unruly members of the congregation
though the agitators were removed by some means, and the doors
relocked; another band of men closed the chancel gates and stood
guard in front of them. The *Church Times* praised the wise and
judicious conduct of the churchwardens. Tooth continued the service at the other end of the church as though nothing had happened. The disturbance was similarly ignored by the priests and
laymen in choir who continued intently devout to the end.

Outside was a crowd of a thousand bent on trouble and already
singing their own version of *The Two Obadiahs* and the National
Anthem (including the words 'Frustrate their Popish tricks') and
an additional verse:

> Three hundred years have fled,
> Since the heroic dead
>   Our noble sires
> Bravely the battle fought
> And for us freedom wrought
> With vict'ry dearly bought
>   Thro' martyrs' fires.

Church Association agitators were haranguing the crowd and distributing tracts addressed to *The Men of England* (one survives in
Mr. Plimpton's collection). Tooth was greeted with hisses and
groans, and his protective bodyguard with shouts of 'Traitors.'
When Mackonochie was recognized there was a furious charge
towards him, and he was only just rescued in time by the police,
six of them. One gang followed him and his curate as far as the
railway station. Almost every newspaper in the country and others
as far away as New York carried some account of the affair during
the next week, beginning with often contradictory descriptions of
the ritual, clouds of incense, types of vestments and musical ren-
derings. As for the disturbances inside and outside the church, even
the usually hostile *Standard* described the crowd as 'roughs of the
lowest class who threatened with horrible oaths to re-assemble

next Sunday.' The same paper described the evening crowds as good humoured with the exception of some stone-throwing adolescents, so it sounds like an eye-witness account. However, there was fighting off and on after the evening service until about half past nine when every one gradually dispersed. *The Graphic* published an illustration of Tooth and Croom anxiously looking through the vestry window at the crowd. *The Daily Telegraph* said that the brawlers were idlers and not the emissaries of the Church Association; but Mr. Albert Jovay replied that from remarks he had heard, 'the Church Association is at the bottom of the matter.' *The Camberwell and Peckham Times* gave definite proof of this. *The Rock* reprinted *The Guardian's* account and made it an excuse for sniping at the Westminster Road Chapel for their choice of music, some tunes having been chosen from the mistrusted collection of *Ancient and Modern*. 'Last night (*New Year's Eve*) there was a *midnight choral service*' (their italics), which evidently they considered the pinnacle of ritualism.

Headlines varied from *The Hatcham Fog* and *The Hatcham Scandal* to *The Contumacious Vicar* and *Now or Never;* and all referring to the extermination of ritualism. Letters poured in from A Satisfied Parishioner, An Aggrieved Parishioner, Old English Citizen, English Churchman, Old Inhabitant, Clericus, E.C.U., A Fair Field and No Favour; this last was the pseudonym of Tooth's deacon, W. Crouch.

There was a slight swing from outside opinion towards Tooth since it was generally agreed, as one wrote, that the 'proceedings were disgusting,' and there was a definite closing of the ranks in support from clergy, many of whom had been far from ritualistic. Also, the discussion in the Press brought every shade of opinion into prominence and softened some of the sharp edges of criticism. Some reporters, who were hazy about the doctrinal and legal issues, praised Tooth for his 'pluck'; for most people saw that the congregation backed up its vicar and considered he was their champion. All the same, the next official step was freely mentioned and considered to be incarceration in Maidstone Gaol.

The anti-ritualists began to organize on a local scale and instituted 'The Hatcham and Protestant Defence Committee,' which gathered strength from now on, and was not dissolved till 1886. M'Clure, a one-time Roman Catholic, and an official of the Church Association (some thought a paid one), took the chair at a meeting in New Cross supported by Protestant parishes in Deptford. They called an open air meeting in the road outside St. James's Church for the next Saturday afternoon in order to compose a memorial to

Lord Penzance. They also made plans for assembling in good time the following Sunday so as to gain admission to the church and 'force an entrance at all cost short of breaking the law.' One of the plans was the printing and distribution of tickets: *Admit Bearer by the north door before 10 o'clock.* It was hoped to have the church full with their own supporters. These tickets were taken by hand from house to house by the Sisters and members of the Defence Committee, and with extreme caution. However, it was impossible to keep it secret from the Protestant party, which retaliated. They ordered several hundred facsimile ones from the printer who in good faith undertook to produce them. By an extraordinary piece of luck, the printers delivered them to Walter Plimpton's house. There was a frantic hustle then to overprint new tickets with the names of Croom and Plimpton and to redistribute them. The result finally distinguished which party ticket holders supported.

On Sunday morning, January 7th, in spite of having an entry ticket *The Times* representative had difficulty in making his way through the rough crowd. By nine o'clock the approaches to the church were already filling up with people who had come to do some dirty work. There was a hubbub when some dissidents tried to gain admission at the west door without tickets. Superintendent Gernon was on duty with a number of police constables and a stout barricade had been erected around the church. All the same, one clergyman was so roughly handled between the main road and the church that he had to retreat into the nearest house for safety. Two more arrived late and the doors were unlocked. At each end of the rows of worshippers, a man was stationed in case there was a rush into the church, and in the front rows were the Sisters. As Mattins started, the voices inside the church were drowned by the uproar outside, and it was clear that this was no usual crowd. The National Anthem, the new version with the additional verse, was roared over and over again. Inside, the service continued uninterrupted including the sermon on the Epiphany gifts. At the moment of the consecration there was a tremendous crash outside. The barrier round the church had given way to a crowd who had climbed the wall by the school where they overwhelmed the three policemen guarding it. A thunderous assault on the doors followed. Women stood up fearfully and the men rushed to barricade them with benches and forms and chairs. At this point the police, who were mounted, drove the mob from the doors but not from the adjacent roads and grounds of the church and vicarage. Its size was variously estimated as between five thousand and eight thousand; some accounts say it was well dressed and others poorly dressed, but there was room for both to be represented. Inside the church the service finished just after midday; first Crouch (the deacon) and then Croom spoke to the people, since no one was able to leave.

'Men and brethren,' said Croom in apostolic style, 'please keep your seats. There is no need to be afraid. The police are in charge of the church and grounds. If you left now you would only irritate those outside, so please keep your seats until we know it is safe outside.' Crouch said much the same and asked them to join in the Litany, and later in Evensong, described as a 'supplementary service' by one reporter. Outside the church the words of the Moody and Sankey hymn of 'Hold the fort' penetrated to the congregation, a sentiment which those inside devoutly echoed.

By this time, it was after one o'clock and most had been inside for over three hours. Looking through one of the windows, it was obvious that reserves of police had arrived and Croom gently opened the west door. In single file and to shouts and jeers the worshippers emerged. One of them was Thomas Fry, described as the legal representative of the Church Association, who seemed pleased with the uproar. Cat-calls, groans and derisive laughter followed the clergymen as they came out. Tooth, strongly escorted, was greeted with a torrent of hisses. In reply, he bowed as ostentatiously and sarcastically as he was able. This enraged the crowd, who countered with shouts of 'Fire will get you,' 'We'll see you in Newgate.' 'This way to Rome' and 'Out you shall come if we swing for it,' as well as a 'shower of blasphemies and oaths.' Meanwhile, since the church was locked and the police in control, the enormous crowd swept up the main road, knocking over an old woman's apple stall, and charged the railway station. On the platform were men and women who had come from town to support Tooth. One account hints that this mob was chasing two clergymen whom we know as Mackonochie and his curate, since they were easily recognized. Suddenly, the word went round that Browne, the inhibited curate, was going home, and they tore after him in the opposite direction; but with skill and luck and the aid of the police he reached home safely. There was no service in the evening and gradually the crowds dispersed.

One parishioner had no doubt that the gangs were organized, for 'bodies of roughs sent back by the police were only to be led on again by ringleaders . . . a train by the East London Railway was packed with them . . . men received one pound each and boys a shilling.' And the writer reports that a 'clergyman coming up to St. James's was set upon by the mob and literally pounded with clenched fists. . . . Another was placed in a barrow, treated to a ride, and rolled in the mud.' Two others, evidently Mackonochie and his curate, Hogg, were hunted from the church to the railway station and only escaped by the exertions of the police. 'The fury of these hired villains was terrible.' If a 'deeply laid conspiracy exists against the clergy and people of St. James's Church,' as this parishioner asserted, 'the methods of its promoters achieved both notoriety and obloquy on the one hand and sympathy and prayers on the other.' And, of course, there was no possibility of compromise; the situation was bound to become worse. *The Rock* disclosed that 'forty dockyard lambs (or labourers) received 10/- each together with seats in the church and that the whole body, police and lambs included, were fed at 1/3d a head by Mr. Page of New Cross.'

Two local incidents followed. A parishioner complained that he had been refused entry at St. James's Church contrary to the law of the land. On learning it would cost him £1,000 to take proceedings he abandoned the suit. An ordained minister of the Church of England left the Established Church in his old age because of 'Romish practices' and took over the South Island Place Chapel, Clapham Road, built of zinc and with a scanty congregation.

VIII

AFTERMATH—SUNDAY, JANUARY 14TH

THERE was plenty to report in the following week when public meetings of violently opposing views were held. The meeting of the English Church Union came first and *The Times, Daily News, The Standard* and *The Guardian* included long accounts of its deliberation; *The Times* heading was *Defiant Attitude of the Ritualists.* All the stalwarts of the E.C.U. were present, many of them now old and far from radical in their ecclesiastical views. In fact the President, Charles Lindley Wood, was one of the youngest men in the room. Charles Wood made a scholarly historical review of the situation. As for the Judicial Committee of the Privy Council, he reminded them, 'Mr. Keble said we ought never to rest while it remained.' This was a statesmanlike appeal, for by now Keble was classed as a moderate; he was recognized too as one of the greatest theologians and scholars of the Church of England. Canon Carter moved the first resolution which 'denied that the secular power had any authority in matters purely spiritual.' Archdeacon Denison, an extremely popular figure and always a success on any platform, proposed the second one which supported any priest not guilty of a moral or canonical offence who refused to recognize suspension under a secular court. The third resolution appealed to an interpretation of the Ornaments Rubric placed on it by the Lower House of Convocation of Canterbury. All were carried unanimously with terrific enthusiasm. Tooth and Hatcham were freely mentioned in the speeches; the case was uppermost in men's minds as Lord Penzance's patience was obviously becoming exhausted. The inimical *Daily News* put its finger on the spot when it declared that 'no speeches, no resolutions and no resistance can make the English Church a State Church and a Free Church at the same time.' What the editor did not realize was that the possibility of disestablishment did not dismay high churchmen, who mostly felt they had nothing to lose by this but their chains.

The second meeting was held by the Working Men's Protestant League in the road outside St. James's Church on the Saturday afternoon. By three o'clock the road was full, and the speaker appealed to the audience to leave the pavement clear for the residents. M'Clure spoke from a chair in the middle of the crowd. It was a lovely day and every one enjoyed themselves. The chairman was one of the aggrieved parishioners, a Mr. Holloway, who was

E

a worshipper at St. John's, Deptford. He wished to send a petition to the Bishop of Rochester against the illegal practices at St. James's, including the adoration of Joseph and the Virgin Mary which, he said, was 'against common sense.' The ritualists would have agreed with this misinterpretation of their practices but not with the crude ones that followed, declaring that it was blasphemous to believe in her as the mother of God and giving particular reasons. The meeting ended with three cheers for the Queen, three for Mr. Holloway and three groans for Mr. Tooth. After a bit of scuffling and horseplay the meeting broke up; providentially it had started to rain.

The third meeting had already taken place, and news of it brought to the Protestant League meeting outside St. James's Church was greeted with fervent cheers. Sitting on Saturday morning in his court in the Library of Lambeth Palace, and after hearing evidence through affidavits, Lord Penzance said, 'I have no hesitation in pronouncing that Mr. Tooth was contumacious and in contempt in not obeying the orders of the court.' He said a great deal more about Tooth's 'delusions' and entertained a few of his own when he pointed out the Acts of Parliament of Edward VI and Elizabeth I under which, had Tooth offended three times, he could have been imprisoned for life; a course obviously acceptable to Lord Penzance. Costs as always were awarded against Tooth. The next step was a *significavit* addressed to the Queen in Chancery which would be answered by an order committing Tooth to prison.

There is no public record of the meeting of the Hatcham Defence Committee which had met at the vicarage earlier in the week. The members decided that on Sunday Tooth would hold two low celebrations of Holy Communion at five and six o'clock with Mattins between; this was done and there were sixty communicants. How the scurrilous *Rock* knew that Tooth wore 'a handsome green vestment' cannot be guessed.

At a quarter to nine the Bishop's apparitor arrived and posted a notice on the door that no service would be held. Tooth had received the notice at the vicarage the night before, presumably by hand, and had acted accordingly. The rest of the congregation went as a body to St. Paul's, Lorrimore Square, Walworth, where they recognized some of the faces of men who had been disturbers of the peace at Hatcham bent on trouble again. In Hatcham a crowd of eight thousand, a large part of them roughs, gradually gathered round the church of St. James's; but it was closed. There was no shortage of police; three hundred in readiness, two hundred on duty and many mounted. There was an organized rush to read the official notice from the Bishop of Rochester. But after that, although there was a good deal of stone-throwing and shouting, reserves of mounted police kept order without difficulty, moving the crowds all the time. Suddenly it started to rain heavily and they melted away, many apparently into adjacent public houses. So the day ended in comparative peace.

As for Tooth, he had been ill and living under a continual strain; he left his address with his curate and went off to Tunbridge Wells. It was the most sensible thing to do, as the writ committing him to prison might not be served for another two or three weeks. The *Church Times* reporter managed to see him and thought he looked well enough, saying, 'in any case he has the appearance of an ascetic.' He also elicited the fact that communicants in the nine years of Tooth's incumbency had increased by three thousand a year, from less than two to nearly five thousand. *The Western Morning News* whose reporter could not see Tooth, while it disparaged the size of the Defence Fund noted that 'his stipend is the truly princely one of £150 a year'; and 'if you argue with him the chances are that you will be worsted.' Rumours ran round the parish like wild-fire that the vicar had run away; that he had the chain on the door to bar intruders (so did many others in the road, having seen the mob and had their gardens ruined); that he was appointing someone to take charge of the parish in his place; that the Bishop would do the same.

All the newspapers, having sifted the affair till nothing remained but the deadest of chaff, now tried to find something new and enlivening; some changed their tune and admitted doing so. After all, the *affaire* Tooth begun nearly seven months ago had hardly been out of the news since. At the end of St. James's little cul-de-sac, the church stood unlit, empty and locked, its own silent protest against a legal system which drove a sword between good men in all ranks of life.

IX

IMPRISONMENT—SUNDAY, JANUARY 21st AND MONDAY, JANUARY 22nd

ONE of the key figures in this controversy was Bishop Claughton of Rochester. Sitting in the comfortable peace of Danbury his resolution against defiant Hatcham and its vicar hardened. He decided he must exert what authority he had in order to subdue the ritualism inside the church and the rioting outside, so he enlisted the aid of the police force and Superintendent Gernon of Deptford. At 10 p.m. on Saturday evening, January 20th, Gernon, accompanied by the Bishop's apparitor, fixed a long notice under his seal and signed by the newly appointed curate-in-charge of St. James's, Richard Chambres. This declared that Chambres, having been appointed by the Bishop, had not been able to gain access to the church because the vicar and churchwardens refused to give up the keys, and he therefore ordered that the church should be closed for the whole of Sunday, January 21st. To enforce this the Superintendent detailed Inspector Hamblin, a sergeant, and twelve men with three hundred police to be posted in reserve outside from midnight to midnight. The Sisters had distributed notices to the regular worshippers during the week with news of a six and seven o'clock celebration as before, and this had been noted by the opposite faction. It was, therefore, fair to assume that the same procedure would be followed as on the 14th. Some friendly priest would celebrate early in the morning, since Tooth was in Tunbridge Wells and Browne inhibited; and this was carried out. Soon after five o'clock in the bitter cold of a freezing fog an unknown priest with Browne, the inhibited curate, Croom and Plimpton and 'thirty to forty ladies and gentlemen' (others said fifty to sixty), presented themselves at the church door and were 'courteously refused entrance.' Mr. Croom, who was no weakling, asked Inspector Hamblin what he would do if the fairly solid group pushed him aside.

'I should at once take you into custody,' replied Hamblin. Even Croom was unprepared for this and is reported as answering in a less bellicose tone.

'Do you really mean you will stop us entering to carry on a service?'

'Any gentleman who attempts to do so will most certainly be promptly taken to Peckham Station-house and charged with obstructing the police in the execution of their duty,' was Hamblin's official answer.

No reply to this was possible, so the shivering congregation dispersed and later joined the worship at St. Stephen's, Lewisham. When the anti-ritualist crowds began to gather from eight onwards there was not much to see or do; and though hundreds were arriving during the morning, others were leaving. The police were well in evidence with reserves stationed in the school. Later the sun came out and it was a beautiful, cold, dry day, with nothing to mar it for the curious crowds except an empty church, a witness to the supremacy of the civil power.

The next day, Monday, January 22nd, Tooth returned to London and went to the house of Layman who evidently knew that the order committing Tooth to prison was about to be served. Tooth would have preferred to be arrested in Kent and sent to Maidstone Gaol but this did not happen. When the sheriff's officers of the court arrived to arrest him, Layman, as one of his legal advisers, accompanied Tooth to the forbidding Horsemonger Gaol at the approach to London Bridge, where he was put in the debtors' part of the prison. As Tooth was the first of the five parish priests in the next ten years to go to gaol, every newspaper in England carried some report of the arrest either first or secondhand. Opinion was divided between just and rich deserts, or suffering for conscience's sake. *The Rock* had made a scoop when it acquired confidential minutes of a meeting (a Chapter) of the Society of the Holy Cross together with the *Rule of Life,* and the details of the brethren's ascetic practices. Having no compunction about private documents, it published the account *in toto* in its next number describing the S.S.C. as 'one of the most formidable of those secret societies set like so many gins and snares in the pathway of our Protestant Church.' It declared that the 'canker of asceticism has entered the church.' It could be that its taunts at episcopacy roused Bishop Claughton, when it derided him for 'shrinking from the post of danger' and not showing himself at Hatcham as though he was afraid to act through the civil power and close the church. *The Western Morning News* hoped that imprisonment would compel Tooth 'to withdraw from the church and set up his gee-gaw shop at Rome, or, like a Dissenter as he is, in a Free Church.' This was a point made by many columnists, among them the writer of the editorial of *The Times:* 'he can emancipate himself at any moment. If he is a martyr it is for a mere triviality . . . which he is perfectly at liberty to enjoy under certain conditions.' But to Tooth it was no triviality. As far as he was concerned the court of

Lord Penzance had no authority at all and he was demonstrating this, as others would do later, by the only means in his power. He ignored it.

On the whole *The Non-Conformist* deprecated the situation as a type of persecution similar to their own position in the past. The writer did not anticipate disestablishment, a course which seemed logical but not one unanimously desired by all high churchmen. 'Let them form a Free Church,' declared the *Sunday School Chronicle*. *The Standard* wanted to know how Tooth, once in, was to be released, for 'every day . . . will tend to lessen his original offence and bring him one step nearer to the coveted position of martyrdom.' *John Bull*, under a heading *The Quasi-modo Court of the Arches*, and ever the mouthpiece of the under-dog, tried to speak for the 'inexpressible disquietude of the church! For one that sympathized with Mr. Tooth's ritual there will be ten thousand to deplore his imprisonment'; and it tilted at the broad church paper *The Guardian* which had come down on the side of authority, to the disgust of *Church Times* readers and the exultation of *The Rock*. The *Leeds Courier* said, 'Tooth deludes himself that he is not a notorious breaker of the Law' and the *Midland Courier* that Tooth had submitted 'with a *fairly* good grace to the penalty of his foolish obstinacy.' What the *fairly* qualified is a mystery. Most local papers were sympathetic or non-committal. *The Camberwell and Peckham Times* wrote: 'Mr. Tooth in gaol with keys in pocket, Bishop Claughton at Danbury with sealing wax and parchment, and one of the most respectable congregations in South London having to go and cadge sacramentally on other local churches, are sights for gods and men.'

Then there were the cartoonists and the punsters. *Spy's* cartoon, *The Christian Martyr*, showed the long, slightly lugubrious Tooth behind bars. *Fun* had a design for a ritualistic stained glass window: the bewigged figure, *Law* was shown ready to whip the vested and haloed martyr, with the sub-scription *Saint Tooth Ye Martyr—Hys Flagellation*. *Punch* had already had a cartoon showing a kindly Lord Penzance vainly trying to pull a savage faced Tooth through the key-hole of the Court of Arches. *Funny Folks* showed a benign judge with an instrument labelled *Writ* extracting a fanged tooth 'OUT' from an old dame beside whom was a large bag, *Endowments*, and the words 'Even though the operation might have been painful the patient will be all the better for it.' There were also some rather feeble puns on Hatcham (such as a goose shown sitting on two eggs, one Romanism and the other Ritualism); and there were many attempts at verse, of which the following ones from *Punch* are a typically heavy-handed example.

Two of a Trade
Toole in his gaiety, Tooth in his gravity,
The Town to amuse at this time of depression,
Though with different art, both play the same part,
In the Strand and at Hatcham—*The Man in Possession.*

Dens—a Tooth.
A Theological Authority in the Church of Rome not of
England.

If your ritual eggs at home
You'd not smash, from that risk snatch'em
As you cannot bring Hatcham to Rome
By going to Rome to Hatch'em.

And from *Fun,*

Why didn't the most recent Ritualists keep their
plots and practices dark—say at Deptford?
Because that wouldn't have been the way to Hatch 'em.

Every one up and down the country read and knew about
Hatcham and Arthur Tooth, and many were avidly waiting for the
next instalment from Horsemonger Gaol.

THE TOOTH THAT WON'T COME OUT.

Reproduced by permission of "Punch"

X

CHRISTIAN MARTYR

TOOTH was received by a warden and taken to the Governor and then housed in the debtor's wing. It was probably Layman who asked whether he could be put in the better part set aside for 'first class misdemeanants,' but that section was only reserved for criminals and this class did not, as yet, apply to him. At first he had a rather squalid cell but was allowed to change it for another, and he said it was adequate. The furniture, which included a canvas bed, was minimal, and Layman arranged for a couple of chairs, books and a better mattress, possibly a feather bed, to be sent in. Meals were brought by the Sisters, and the cleaning was done by a prisoner anxious to earn a little extra cash. Outside there was a waiting room divided into partitions like a large cage; there he could receive visitors three times a week, following the daily service which he invariably attended at three in the afternoon. In spite of a small fire, the cold was intense, and Tooth wore his muffler and heavy coat and, some accounts say, his hat too. (An illustration shows him doffing it as he received visitors.) 'The routine is oppressively monotonous,' said *The Daily Telegraph;* so was the damp chill. Browne, the inhibited curate, arranged the rota of visitors and there was no lack of them. One of the first was a courtesy call from Canon Liddon who was not a personal friend; another was Tooth's old vicar, Canon Gregory, who brought a brace of pheasants; Bishop Tozer, Bishop Jenner, Canon Carter and A. H. Mackonochie followed. The sympathetic public longed to show their support, so when Tooth wrote to the Press appealing for funds for his Orphanage which had received a good deal of publicity, the money poured in for it, as well as for the Defence Committee; so did addresses of sympathy from parishes and public meetings including one from St. James's parishioners. Back in Hatcham the tireless Defence Committee organized two addresses to the Bishop. Not all the Press accounts were sympathetic; some pretended that imprisonment was the equivalent of a sybaritic retreat as in this account from *The Rock:* 'A well-dressed, well-fed ecclesiastic, holding levées and receiving bouquets of flowers from his lady admirers, and hampers of game from his male friends, was felt to have as little claim to be dubbed *Martyr* as summer excursionists in first-class carriages to Lourdes have to rank as pilgrims. If *Spy* had cared to do his duty he would have drawn

Mr. Tooth seated in an easy chair in a carpeted study, with his table covered with books and flowers and the cards of his worshippers . . . ' It was extremely galling to Parliamentarians, such as Lord Shaftesbury, and to Erastian bishops like Claughton and Tait, that the eyes and ears of the world were focused on Horsemonger Gaol. The strong were far from claiming victory in a battle which was to some extent a war of nerves.

No one mentioned the long and leaden hours from three o'clock on Saturday afternoon to Tuesday morning when Tooth was allowed to receive visitors again, nor his anxiety about the parishioners and the future of St. James's. For on the following Sunday, January 28th (Septuagesima), the church was closed all day against the Bishop's curate-in-charge, and guarded by a strong contingent of police. Croom and Plimpton had not been able to take possession, and persisted in their refusal to give up the keys which they claimed belonged to the rightful vicar and no one else. They arranged for the congregation to attend the Choral Eucharist at St. Stephen's, Lewisham, a mile or so away, where Bishop Jenner, former Bishop of Dunedin in New Zealand, was to pontificate. This led to a most amusing situation. A violent account appeared in *The Rock* which described with horror the advanced type of service at St. Stephen's. It began with a description of the altar as 'a most gorgeous affair with flowers and a large brass cross and in the wall behind a gaudily-coloured carved representation of the Last Supper' (a biblical enough scene one would have thought). 'A long procession of choristers in purple cassocks and short white surplices filed out of the vestry followed by the cross bearer, then a mace bearer (*do they mean this?*), then the Bishop's pastoral staff followed by three clergy in eucharistic vestments . . . before reading the Lessons (*sic*) the curate made the sign of the cross on the book and crossed himself. The *Agnus Dei* was sung. After all had communicated the priest rubbed the paten with his finger to collect every crumb of bread. Then came elaborate rinsings of the chalice, the celebrant turning it round and round so as to get every drop, and within a few feet of the inhibitor of Mr. Tooth. . . . *The Bishop of Rochester,* who certainly looked very effective when he took his crozier in one hand, and with the other gave his benediction with first two fingers raised making the sign of the cross in the air. . . . But to crown all at the end of the list of the sick to be prayed for, came in a loud voice the following words: "And for the Reverend Arthur Tooth, now in prison for conscience sake and for the congregation committed to his charge" . . . ' As there was to be a confirmation in the afternoon the writer, 'A Lover of Consistency,' wanted to know 'whether this is the kind of thing the candidates are going to be confirmed in.' Yes, it was.

On reading this, one of the evangelical clergy was moved to write to *The Times* who gave it the headline QUIS CUSTODIET? It was printed in full outside the correspondence page with the comment, 'In our own account of these ceremonies at St. Stephen's Church, Lewisham, it was stated that the Bishop of Dunedin, New Zealand, in his full bishop's robes, brought up the rear of the procession. For Bishop of Dunedin, should be read Dr. Jenner, former Bishop of Dunedin.' Dr. Jenner was a member of the Society of the Holy Cross, and the friend and supporter of Tooth and Mackonochie.

Press comment barely diminished during the following week and comments, often in the form of weak puns, continued. 'Your riddle upon Mr. Tooth is the Tooth-ousandeth joke we have received upon the same subject'; and 'The Church of St. James has been shut up. So has the incumbent. Serve him right till he consents by shutting his mouth, to open his prison.' Another reporter wrote,

> The sympathy of the English Church Union with Mr. Tooth may be heightened by a feeling, peculiar to Englishmen, of admiration for an offender who shows himself game. Undoubtedly the contemner of the Court of Arches is game to the backbone: but the game is too High.

Local opinions varied. 'The reverend gentleman is merely a wrong-headed and strong-headed person who appears to have a morbid taste for notoriety. . . . He is no prisoner for conscience sake. He has broken the law. He is a mischievous man. He has sown dissension . . . ' And 'The Reverend Mr. Tooth remains as incalcitrant as ever in the jail as he did in the vicarage.' The sympathizing *Camberwell and Peckham Times* concentrated on the good work of the Orphanage and asked 'Is it to be broken up because the founder is in prison?' and went on to describe Tooth as 'our good friend.'

All over England meetings were organized by the Church of England Working Men's Society and the English Church Union with resolutions by the hundred. Tooth himself had replied to his parishioners with an appreciation of their loyalty: 'There is no unhappy remembrance to cloud the time spent together: I have no longer an opportunity for the exercise of my office, and our church is closed against you, but you once more rally round me with words of kindness and hope.' The Hatcham Defence Fund was satisfactorily swelled, as was the appeal for the Orphanage. Small and large contributions poured in from far and wide.

The church was closed again on February 4th with a strong contingent of police again at hand from midnight. A large number of curious visitors paraded up and down, but except for an argument between two opponents about the Book of Common Prayer, all was quiet. The old congregation divided itself between various churches; three hundred went by train to St. Peter's, London Docks, led by the churchwardens, Croom and Plimpton.

The Bishop of Rochester had been inundated with letters, to many of which he replied non-committally, as in this to 'A Working Man': 'My Good Friend, I have a great respect for those who work for their daily bread, but I think it would be well if you, whose time is so much occupied with other things, would trust a little more to the wisdom and true faith of the Bishops of the Church of Christ. To My own Master I stand or fall, and to him I commit my conduct, my whole soul and all my doings. With me it is a very small thing that I am judged of you or of men's judgement.' The last sentence expressed precisely the same attitude as that of the ritualists, including the incarcerated Tooth. But obviously some action had to be taken by someone. A local reporter wrote: 'as to that good man's flock, his Lordship may rely on it that a great scandal is created, and one of which most people feel he is bound to remove.'

XI

THE ARM OF THE LAW AGAIN

DURING the week that followed February 4th, Sexagesima Sunday, Chambres resigned. It was always believed that on hearing the scheme plotted for the next Sunday (Quinquagesima), he would not concur with it. It was also widely rumoured that a priest as curate-in-charge was only found with difficulty and that many including a Mr. Peake refused to take the post. This produced the couplet:

> What lofty Peake looked down on with disdain
> Low lying Dale was but too glad to gain.

Benjamin Dale was a high churchman of the old Tractarian school, an elderly man with a good record of parochial experience. He accepted the charge of the parish and immediately served notices on the churchwardens and Tooth for the keys of the church. He was politely refused in the usual way. At midnight on Friday and unobserved, he brought locksmiths to pick the lock; but they were not successful. On Saturday morning, much earlier than usual, the police took charge and kept sightseers away. Just before five o'clock in the afternoon this Bishop's deputy apparitor arrived with the foreman and two locksmiths from the safemakers, Messrs. Chubb; they were accompanied by Inspector Rolfe, presumably to give the process respectability.

Chubb's men set to work with a will on the vestry door, so that the noise aroused the local inhabitants on each side of the church. As it was pitch dark, nothing could be seen, but Mr. Plimpton, next door, soon realized that something was afoot. He could hear the resounding attacks from hammers on six iron wedges which were driven into sockets cut into the solid stone. By this time a substantial crowd was following the proceedings, with feelings that varied from the jubilation of Mr. Dale to the dismay of Plimpton. Eventually the masonry gave way, but when the door crashed open there was a new obstacle in the shape of a solid iron chain which could only have been removed by being hacked in two. There was an easier way to dispose of it, and one of the workmen grabbed a skinny little boy out of the crowd and, explaining what he had to do, edged him through the narrow opening. In a second the boy slipped the chain and the church was open. Plimpton stepped forward and demanded to know by what authority this had been done; he was courteously but firmly refused admission. He left and consulted Layman, who advised him to return and take down the names and addresses of those responsible, including that of the Inspector, hoping to charge them in court. The police remained on duty all night (February 10th) and the St. James's churchwardens retaliated by refusing them the use of the school as headquarters. Instead the old station on the north road was taken over, though it was not so conveniently situated. Notices for the next day were posted, giving the times of services as 10.30 a.m. and 3 p.m.

Meanwhile, inside the church as many offending ornaments as could be were removed by Dale; the large gilt candlesticks flanking the altar, the flower vases, the chalice veil. The lace super frontal and frontals were replaced by a 'common green baize cloth.' The banners were taken into the vestry, even the small pulpit hanging was removed. A cross and two candles were left on the altar with the consequent display of 'the fine slab of Parian marble,' usually concealed, and completely noncommittal so far as ritualistic practices were concerned. Dale also removed the six figures of angels, stripped the side altar, and locked and boarded up the organ.

The next day (February 11th) Mr. Dale took Mattins in surplice, scarf and hood. He also read 'that portion of the service announcing a celebration, the prayer for the Church Militant and collect.' So it looks as though there was no celebration, although another newspaper spoke of 'after the Communion Service.' He read the statutory declaration prescribed by law and asked Croom and Plimpton as churchwardens to sign this, which they courteously refused to do, making the excuse that they had not heard it all. Two others from the Protestant League Committee, of which there was present a large representative contingent, obliged. There was some scuffling and shoving after the service both inside the church and out, mostly from over enthusiastic sightseers. When Dale announced the services for the week following, prayers on Wednesdays and Fridays and a celebration following Morning Prayer alternately with one at half-past eight on Sundays, someone audibly thanked God. Locally, it was reported as follows:

> Sunday morning. At church again 9.30. Doors open at 10.15 and the sound of the church-going bell is heard. We enter. Dust on seats. Police evidently in search of spiritual instruction. Glad to note it. At 10.30 two clergymen come in, Mr. Dale and Mr. Craig, and the service is gabbled over helter skelter. No organ. No hymns. Altar stripped of everything but the Cross and two candles. A dingy bit of green bunting stuck anyhow over the holy table. All the altar frontals removed, but not by the Bishop who, at Danbury, uses the colours and burns lights on his altar in his

private chapel. Annoyance of a Protestant Clique because Mr. Dale will persist in kneeling in front of the altar. A gentleman gets up during the service and goes and has a good stare at him. Sermon tolerably erudite and singularly avoidant of annoyance to anybody. Curate reads himself in. People smile. Churchwardens asked by him to sign as usual. Churchwardens blandly say 'ta ta, no thank you.' Service over, row begins outside. . . . Uproar. Lots of 'you're another' and 'So are you.' Edifying spectacle just outside the house of God. Inspector Rolfe, at the head of 100 men, 'Now then, gentlemen, I've my orders. Please move on.' Tableaux. Curtains down. Red fire and soft violin music.

The news of Dale's intrusion was conveyed to Tooth in a letter by his curate, Browne, as visitors were not allowed on Sunday, and we can imagine his feelings. It was fairly certain he thought he would never regain possession of his church. Perhaps years later he ruefully contemplated the keys once so carefully protected, and now so useless as many were quick to explain.

Mr. Tooth keeps the keys of his church but they are now only curiosities. . . . These keys should now be sent to the Tower to be put with thumb screws and headman's blocks, as curious historical relics. . . .

It is not difficult to follow the sub-conscious train of thought.

The afternoon service was orderly and the church was cleared speedily. Police remained on duty all night until Chubb's men arrived the next day to change all the locks and restore the damaged door. The old keys were useless.

Societies were holding meetings all over the country and a Sustenation Fund was set up for those who suffer for 'conscience sake.' Costs in such proceedings could be crippling and the Church Association's resources were limitless as far as one can tell. If anything, sympathy for Tooth was increasing, and public indignation escalating. It reached a grand climax the following Friday when the Church of England's Working Men's Society held a 'triumphal' meeting of over two thousand, with an overflow of nearly the same number, at the Cannon Street Hotel. They had held dozens of meetings in the past weeks and this was the final one and it impressed many people, not least the civil authorities. Colonel Fraser reported to the Home Office that 'it would be advisable to release Mr. Tooth to avoid serious consequences' and plaintiffs in the suit were told this. Mr. Hudson, however, had declined to make an application for Tooth's release.

Nevertheless on Saturday, February 17th, Lord Penzance sat at 10 a.m. not at Lambeth Palace as was customary, but in his room in the House of Commons, to hear an application for the release of Tooth on behalf of the three aggrieved parishioners, and notwithstanding Mr. Hudson's previous unqualified refusal. Lord Penzance now granted his application to set Tooth free from prison. There must be some justification for the view that the Church of England Working Men's Society influenced authority since on the previous Tuesday Hudson denied that he and his fellow prosecutors were anxious to have Tooth released. Yet in three days they had altered their view.

Charles Powell conveyed the news to Tooth in Horsemonger Gaol and then to his close friend, Thomas Layman, who set out for the prison. Tooth and Layman hastily left the gaol but immediately returned so that Tooth, having ceased to be a prisoner, could call on the Governor whose kindness he had much appreciated. Arrangements were made for packing up his books and other belongings. Two hours later, a white muffler round his neck, he went to Layman's home, first calling on Charles Powell. It looks as though he too believed that the influence of the Church of England Working Men's Society had had some effect. After that he met a few of the congregation at Baldwin's Gardens where they discussed future action. Tooth was more debilitated than any one realized, in spite of his spirits. However, he paid a fleeting visit to the Orphanage, always a first concern; probably he went there after dark as the sightseers lining St. James's Avenue were disappointed at his non-arrival and had drifted away. He then made his way to Brighton to his brother's for some fresh air and rest. The inhibition was still in force, and costs of over £300, which rumour incorrectly estimated at about £1,000, had to be paid. Fortunately, money was the least of Tooth's problems, and up to a point this gave him a measure of security and independence denied to many of his brother priests. There was no way of obtaining possession of the church now other than by a stronger display of brute force, and evidently he dismissed this. The effective ministry of Arthur Tooth at Hatcham was at an end, and in that sense Lord Penzance had won the day.

XII

LENT 1877 AT ST. JAMES'S, HATCHAM

BENJAMIN DALE did not make the mistake of Richard Chambres. He took rooms at 366 New Cross Road and settled in as the authorized priest-in-charge. He stayed three months, and they were not happy ones. Perhaps at the distance of nearly a century it is possible to take an objective look at his brief ministry and the painful local situation.

Dale was an old-fashioned high churchman of the 1840s. But by the 1870s only Pusey, among leading figures, and a few early Tractarian followers remained as a link with the days of the Assize sermon. To Dale 'high' doctrine could well find expression without ritual which was to him unimportant; and he respected and valued the Establishment with the traditionalists. Dale hoped to revert to the 'high and dry' tradition of the Granville days. He intended to do his best for both parties, for he was of the compromising temperament. The result was that he pleased no one. He could conceivably have been successful had Tooth not been committed to prison, but this induced tremendous emotional overtones of loyalty to their vicar from the Catholics, and intense aggressive resistance from the Protestants. He entirely misunderstood the position of two violently opposed factions, neither of which would deviate one inch. On one occasion when he extended his fingers for the blessing a Protestant said audibly 'This will not do.' *The Non-Conformist* advised its now jubilant friends to be extremely careful. The Hatcham Defence Committee met and only allowed the Press to report the main resolutions in the following terms. They affirmed their loyalty to Tooth as the only priest lawfully authorized to minister in the parish. Secondly they absolutely refused to recognize the Reverend Benjamin Dale as curate-in-charge and resolved to withhold from him all support, moral, personal and financial. They protested against the breaking open of the church. They also decided to open a St. James's House for the purpose of societies such as the Confraternity of the Blessed Sacrament, the E.C.U., and the Guild of All Souls, and so to keep the congregation together; they consulted Tooth about this. The other resolutions they sent to the Bishop of Rochester. The rest of the meeting was private and concerned the plans made for the next Sunday; some of them now seem rather puerile and unwise to say the least.

The next Sunday was February 18th and the first in Lent. Both

F

sides by this time had managed to marshal their forces. The Protestant Working Men's League had been distributing handbills urging parishioners to 'support them in thanking God for the reopening of the church and praying that the minister would 'conduct the services with the Protestant simplicity which their fathers have worshipped in since the glorious Reformation.' The adjective 'glorious' was invariably applied to the Reformation although the users were extremely hazy about the historical facts and even ignorant of the other side of the story. In the same way the confessional was always 'vile' and the Mass 'blasphemous and idolatrous.'

By the Sunday, therefore, both parties were ready for a tussle. The members of the old congregation were determined to assert their right to worship as they were accustomed to; their opponents were equally determined to insist on worship as they considered it ought to be conducted in a Protestant church as by law established. It was probably this determination that led to an overt clash at Morning Prayer, which took place at eleven o'clock, the first service of the day. As he entered the church Dale noticed that the prayer desk which stood outside the chancel screen facing the east end ready for the Litany had been reversed so that it faced westwards towards the congregation, a Protestant direction. He unobtrusively but obviously replaced it in its original position, to the discomfort of the Protestants. About four hundred of the 'old' congregation sat in the front led by Browne, to seven hundred of the others. The Catholics largely ignored the service and showed this by their actions; so that when Mr. Dale knelt and his congregation squatted, noted the *Church Times*, Mr. Tooth's congregation stood up. When Mr. Dale's congregation stood up, the others knelt down. 'We think this course was very undignified,' concluded the reporter (and so it was); and it produced a further divisive effect among the parishioners, not all of whom supported this action. Mattins concluded with the singing of the *Old Hundredth*, and the old congregation poured out of the church while the Protestants remained behind. The service of Holy Communion followed, and Dale preached from the text in Psalm 29, 'The Lord remaineth a King for ever.'

No one believed him when he said that opening the doors of the church had opened the doors of Horsemonger Lane Gaol. (The *Church Times* pointed this out.) Dale claimed that he was Arthur Tooth's best friend, and asked members of other congregations to stay away. 'I want the parishioners of this parish to fill the church,' he said. After mentioning the incident of the prayer desk and calling it 'petty,' he castigated the 'ritualists,' who had now left, for gratifying their pique by their unco-operative actions. After this there was a collection, and the service proceeded, but it does not seem to have been followed with much attention. 'About thirty Protestants surrounded the chancel screen and two policemen were summoned to prevent them from entering the sanctuary. Even at the consecration and communion they continued to stand and stare without any sign of devotion.' About a dozen out of the large congregation communicated and, concluded the *Church Times* reporter, 'Mr. Dale no doubt gave a sigh of relief when the service was over and well he might, for he had brought things to a pretty pass. If he thinks that this Hatcham case is all over he is greatly mistaken . . .' Poor Mr. Dale's moderation in every word and action only brought odium from both quarters.

Things went from bad to worse, the situation now having been exacerbated by the conduct of both opponents and their followers. The next Sunday (February 25th), the congregation carried their own devotional books which they intended using ostentatiously instead of following Morning Prayer. The Protestant League had mustered in force, having planned to prevent the ritualists from leaving the church after the Litany and before the communion. There were many fewer of the old congregation present, and when Croom and Plimpton led them from the front seats towards the west door the others barred the way. One side shoved, the other resisted; words and blows followed and as some pushed their way, Croom was thrown through the door and down the steps while behind him the door was shut and locked. Plimpton was forcibly detained inside, with the other half of the contingent outside. Rather pluckily, Croom gathered himself together and made for the door, hammering on it hard with the end of a walking stick and drowning the words of the Epistle. The door was opened and he made his way in, explaining sharply that he had a right as churchwarden to enter and safeguard the fabric which he believed to be in danger. The angry words of reply were clearly audible over the church and Dale stopped until order was restored. But it was impossible to continue with the noise of people standing on chairs and shouting out. Dale then mounted the pulpit for the sermon, roundly expostulating at the unseemly disturbance. He announced that the evening service was cancelled although he held one in its place at three o'clock. The morning service then concluded; there were only seven communicants. As the congregation dispersed, two men had a fierce fight in the road outside and there were threats of summons being taken out the following day. Opinion con-

demned both sides, and Croom wrote up his version of the affair
for *The Standard*.

The Hatcham Defence Committee appealed to Tooth. What were
they to do? Tooth replied and the correspondence was published.
He said he understood that the services meant nothing to his
congregation. He rode brutally over Mr. Dale's 'high' observance of
red letter days and coloured offertory bags; he discounted these
since Dale came as an intruder. He reminded them of his declaration on Advent Sunday not to accept schismatical ministrations.
He also explained that he had to continue to stay away as his
health was extremely poor and he could not ignore the doctor's
instructions. He now asked his congregation to abstain from attending St. James's until he took charge of it again, which he promised
them would be at the earliest possible moment.

It was advice that brought death to the type of churchmanship
Tooth had introduced at Hatcham. So much dissension again
divided and diminished the Tooth adherents, and some of the congregation did not come any more. The correspondence columns of
The Standard show how high feelings ran. It was conceded by the
Press that on the whole the ritualists behaved with 'exemplary
moderation.' One writer said he left the church 'by no means impressed with the good sense, sincerity or tolerant spirit of the
Protestant party. What does Protestantism mean but liberty of conscience and liberty of worship?' So the Protestant side was splitting
too.

When Arthur Tooth's letter was made public, comment poured
in from far and wide and rumours mounted, especially as the news
of the opening of Saint James's House in Lewisham High Road
was now public. One letter in *The Church Review* advocated the
use of an 'iron church' or an 'upper room' or 'a ministry in the
catacombs or the formation of a new communion.' But this would
only have initiated a schism, as would the use of an altar in the
National Schools. The Defence Committee, after due consideration,
decided in view of their vicar's wishes to take the whole congregation by train to the most accessible ritualist church, St. Peter's,
London Docks, being the most suitable. Ideas on disestablishment
and the abolition of the *congé d'élire* were freely aired by the
Liberation Society and the English Church Union. Meetings were
taking place all over the country to discuss the consequences of
Tooth's imprisonment and inhibition and the seizure and possession of the church by the 'curate-in-charge.' Other legal cases
were pending and fuel was added to the flames when it became
known that Captain Lowrie, the Governor of York Castle (the

Gaol), had publicly expressed sympathy with Tooth at an E.C.U.
meeting. This statement was treated as 'insubordination, if not
treason,' by the visiting justices. They made it clear that they feared
lest any future clerical misdemeanant under the same Act committed to York Castle under Captain Lowrie with his 'enthusiastic
religion' might receive preferential treatment, and suggested that
any chaplain he recommended would be suspect as a crypto-
ritualist. When three army chaplains supported Canon Gregory's
lectures on the Prayer Book, *The Rock* said they ought to be
cashiered.

The result of Tooth's appeal to his congregation was that only
fourteen or fifteen of the old congregation attended St. James's on
the next Sunday, Lent III, and there were no incidents. There were
only three communicants at 8 a.m., but the church was 'fairly full'
said one reporter, for Mattins and the Litany at 11 a.m. There was
no second service of Holy Communion.

Wild stories of ritualist horrors were now being whispered about
and sometimes uttered publicly. This, for instance, was what
Robert Fleming, the churchwarden of St. George's, Hanover
Square, and a hotel keeper, heard in Clarges Street; he repeated it
to a Mr. Bannister who again repeated it at a Church Association
lecture at Christ Church, Somers Town. At Mr. Fleming's hotel,
two ladies clothed as nuns came on a visit to their mother who
was aged eighty. On entering the room they at once threw off their
hair jackets, which they were bound to wear, and on leaving after
a few days' visit they ordered every kind of finery to be placed in
their portmanteaux. On being asked what they wanted with things
of that kind at a convent, they replied that they were generally
habited in black, but that they always put on grand dresses when
the *holy fathers come to the convent.* 'This is going on in our midst
and the Church Association is determined that it must stop,' said
Mr. Fleming. Tooth's portrait model was put on view at Madame
Tussaud's along with the late Mr. George Odger, a criminal, 'Uncle
Tom' and the radical General Ignatieff. By this time Tooth was
abroad and very ill.

Meanwhile everything was quiet at Hatcham on Passion Sunday. There were only four communicants at the early communion
and for the first time there were no police on duty. The Protestants
had decided to take themselves elsewhere, on the grounds that
Mr. Dale's services were not of a 'truly Protestant character.'
Rather daringly Mr. Dale had managed to produce a small choir,
using the harmonium to accompany them. At the same time Tooth's
three months' inhibition came to an end, although it was to con-

tinue indefinitely if he failed to conform to the ruling of the court. On the eve of Palm Sunday there was a choir practice in St. James's Church for Easter Day, and after the last three choristers had left the police discovered the north door in the baptistry was open. They called Dale and the church was searched, but nothing seemed amiss. The verger said he had tried all the doors before he left with the exception of the baptistry door as that one was never opened. The next morning Dale was horrified to discover that Tooth's paintings on the chancel screen had been hastily daubed out with thick black paint, as had also the board with the roll of members of the Confraternity of the Blessed Sacrament. These panels, depicting scenes from Dante's Inferno, were for some reason a source of much irritation to the Protestant party. Dale always believed he knew the perpetrator, the violent Orangeman in the Protestant League called M'Clure, who probably distributed the handbills in the seats of the church calling for the election of a Protestant churchwarden in place of Croom at the next Easter vestry election. (Dale promptly removed the leaflets and threatened action.) *The Church Review* risked a description of the men involved, three in all, and said they were known as the 'nuisance of the parish.'

Holy Week began, therefore, in a highly charged atmosphere unconducive to spiritual devotion. On Good Friday the Bishop of Rochester put in an unobtrusive appearance. He came without notice, but his apparitor had rather surprisingly sent Fry and Holloway a telegram to tell them of his arrival. As these men were two shining lights in the Church Association one wonders how it was that they were notified rather than the churchwardens, Croom and Plimpton, whose term of office was drawing to an end. Bishop Claughton arrived in good time and had a long interview with Dale. After this he took Morning Prayer without the Litany, and then ante-communion as far as the Prayer for the Church Militant, when he dismissed the congregation 'in the episcopal mode,' the right hand with thumb and two forefingers uplifted. He preached for twenty minutes on the text St. John 17: 4, and began with the collect for Easter Eve, though no one could understand why. The congregation was scanty and all were new-comers who 'squatted' throughout the service.

A 'high church observer' sent an account to *The Greenwich and Deptford Chronicle*, remarking on the ironical inclusion of the offertory sentence 'What a man sows that shall he reap.' He also noted that the Bishop 'indulged in a fancy ritual of his own.' None of the three aggrieved Protestant parishioners, Hudson, Gunston and Gardner, was present, nor had they been inside the church since Dale's arrival. Fry and Holloway were much in evidence. Holloway, especially, made himself extremely officious, preceding the Bishop round the church and pointing out the confessional, the crucifix on the rood beam, which he said must come down before the people would come to church, and the desecrated altar in the lady chapel.

Then, with a great flourish, he declaimed in clear tones heard by every one, 'Finally my Lord, the triptych of the Confraternity of the Blessed Sacrament.' The Bishop peered at the blank, black painted panel, but it revealed nothing. As to the screen whose scenes were similarly obliterated, Holloway muttered that it was sad to see and he could not imagine who had done it; an almost certain lie, which he made worse by adding that he thought it had been painted out by order. Dale believed that Fry had connived in the act. The Bishop 'shook hands warmly' with Fry and Holloway on his departure and said, 'God bless you.' He did not attempt to meet any members of the old congregation; nor did he enquire for Croom or Plimpton; nor seem surprised that the churchwardens were not present to meet him. He never made any conciliatory approach to the Tooth supporters. At the end of his visit one of the old congregation evidently spoke to him and explained that Fry and Holloway did not represent them, adding that had the Bishop sought a personal interview with priest and people months ago, much of the trouble could have been avoided. This last statement is doubtful, but all the same it might have been a course worth pursuing. 'The Bishop has not played the man, but has shown himself most lamentably weak, staying away from St. James's when his presence might have conciliated, and then coming at a time when he knew those who cared for St. James's would not be there,' said one of those present. Claughton is not an endearing personality and he is no more than a name to-day. When in a few months he was translated to the new diocese of St. Albans few parishioners lamented his departure. And a member of the St. James's congregation smoothed ruffled breasts with some mild ridicule by posting up the following in St. James's House.

A LAY OF HATCHAM—GOOD FRIDAY, 1877
(With apologies to the Author of *Alice in Wonderland*)
The Prelate and the Protestants
Were walking to and fro,
They wept to see the Altar screen,
Their tears began to flow.
'Tis very sad,' the Prelate said;
'Dear Tooth—I loved him so.

'If I should send another friend
  To stay for half a year,
Do you suppose,' the Prelate said,
  'That Arthur would keep clear?'
'I doubt it,' sighed the Protestant,
  And shed a bitter tear.

'Oh, Benjamin! come talk with me,'
  The Prelate did beseech;
'For you are bold, though meek and mild,
  Of saponaceous speech.
You're just the man, my dearest friend,
  To stand within the breach.'

But Benjamin he looked at him,
  And gently shook his head;
'My time is up next Sunday week,
  And not a tear I'll shed.
Dear Tooth is welcome to return
  To such a nettle-bed!'

The Protestants then coming up
  The Prelate took in tow,
And trotted him all round the church
  Before they'd let him go,
Talking the while both fast and loud
  About their absent foe.

'The time has come,' the Prelate said,
  'To talk of many things,
Of cassocks, and of chasubles,
  Of angels with gilt wings,
And whether lessons should be read,
  From Apocrypha or—Kings.'

The Protestants they turned on him
  With many a baneful frown,
And vowed that every ornament
  In the church must be pulled down,
And that such pious folk as they
  Must be preached to inner gown.

They wouldn't have no Tooth nor Dale
  Nor any of their crews,
No Ritualists, no High Churchman,
  Nor any E.C.U.'s;
They had no great objection to
  Mohammedans or Jews.

'I weep for you,' the Prelate said,
And shook them by the hand.
'God bless you, friends, your pious griefs
I fully understand;
May England's Church be always served
By such a noble band.'

The Prelate sadly turned away,
His mind was not at ease,
For though his conduct had been ruled
The clamorous to please,
He thought perhaps 'twould hardly 'take'
In his diocese.

E.E.C.
St. James's House, Hatcham, S.E.
April 9th, 1877.

The churchwardens arranged for a St. James's celebration on Easter Day at 9 a.m. at St. Peter's, London Docks, the celebrant to be W. H. Browne, the curate whose period of inhibition had ended. Walter Plimpton sent out the notices and distributed eighty tickets on the station for the 8.48 a.m. train. Others swelled the congregation of St. Stephen's, Lewisham, where there were seven hundred communicants, a large number for a new church; those on the north side of the parish went to St. Paul's, Lorrimore Square. It was this policy of dispersion that lost the Catholics the church of St. James.

On Easter Day there was an interruption from the unwearying Church Association at St. Paul's, Lorrimore Square, where some Toothites were present. *The Rock* reporter described it 'as a high celebration with the officiating priests wearing rich vestments with stoles and hats to match. A young priest' (they probably meant the crucifer, spelt cruciger in one account), 'walked in front having a golden image of the Saviour on a large cross and on either side an acolyte with a lighted candle. In this order they walked slowly round the church singing the *Gloria in excelsis.*' This is possible but seems rather improbable.

At St. James's on Easter Day, Dale unbarricaded the organ as he now had an efficient choir. Unfortunately there were present about a dozen members of the Protestant League, to whom singing was distasteful, and they spoke the responses 'in a very loud voice' as the choir sang them with the organ. 'The choir and organ maintained their ground but the confusion was considerable,' said *The*

Daily News reporter. The total number of communicants was twenty-two, which speaks for itself. Two more had made their Easter communion on Holy Saturday but no light is thrown on the ecclesiological principle upon which this action was based. Had sufficient 'Toothites' been present instead of dispersed, the voices of the twelve would have been unnoticed and the ritualists could have established their claim to be the rightful congregation.

XIII

EASTER TO WHITSUN, 1877

THE Easter Vestry meeting for the election of churchwardens was called for noon on Tuesday, April 3rd. Dale was said to have altered the time to 10 a.m. There were comparatively few churches in those days where the election of churchwardens by the ratepayers aroused any interest at all. In parish after parish it was a formality that took place with a handful of people present, usually the old churchwardens and sidesmen. However, since the sharpening of party strife, both sides were sensitive to the importance of the office of churchwarden. It is true that the vicar's nominee was treated as an appointment as it still is sometimes, though only by courtesy, to-day. The other churchwarden could be elected by any parishioner regardless of the voter's religious tenets, or the lack of them. The law simply required him to be a ratepayer. This situation no longer prevails. It was open to the worst possible abuses. The members of the Church Association had canvassed for their own candidate, Fry, by delivering handbills throughout the parish and leaving them on the seats in the church. When Easter Tuesday came excitement mounted beyond reason. Each faction had taken the precaution of summoning the parish overseers and collectors to attend with the rate books, so that only qualified electors could gain admission to the vestry in the north transept. Long before 10 a.m. the cul-de-sac at the end of St. James's was packed with a milling crowd. After a good deal of scuffling and pushing two hundred packed into the vestry. Dale came forward to the table in front and appealed for order, but his words were drowned by the uproar from those who had not been admitted because of their legal disqualification. A great many of these cries came from poor parishioners who were ineligible; they were clamouring for Croom who, himself, was excluded since a reorganization of parish boundaries had put him outside them. Dale said afterwards that had he known of his exclusion, he would have protested as Croom, still churchwarden, had a right to be present.

Order was at length restored and Dale called for the minute book which was in a locked tin box, the key of which was in Plimpton's care. There are various accounts of the next incident. One is that Plimpton refused to open it and that Dale said he would have to resort to force, at which Plimpton gave way. The other is that Plimpton opened one lock but did not possess the key to the other.

When the police appeared it was broken open; apparently the second key had never been in Plimpton's possession. The minutes of the last year's vestry meeting were minimal. It transpired that at 8 o'clock in the morning with six persons present, Croom and Plimpton had been re-elected churchwardens. There was loud laughter but it was not an unusual situation. Nominations then followed. Plimpton, for the ritualists, was greeted with hisses by Fry's supporters. Fry was proposed by Holloway for the Protestants and elected by a large majority of 180 to 20. Mr. Dale then put forward a candidate, Robert Webb, on the nomination of Tooth the vicar. This was generous and even courageous of Dale and he was immediately shouted down. When he said that he would then nominate Webb there was a furious outcry. 'An uproar ensued which lasted a considerable time,' says one report, and there were groans and hisses and insults and cries of 'He's a Papist,' 'Popery' and 'Go to Rome.' Dale seems to have been unperturbed, while the two new churchwardens nominated their own sidesmen, a new procedure. Fry nominated two Protestants, Sanders and Soliague. Holloway, who had nominated Fry as churchwarden, and Soliague, his seconder, were both St. John's, Deptford, worshippers though ratepayers in Hatcham, as were several others present, Werter Smith for one. Webb nominated Plimpton and Layman as his sidesmen; Layman was not a parishioner although a ratepayer and had been a manager of the Schools and a communicant since Granville's day.

The meeting closed after forty minutes, and Dale refused to answer questions from the Protestant party about the time which he had chosen for the meeting. Meanwhile, M'Clure of the Protestant League was outside the church making speeches. He gave a fiery oration, declaring that the battle had only just begun but that with himself at its head the Protestant League was ready to do much more. He managed to inflame his hearers to such an extent that when Plimpton went into his house next to the church with Croom beside him, the crowd hooted and groaned and hissed. A reporter also noted that no one thanked the chairman for his offices, a tribute he deserved, even though it was no more than a formality. It was a formality no one would observe for the next eight years.

After the vestry meeting at Hatcham, which was reported far and wide in the press, sometimes with much exaggeration, letters poured in from the chief participants in the affair. Dale wrote to *The Standard*, a paper hostile to Tooth, saying that those who issued handbills gave the time of the vestry as noon. He and the churchwardens had always given the time as 10 a.m. in the notice on the church door. He added that he knew the person who had altered the time on the notice with a pencil, the person who tore down notices in the church on February 11th without authority (the day when Dale first ministered in the church), and also the man who caused the 'scandalous confusion' on February 25th by 'pushing aside an old gentleman (Croom) in the church,' as well as the unauthorized distributor of handbills in the pews. He said he had not discovered the sacrilegious dauber but believed that the police would bring him to light. He exonerated Plimpton from any lack of co-operation in opening the box containing the church records, as he had only possessed the one key. He apologized to Croom for his exclusion and paid a tribute to his courtesy. Finally, he praised Fry as a broadminded man of Christian charity, common sense and legal information.

Evidently the cap fitted, for M'Clure replied saying he had been consulted by members of the Working Men's Protestant League; he intimated that certain other notices in church should be removed. These were the ones on the pillars asking people to remain seated during any disturbance, and the list of names requesting prayers of the congregation for the departed, inflammatory material to the Protestants.

Fry, the new churchwarden, asked where the 1,200 odd parishioners were who supported Tooth and why they did not attend the vestry, drawing the conclusion that 'the vast bulk of the parishioners are entirely opposed to that party who are endeavouring to assimilate the doctrine and service of the Church of England to the Church of Rome.'

Walter Plimpton replied, saying that after a Bank holiday the day and time was worse than inconvenient and that in any case churchwardens had such limited powers that after all it was hardly worth creating a violent opposition. He drew attention to the presence of Hudson at the vestry meeting, the chief promoter of the suit against Tooth. Hudson had been heard to say that he had no intention of worshipping at St. James's but preferred All Saints', Hatcham Park, which was five times farther away from his house. Plimpton added, 'This man was a voter at the St. James's vestry meeting.'

No one mentioned the real reason for the small band of ritualist voters, which was that there were very few ratepayers among the poor, and very few parishioners among the rich who came from surrounding parishes even as far away as Kensington and Bloomsbury.

Hatcham was still news throughout the length and breadth of the country. When there was a disorderly mob at Camberwell and a row over a faldstool in a church at St. John's, East Dulwich, these scenes were compared with the ones at Hatcham without any qualification, and every one knew what was meant. Meanwhile new rumours flew thick and fast, most of them baseless. Tooth was at Southend (he was in fact at Siena). He was to be received by the Pope (although he received an invitation, he refused).

> Come and call says Pio Nono;
> Tooth replies, 'I thank you, No, No.'

There was another report that he would shortly resign; this Tooth himself denied. The fact was that Benjamin Dale was about to resign. Meanwhile each week the *Church Times* listed a steady flow of contributions to St. Michael's Orphanage and the Hatcham Defence Fund. *The Rock* exacerbated rage with its insinuations against ritualist tendencies and the Church Association increased its prosecutions under Lord Penzance's Act. Mr. Bodington in Wolverhampton, T. P. Dale of St. Vedast's, and old Mr. Rodwell of St. Ethelburga's, Bishopsgate, were all victims; Mackonochie at St. Alban's, Holborn, was well aware that he was not to be left alone for much longer. Both sides were organizing meetings up and down the country to gain support. The Church of England Working Men's Society, with its 150 branches, was campaigning for the repeal of the Public Worship Regulation Act and receiving firm support.

On hearing officially of Benjamin Dale's impending resignation, the Hatcham Defence Committee met and drafted a letter to the Bishop of Rochester who was still in control of the diocese. Sent by Robert Webb it asked the Bishop to allow Tooth to nominate his own curate-in-charge who would represent the four to five thousand communicants of Tooth's last year. This would bring peace, he said. Claughton replied brusquely in the negative. He could only give the same answer that he had given previously to Croom and Plimpton; 'I can give you no other answer than that which I gave to them.' He then rounded on Webb in a completely unjustified attack:

> If it be true that, immediately on your nomination *(as church-warden)*, you named Mr. Plimpton as your sidesman I think you erred in judgment, not as regards that worthy man himself, but because he has been one of the foremost in a fearful warfare which ought to be forgotten. . . . In the interests of peace you ought not to have named him.

He made no mention of Fry, who had organized and schemed and abetted the opposite side, whipped up supporters, provided handbills and subscribed to the Association which paid M'Clure for his minions, 'the roughnecks.' Claughton's every gesture of support was to the one side only, and every act and word of harshness to the other.

Webb wrote an extremely good letter in reply, which suggests that Layman had been consulted. After assuring Claughton of his desire for law and order he continued:

> I understand that your lordship wished that a member of the old congregation should be supported as vicar's warden, even supposing that Mr. Plimpton had been nominated to that position. That being the case, I could not have supposed myself acting contrary to your lordship's wishes in nominating Mr. Plimpton as one of my sidesmen. I have no idea that nominations have taken place in this parish. . . . I had no time but to appoint the first two gentlemen that I could find willing to support me in my office, one of which happened to be Mr. Plimpton. As you say the warfare in which he was engaged ought to be forgotten. I presume there is no occasion to allude to it. Your remark on what you told Messrs. Croom and Plimpton is not quite clear to me. In their case, I understand you asked for the keys of the church before you could accede to their application. As they were unable to produce the keys, you must pardon me if I do not comprehend how such a reply can answer my request and must beg you to explain what I am to understand from that passage in your letter—I can give you no other answer than that which I gave to them. The position I have to occupy is not of my own seeking but having undertaken it I feel I should not be doing my duty if I did not urge upon your lordship the importance of telling me whether you will accede to my application or not. . . .

The Bishop's reply was terse and simple.

> My answer to Messrs. Croom and Plimpton when they asked me to license to the charge of St. James's, Hatcham, one nominated by Mr. Tooth was simply this, that I could appoint no one to that charge who would not obey the law.

To which Webb replied:

> My Lord Bishop,
>
> Am I to understand that you will license a nominee of Mr. Tooth's providing he will obey the law? To put the matter in a practical form, supposing Mr. Tooth mentioned the names

of five or six clergymen, would your lordship select one and license such clergyman as curate of Hatcham providing he gave you an undertaking that he would obey the law?

If you can give me an affirmative reply to this, I will at once communicate with the vicar of Hatcham with the view of getting this arrangement carried out?

But Claughton showed that he had no intention of making any concession at all.

Sir, there are reasons *(which of course he did not state)* why I cannot pledge myself to accede to your proposal.

Webb very courageously continued the correspondence with a last letter on April 26th:

I deeply regret your inability to consider the claims of the really aggrieved parishioners of St. James's, Hatcham, more than one thousand of whom asked your lordship not to sanction the proceedings against Mr. Tooth. Had you the same consideration for them as for the *three* parishioners engaged as the instruments of the persecution (who have not attended the church since Lord Penzance's commands have been obeyed) Catholic Churchmen would not be so strongly convinced as they are that it is the bishops (with some noble exceptions) not the priests of the advanced school of thought in the Church of England, 'who alienate the laity'); and that it is your lordship, not the so-called Church Association, who is responsible for the present distress in this parish.

And Webb sent the correspondence to the Press.

XIV

TOOTH REDIVIVUS

BENJAMIN DALE left the first week in May and there were no regrets. He was an honest and moderate man, who said he was sorry to leave as it unsettled things, but he cut no ice with either faction. In a letter to Archbishop Tait's chaplain dated June 14th, and giving the impression that it is an answer to one from him, he asks what was he to do. It is doubtful whether he ever had the opportunity to give the Primate the unbiassed information he was willing to offer.

Fry, the people's churchwarden, was now moving heaven and earth to obtain the destruction of the confessional and the crucifix on the rood beam. This was not the cross on the screen but the crucifix with stands for the Mater dolorosa and St. John on each side of it, and in front of the screen. On the day after he left, Fry opened the church accompanied by a local carpenter who demolished the altar, or communion table, in the side chapel. The pieces were then carted into the vestry and stacked on top of each other. Since Tooth's departure the altar had been covered over and unused.

On the following day, May 6th, Rogation Sunday, a clergyman from Milton-next-Gravesend officiated, and there was a good sized congregation but only two remained to the Holy Communion which followed Morning Prayer. But with Dale's departure Tooth arrived to take possession again of his church and parish and vicarage, as he had always said that he would. The secret was well kept, for plans had been laid at much longer notice than a few hours. Tooth had been staying in Brighton but on Saturday arrived unseen in Hatcham. The letter which he sent to Webb was dated May 12th but the 'old' congregation had been informed much earlier. It was also the day of the long awaited judgment on the Ridsdale appeal on ornaments at St. Peter's, Folkestone, which were declared illegal, although the eastward position was allowed. This was small comfort to ritualists. Tooth's letter to Robert Webb, the vicar's churchwarden, ran:

> I have returned to London to renew my claim to my position as the lawful and canonically instituted vicar of this parish; secondly to assert that all services which have been conducted here since my removal from my parish have been schismatical;

G

thirdly that the various appointments to the cure of souls which have been forced upon my parishioners, from the nature of the case, must be null and void.

He asked Webb to make it known that he would celebrate the next morning at 8 a.m. and ended:

I wish it to be understood that I reserve it as a matter for my own discretion to say when I shall repeat my ministrations, not elsewhere in my parish but in my own pulpit and at my own altar.

It was always believed that early on Sunday a south aisle window of the church was broken, and Croom's son insinuated inside where he undid the chain and turned the key. Fry lived in St. James's and he was amazed to hear the bell ringing with what one old St. James's member called 'as no Protestant ring.' The *Church Times* described the scene exuberantly. Fry promptly dispatched his maid-servant to find out what was the service and who was the minister. We only know that her news did not soothe him, and he rushed out of the house 'completing his toilet on the way,' somehow having obtained the services of two policemen. As Tooth turned to the congregation for the absolution, he observed them peering through the curtains at the west door, and he paused for the interruption. He watched Fry bound up the nave followed by the two constables; the men in the congregation rose as one and barred the chancel gate, engulfing the three latecomers.

'Mr. Webb, Mr. Webb,' called Fry. To which Webb, his co-churchwarden who was standing beside him replied, perhaps ominously, 'I am here to do my duty, Mr. Fry.'

'I give Mr. Tooth in charge,' shouted Fry, 'take that man into custody.'

'You'll do nothing of the sort,' retorted Webb.

'What! you won't support me?' said Fry incredulously.

'No,' answered Webb, 'and *you* can't do anything without *me*.'

For one churchwarden could not act on his own. Fry, nothing daunted, turned to Tooth, who was impassively and silently facing the congregation, and called out,

'Mr. Tooth, will you speak to me?' But not receiving any answer, he continued, 'Mr. Tooth, you are prohibited from officiating and I, as churchwarden, call upon you to desist.'

But Tooth might have been deaf for all the notice he took, though what puckish elements of satisfaction he nurtured inwardly, no one can guess. Fry and the police then left and Layman asked every one to resume their seats; at which Tooth continued the service by giving the absolution, not perhaps inappropriately.

At the next interruption Fry returned with Sanders but no one stirred, and they ignored the remarks made by Fry and Sanders from the gate of the chancel. On Tooth's return to the vestry Fry and his friend followed, and the ensuing conversation took place.

'I protest against you being here.'

'Yes.'

'You have been inhibited from performing any service in this church.'

'Yes.'

'I protest against your action.'

'Yes.'

Eight or ten men who had followed Fry and Sanders into the vestry showed such impatience that Webb, always temperate and fair, told them Fry had every right to protest even though he, Webb, disagreed with his views.

By now the rest of the congregation was lining up outside, some three hundred in all. Gathering up the vestments Croom accompanied Tooth along the path to the vicarage, while behind them Fry locked the doors and set off for the police station to demand a watch on the church, which was in fact kept night and day for some weeks afterwards. Fry also determined to have his revenge, which he took in the afternoon of the same day by hacking bits off the very solid confessional, until someone intervened and made him stop.

On the following Tuesday evening, leading a party of workmen into the church, he completed the destruction. With the help of ladders, ropes and saws they detached the crucifix from the beam and let it fall to the floor where it was damaged beyond repair. The noise was considerable. Joseph Plimpton heard it, and he also heard them boarding up the windows with the wood from the side altar so that no untoward entrance could happen again; but he was powerless to interfere in the situation. It is just possible that this oak cross is the one at Walsingham, known as the Hatcham Cross. Webb lost no time in obtaining a declaration from Archdeacon Grant that Fry's actions were illegal and that he was liable to prosecution. But Fry was himself a lawyer and behind him were the funds and backing of the Church Association. He had very little to fear. When Webb sent the correspondence to the newspapers, Fry replied that Lord Penzance, in the case of Hudson and others v. Tooth, said *inter alia:*

> A crucifix has been set up on a beam crossing the nave of the

church, and a second communion table has been placed in the south aisle and as no faculty has been obtained for these additions and alterations I must order them to be removed.

Fry then claimed that following the judgement of the Ridsdale appeal he was entitled to remove the crucifix according to clause 14 in the Public Worship Regulation Act: 'that it shall not be necessary to obtain a faculty from the ordinary order lawfully to obtain any monition under this act.' He therefore asserted that his removal of the communion table in the side chapel was also protected and sanctioned. The comment of the *Greenwich and Deptford Chronicle* on the destruction of the crucifix was to the effect that Fry, whatever his feelings, would have done better 'to avoid treating the semblance represented, with contumely,' a sentiment echoed by many moderates.

When Webb cited Fry in the Chancellor's Court, Dr. Robertson (the Chancellor) refused to issue an injunction. He claimed, however, that it was solely on the score of age and infirmity and the lack of a court and not any other grounds. They learnt later from the lips of Tait himself that they could have compelled the Chancellor to hear the act by issuing a *mandamus*. The suit was eventually consigned to Lord Penzance's court and subsequently condemned, a not unexpected result. In any case the cross was now shattered and useless.

XV

SUMMER AT HATCHAM

ARCHBISHOP TAIT was now in charge of the diocese of Rochester until the appointment of the next Bishop. At Hatcham on Whit Sunday when a Mr. Soden of Homerton officiated and there were less than a dozen communicants. Soden was followed by Mr. Gardiner, a curate of St. Pancras Parish Church, Euston Road, whose vicar was Antony Thorold. He wrote to the Archbishop's chaplain, as though in response to an enquiry, to say that the services at St. James's were tolerably well attended, 350–400 in the morning and fewer in the evening, equal men and women, adding that there was none of the upper class present. These numbers were poor compared with the days of Tooth, but that it was a middle to lower class congregation showed that all were parishioners. Gardiner added that there was no unseemly conduct except that a few persons strolled into church during the service. He stressed the anxiety and care of the churchwardens for his welfare. Webb had described to him how some person or persons had removed the cross and candlesticks from the ledge behind the Table and taken down the side curtains which had been thrown carelessly behind it. Fry had apparently expressed indignation that this should have been done, but though he may not have been implicated he almost certainly knew the offender. These ornaments were rediscovered in the time of Walker. Gardiner ended by saying that the activities of the Protestant League are 'quite distasteful' to the representatives of the parishioners. He described the confessional box as 'grievous to see for it has been mutilated by having pieces broken off and otherwise damaged.' Archbishop Tait's interest was stimulated by a request from both parties for a hearing. He had also received letters from individual members of the congregation. One came from Miss Jane Vaughan, an old inhabitant living at 20 St. James, who had attended the church from the day of its consecration and was responsible for much visiting. She made a long and impassioned appeal to the Archbishop to see her point of view. In an angular and educated hand, she wrote:

Those who waited on your Grace have never attended the services in the church or entered the doors before the prosecution when they came to act as spies and scoff. They have never given a farthing for the support of the church and parochial charities and the drop in communicants.

Next door to Fry a Miss Augusta Duncan wrote to the Arch-bishop also asking for an interview. If she was one of the Protes-tant supporters of Fry one would suppose that she would have been content to leave it to him, so it is not unreasonable to place Miss Duncan along with Miss Vaughan as old members of the original pre-Tooth era who had accepted his changes with acclamation and profited by them.

It does not seem to have occurred to Tait that this was the moment to call a round table conference, as Walker later did. He did, however, consent to receive both sides. The Protestants went first and asked for the following points to be considered: the sequestration of the living of St. James so that a curate could be paid: the appointment of a curate: the management of the parish schools which were in the hands of an all-ritualist committee; and finally a faculty to remove certain articles, one of these was the confessional. The Archbishop said that as future guardian of the diocese he would give these matters the most careful attention. The ornate confessional was a particularly irritating reminder of a doc-trine abhorred and detested by the Protestants who constantly denounced it as 'vile,' and commented on the dangers from the practice of confession which beset 'wives, daughters and servants.'

The confessional was rather like a sentry box with a prayer desk on each side. It is plain that the doctrine and practice of confession were understood at St. James's by 1874. It was an exhibitionist action on the part of Tooth to import this style into an English suburban church when all that was necessary was a kneeling desk and a seat for the priest, though penitents are often grateful for curtains as a screen. Tractarians who struggled to revive the prac-tice of sacramental confession suffered many embarrassments in doing so. According to their own witness they were absolved in the most inconvenient places, such as vestries and private studies. Tooth therefore, having no pattern to guide his taste other than in churches abroad, may have purchased and imported this solid contraption to give to penitents the privacy which on the whole the Church of England has always denied her followers, some of whom cherish anonymity. The subject of sacramental confession was to become even more prominent a week later when Lord Redesdale made his disclosures in Parliament about the book, *The Priest in Absolution.*

The second deputation was led by the ritualists headed by Robert Webb, the churchwarden nominated by Tooth. Webb brought with him a memorial in favour of Tooth signed by 1,200 parishioners; the signatures of women and children, said Fry patronizingly. The deputation included Layman, and Hill of the E.C.U., and Joseph Plimpton. The points they made concerned Fry's destruction of the second altar and the crucifix, an unauthorized action committed during a period when Benjamin Dale was temporarily in charge of the church. Dale, evidently, had given Fry the church keys, and in a letter to the Archbishop said, 'Fry took the meanest advantage of the trust I reposed in him.' But his letter produced no reaction from Tait. Their second point was that Fry and his friends did not support the parish schools and that they were being managed by an independent committee and would not benefit by any change. Thirdly, and this was the heart of the matter, they prayed the Archbishop to license a curate nominated by Tooth, and to secure the services of a priest to minister to the large number who supported Tooth, and who could not conscientiously accept other ministrations.

They pointed out that Holloway, who had been one of Fry's deputation, was the churchwarden of St. John's, Deptford, and 'is not nor has ever been an attendant' at St. James's: that Hudson, the principal promoter of the suit against Tooth, did not attend the services and was churchwarden of All Saints', Hatcham, and that Gunston and Gardner, the other two plaintiffs, were not parishioners at that time. They also made the point that none of the Protestant delegation subscribed either to the funds of the schools or any of the parochial charities.

Tait replied that he could consider the question of the curacy. He offered no solution except the suggestion of a *mandamus* to compel the Chancellor to hear a case against Fry. In spite of the Archbishop's avowal to consider these points the deputation felt that it was not a satisfactory interview from their point of view. They called together the Defence Committee for the following week at which the members were highly appreciative of Webb's delegation, but apprehensive about the removal of the chancel screen. They still hoped to succeed with their suit against Fry, and they wondered whether they ought not to remove the confessional to prevent its destruction, removal or damage by others. The news that Tooth had received sympathetic messages from churchmen as far away as America and Australia was received with great gratification; one came from Dr. J. H. Hopkins, the son of the Presiding Bishop of the Episcopal Church in America.

After the first meeting with the Protestant delegation, Tait dispatched a letter to Tooth by the hand of one of his chaplains, either his son, Crauford, or Randall Davidson, summoning him to Lambeth for an interview. Tooth attended the following day. It is tempting to try to reconstruct this meeting, the only one that took place between these two dissimilar characters. Where did Tait receive Tooth? How did he greet him? And how was he dismissed? Tait drew Tooth's attention to the Convocation Resolutions of 1867 which conclude with the words 'that no alterations from the long-sanctioned and usual ritual ought to be made in our churches until the sanction of the Bishop of the diocese has been obtained thereto.' This was interpreted at the time as applying to *further* alterations; and not to those covered by the Ornaments Rubric. Tooth evidently demurred that the authority of the Archbishop's court could be reversed by the Judicial Committee of the Privy Council, a secular court he refused to recognize in matters ecclesiastical. He also refused to recognize the Resolutions of Convocation, claiming that they were only expressions of opinion since they had not received, and in fact could not receive, the Royal Assent, since it was prohibited by a statute of Henry VIII. He differentiated between the assent of Parliament and the assent of the Sovereign.

Tait for his part could not give chapter and verse for the utterances which he claimed as 'the living voice of the Church.' The conversation must have been further complicated by references to decisions in the Archbishop's court, such as that on the legality of eucharistic vestments which had been reversed by the Judicial Committee of the Privy Council. Tooth himself claimed to be loyal to the synodical Acts of Convocation as declared in 1661 to which he had subscribed at his ordination. A long correspondence followed but was not yet made public.

Activity among the two sets of opponents intensified from now on, and a series of enthusiastic meetings followed. The first was held by the Men's Protestant League on the Friday after Tooth's return in the road outside the church, a favourite rendezvous; and the ritualists attended in full force. The Orangeman, M'Clure, was present but did not take the chair. Proceedings opened with prayers taken by a working man, Mr. Noble. As the Protestant League was supported by a committee of titled supporters and Members of Parliament, it was constantly derided for its unrepresentative character. It was certainly very different from the Church of England Working Men's Society which organized and ran its own affairs without support from the rich or influential. So when Mr. Noble took the prayers the ritualists rather unkindly jeered openly. As the first resolution was proposed condemning Tooth's defiance of the law by his recent 'illegal' entry, a din broke out which developed into a fierce scuffle. The few police were powerless to keep order.

The chairman declared the resolution carried in spite of the fact that no one was given an opportunity to vote against it. The second resolution protested against Webb's conduct, presumably in assenting to Tooth's entry. By this time there was free fighting throughout the whole assembly which drowned M'Clure's voice as he tried to read extracts from the 'impure literature of the ritualists.' Several people were hurt, and the meeting broke up in disorder as fresh reserves of police arrived. On Sunday, however, everything was quiet, as the police were well in evidence. Tooth did not put in an appearance, and the services were taken by Mr. Soden again.

In Folkestone, Ridsdale of St. Peter's, after losing his appeal, preached a long and carefully reasoned documented sermon to his congregation. He regretted apparently ever having appeared in court, and denied that by so doing he had acknowledged its authority in spiritual matters. He then differentiated between certain ritualistic practices which he would abandon; the crucifix and the stations of the cross, because he held no faculty for their use; the *Agnus dei* and the procession. He retained the mixed chalice, two altar lights, wafer bread and vestments. He gave a hint at the end of his sermon of the course he proposed to take: 'Whether our Bishop . . . will give any dispensation from the law of the Church which it would be right to accept, or otherwise meet our conscientious difficulty remains to be seen.' As we know, he asked the Archbishop, who was his diocesan, for a dispensation and abandoned these other practices as well, rather cleverly establishing the principle that such practices were possible, even though disputable and unacceptable, since their non-use could obtain a qualifying exception from ecclesiastical penalties.

The English Church Union, which had enrolled three thousand and five hundred new members during the preceding twelve months, held its annual meeting under the presidency of Charles Lindley Wood. When Tooth entered he was recognized at once and was received with tremendous and loud applause. There was a good deal of ironical amusement at the dispensation granted to Ridsdale, and it was suggested that Tooth might try the same course. Tooth's speech was, however, quiet and even eirenic. A clue to his position lay in his claim that so long as the word 'priest' appeared in the Prayer Book, he would believe it meant a person endowed with sacerdotal power and not a layman commissioned to undertake certain ministerial duties. Charles Lindley Wood made the issues of ritualism clear when he said, 'The pretext for aggression is only a matter of ceremonial. But of what ceremonial? Of ceremonial that touches the very centre of our religious life, the celebration of the Blessed Sacrament. Nothing short of an actual attack on the faith itself could affect us so keenly, for it is neither less nor more than an attempt to deprive the Church of England, by a non-natural interpretation of her rubrics, of those externals of worship which witness to the fact that she is the church that flourished since the days of St. Augustine.' He went on to say that the service of Holy Communion is the old service of the Mass translated into English, as Elizabeth I had once put it to the Spanish Ambassador.

The Church Association also held its annual meeting and disclosed its own position in its printed report. It declared that its first effort was to unite loyal churchmen of all parties in what was a common necessity, since new excesses of ritual were announced yearly, and that protest after protest against these appeared but to no purpose. The Church Association was originated to save the Church! The report then dwelt with satisfaction on the judgements in the Charles Ridsdale, Thomas Pelham Dale and Arthur Tooth prosecutions, and made it clear that the 'consideration of further proceedings in consequence of this breach of the law (*Tooth's ministry on May 13th*) is before the legal advisers of the council.'

Two further occurrences, one local and one national, added fuel to the flames. Some repairs to the gas system in St. James's were necessary. As workmen excavated near the north door and four feet down they discovered two large stone slabs in a 'kind of vault.' These turned out to be the gaudy half-finished tablets which had disappeared since the days of Granville's departure. Indignantly they were temporarily placed each side of the altar until they could be fixed to the walls. Counter-indignation swept through the parish of Hatcham, and it was a difficult situation for the Tooth-ites to explain away at this moment. Mr. Gardiner informed Archbishop Tait that they had been replaced on each side of the main altar. The national occurrence was the translation and publication by the Society of the Holy Cross of the Abbé Gaume's moral treatise *The Priest in Absolution*, compiled by J. C. Chambers. The Abbé Gaume was a saintly man to whom Henry Wilberforce had turned in his hour of need when he left the Church of England. He was a moral theologian of considerable ability as well as an expert spiritual director. He had written this treatise on moral theology; and Chambers, an Anglican priest, translated, adapted and added some advice on certain points of theology, and dealt with some pathological problems. Anglican priests at this time had almost no one in the older generation to guide them on this matter except for a few individual outstanding personalities.

Due to one of those unaccountable accidents following Chambers's death, the remainder of the edition fell into other hands over which the S.S.C. had no control, and Lord Redesdale raised the matter in the House of Lords. Randall Davidson, Tait's chaplain, described Redesdale as an old-fashioned high churchman of the 'high and dry' school. This is not a term a member of the S.S.C. would have used, although they would have agreed that he was not an evangelical of the Church Association type.

Lord Redesdale made a speech and quoted passages in the House of Lords. He was followed by Tait, who said, 'No modest person can read the book without regret and it is a disgrace to the community that such a book should be circulated under the authority of clergymen of the Established Church.' Phrases such as 'the filthy character of the confessional,' 'indecent and abominable book' were used to describe questions which might be put to women and children. No man among the opposition ever conceded that they could possibly be addressed to him for none would admit to a condition of guilt which would need such a ministry; and part of the antagonism to the practice of confession was obviously a rationalization of this position. Under the circumstances the Master of the Society of the Holy Cross, Francis Bagshawe, acted with firmness and dignity, and a representative gathering met the Archbishops of Canterbury and York, and the Bishop of London. They stated that 'all, or nearly all, of our members have found the blessing of confession; and very many of them were constantly applied to by those who desired to share in that blessing. . . . They felt the need of guidance in the ministry to which they believed themselves called.' This was countered by a statement in which the ritualistic confessional was said to have been used for the vilest purposes. The bishops were shaken to learn that the ministry of the late J. C. Chambers as a confessor extended to 'members of both Houses of Parliament, clergy, barristers, merchants, tradesmen and costermongers.' One of the distasteful features of this incident was the method by which a brother of the S.S.C. passed on confidential material from the meetings to the opposite side, so that the opponents of the S.S.C. obtained information obviously not intended for non-members, and made use of it in public.

In the end the Society decided by a fairly narrow majority not to condemn the book, but that no more copies should be supplied. This resolution did not satisfy the Upper House of Convocation when it met in July and in committee to consider the whole subject. The bishops as usual acted together; Bishop Moberly of Salisbury alone spoke in favour of confession, though condemning the book. Finally, the Bishop of London, whose consistently callous attitude to Mackonochie was well known, after noting that the Society had neither repudiated nor withdrawn the 'obnoxious' book, proposed that the House should condemn a practice of confession that rendered such a book expedient. Claughton, now Bishop of St. Albans, supported him. (His speech is interesting because he declared that Tooth had made him pass the most miserable weeks of his whole episcopate; but he said he forgave him.) Claughton ended by saying that when he went to Hatcham and saw 'a confessional box, like that in the Church of Rome as seen abroad, he was awakened to a sense of danger within the Church of England and felt it was time restraint should be placed upon the doctrine.' He was not prepared to concede that the practice had never completely lapsed and was still upheld by Anglican doctrine in the Book of Common Prayer. The practice, though suspect, had spread slowly and steadily among the Catholic party but was not confined to ritualists and advanced churchmen, as we can tell from Liddon's letters. When Manning began to hear the confessions of his friends in the 1840s, Henry and Mary Wilberforce for example, he was far from being an extreme ritualist.

Eventually, after lengthy and prolonged meetings of the Society in synod, some of which Tooth must have attended, the S.S.C. continued with a much diminished membership. The disclosures did, however, divide the Society; the Master resigned and was succeeded by Canon T. T. Carter, the chaplain of St. John the Baptist's Convent, Clewer.

The Bishop of Peterborough, William Magee, wrote to a friend saying:

> You will see that I attack *The Priest in Absolution* not on the ground of its indecency which I have always thought a false issue and more so now that I have carefully studied it, but on the ground of its Roman doctrine of Confession.

Magee was a firmly Protestant Irishman who was eventually translated to York as Archbishop but died shortly after his enthronement. He admitted in the letter to his friend that he feared being praised in *The Rock* or *The Record*, which is an interesting comment from a wholehearted Protestant, and adds: 'Oh how we bishops have need to pray St. Paul's prayer for deliverance from unreasonable men.' At the same time he ends his letter with the words: 'I am rejoiced that you think my letters and my line of attack on the Rits. (*sic*) are sound.'

At the time, however, the debate on *The Priest in Absolution* did harm to the Catholics, and nowhere did it inflame the passions of disapproving Evangelicals more than in Hatcham. There, that very structure so disapproved of by Claughton, was plainly visible to all and a constant reminder of the dreaded horrors of the confessional. 'If Wilkinson of St. Peter's Square (and later Bishop of Truro) is not a Ritualist' spat *The Rock*, 'he sails as near the wind as he can and, far worse, unblushingly advocates the confessional.'

Feeling was further inflamed when Tooth applied to the justices of the Queen's Bench in the Divisional Court of Westminster for the former proceedings against him to be quashed on a technical point; namely that the proceedings were void having been heard at Lambeth Palace instead of in the diocese of Rochester or in London or in Westminster. The justices allowed the application to go forward and granted a rule nisi, which meant that counsel's opinion would be sought. (It was another four months before the final judgement was given.) So the case again became hot news. On the same day the energetic Mr. Fry applied for a faculty to remove various offending articles from St. James's and to replace the stone slabs, a suit which given time would certainly have succeeded. Some members of the Protestant League could not wait, and decided to anticipate the judgement of the Archbishop's court.

On July 15th a policeman, hearing sounds of hammering inside the church, went to the north door where he saw a man looking out, who immediately shut and barred it against the constable. The policeman knocked loudly, whereon the man opened the door and was asked what he was doing. To which he gave the innocent and obviously untruthful reply, 'Nothing.' The confessional had been hacked to pieces, and the man, John Elliott, a builder of North Road, owned to two large chisels and an axe with which he had been attacking the extremely solid box. He was charged by Robert Webb with committing malicious damage.

When the case was heard the next day Tooth was in court. Elliott claimed that the church was open and that he did not break in. If this was so, it could only have been left open with the connivance of Fry. At nine o'clock evidence was given that the entrance was locked and the remaining doors bolted on the inside. At 10 p.m. one of these doors was open. The inference was unavoidable. The penalty for damage exceeding £5 could have been penal servitude. The Protestant League immediately set up a committee to receive donations to defend Elliott, who has been 'unjustly charged with breaking up the confessional. It can be proved that Elliott was justly in the church.' Webb withdrew his proceedings and eventually Elliott was discharged by the jury, the case not having been proved, since the confessional was already 'rickety.'

At this point the correspondence between Archbishop Tait and Tooth was made public.

Lambeth Palace,
June 12th.

Revd. and Dear Sir,

In consequence of the investiture of the late Bishop of Rochester as Bishop of St. Albans, the care of the diocese of Rochester now rests with me till the consecration of Mr. Thorold, the Bishop-designate of Rochester. I shall be glad to have an opportunity of seeing you at your earliest convenience.

My Chaplain, who is the bearer of this letter, will wait to hear at what time I may expect to see you here.

I remain, yours faithfully,

A.C. CANTUAR.

The Revd. Arthur Tooth.

The Vicarage, Hatcham,
June 21st.

My Lord Archbishop,

I have considered your Grace's communication to me at the interview I had the honour to have with you on the 13th inst. I have had search made in the *Chronicle of Convocation* and in other books, and, so far, have not been able to discover that any Canon, Constitution, or Ordinance Provincial, or other Synodical act, of such purport as your Grace was pleased to communicate to me, was made or enacted by the Convocation of the Province of Canterbury on the 13th, 14th and 16th days of February, 1867, which were the days to which I understood your Grace to refer, or indeed at any time that I can discover. Neither can I discover that any such Canon, Constitution, or Ordinance Provincial, or other Synodical act, has ever been promulged either by Convocation or by your Grace. I have therefore to request that your Grace will be good enough to enable me to find official and authoritative evidence of the making, enacting, and promulging of such Canon, Constitution, Ordinance Provincial, or other Synodical Act.

I remain, my Lord Archbishop, your Grace's obedient servant,

ARTHUR TOOTH

Lambeth Palace,
June 22nd.

My Dear Sir,

I beg to acknowledge your letter of yesterday's date. The record of proceedings in the Convocation of the Province of Canterbury to which I referred you at our interview of June 14th (not, I think, 13th) is to be found in the Chronicle of Convocation for the year 1866–7, pages 711 and 842.

The resolution unanimously adopted by the Bishops in the Upper House on Wednesday, February 13th, 1867, concludes with the following words: 'Our judgment is that no alterations from the long-sanctioned and usual ritual ought to be made in our churches until the sanction of the Bishop of the diocese has been obtained thereto.

And in Lower House on Friday, February 15th, 1867, it was resolved, by 47 votes against 3, 'That this House concurs in the judgment of the Upper House that no alteration from the long sanctioned and usual ritual ought to be made in our churches until the sanction of the Bishop of the diocese has been obtained thereto.

Let me recall to your memory what passed between us when I directed your attention to the decision of Convocation. Understanding that you demurred to the obligation of obedience to the Court of the Archbishop and the Supreme Court of Appeal, and gathering also from what had passed that you were not willing to be guided in the matter of ritual by the directions of the Bishop of your diocese, I asked to what authority you were prepared to bow, and having been led by your answer to believe that you consider such authority to reside in Convocation, I referred you to the decision of the two Houses of Convocation of the Province of Canterbury, which I have quoted above. I added that I was informed that a similar decision had been arrived at by both Houses of the Convocation of the Province of York (March 20th, 1867).

In your letter of yesterday's date you write that you 'have not been able to discover that any Canon, Constitution, or Ordinance Provincial, or other Synodical act of such purport was made or enacted on the days to which in our conversation I had referred, or indeed at any time.' Further, you state that you cannot 'discover that any such Canon, Constitution, or Ordinance Provincial or other Synodical act has ever been promulged,' and you ask me for 'official and authoritative evidence of the making, enacting, and promulging of such Canon, Constitution, Ordinance Provincial, or other Synodical act.'

I do not know whether you intend to say that you object to the decision of Convocation to which I have referred you because it has not received the sanction of the civil power.

It is certain that in the Act of Submission of the Clergy (25 Hen. VIII, cap. 19) it is enacted by the authority of Parliament that the clergy 'shall not enact, promulge, or execute any Canons, Constitutions, or Ordinances Provincial in their Convocations unless they have the King's Royal assent and licence to make, promulge, and execute such Canons, Constitutions, and Ordinances Provincial or Synodal.' Therefore, except in cases where the civil power steps in, no decision or judgment of Convocation can answer to such conditions, as might be supposed from your letter to be deemed by you indispensable.

As, however, I was led to understand from our conversation that this very intervention of the civil power caused the difficulty which weighs on your conscience, I am disposed to believe that what you ask for in your letter is not proof that the civil power was a consenting party to the decision or judgment in question, but rather a distinct reference, with dates and pages, to the record of that utterance which I understand, according to your principles, you regard as the living voice of the Church.

Believe me to remain, yours very truly,

A.C. CANTUAR.

Revd. A. Tooth.

The Vicarage,
Hatcham, New Cross.
June 30th.

My Lord Archbishop,

I have to acknowledge the receipt of your Grace's letter of the 22nd inst.

I beg to thank your Grace for the reference to certain proceedings in the Upper and Lower Houses of the Convocation of Canterbury, on the 13th and 15th of February, 1867.

Those proceedings, as I have supposed, and as your Grace points out, do not constitute a Synodical act of the Province of Canterbury. I would however add, for fear of being misunderstood, that your Grace correctly interprets my judgment on this subject, by supposing that had the Synod of the Province passed, and your Grace promulged, or put in ure, any such Synodical act, the fact of the State's refusal to recognize it as a Canon would have made no difference in the respect with which I should have treated it.

Your Grace will also permit me to observe that the resolutions to which you refer, taken in connection with the Report of the Committee of the Lower House of Convocation on the Ornaments Rubric in 1866, the preceding year, and with the subsequent action of the Lower House, involve the position that the Eucharistic Vestments, which are some of the matters on which your Grace addressed me, are ordered to be retained and be in use in the Church of England.

I would also remind your Grace, in reference to your allusion to the Court of Archbishop, that the legality of the Eucharistic vestments was laid down by the Judge of your Grace's Court when the matter came before him, and that any subsequent condemnation of them, either by the last Judge of the Court of Arches or by the Judge sitting under the Public Worship Regulation Act, has been passed in mere obedience to the rulings of the Judicial Committee of the Privy Council.

I am, with much respect, your Grace's obedient servant,

ARTHUR TOOTH

Lambeth Palace.
Monday, July 2nd.

My Dear Sir,

Late on Saturday evening, the 30th of June, I received your letter of that day, in answer to mine of the 22nd.

I had been led to hope that you were willing, in the matter of ritual, to conform your practice to what both the Upper and Lower Houses of Convocation of the Province of Canterbury formerly denominate their 'judgment,' passed on the 13th and 15th of February, 1867, and never since reversed.

I gather from the letter I have now received from you that while you do not doubt that this decision of Convocation forbidding alteration from the long-sanctioned and usual ritual of the Church of England without the consent of the Bishop of the diocese was formerly adopted after mature deliberation and published with the records of Convocation you yet feel some conscientious objection to defer to this decision of both Houses of Convocation unless it can be proved to you that it was in the technical sense of the word 'promulged or put in ure.' But thus to 'promulge or put in ure,' unless with the Royal Licence, is, as I have already pointed out to you, the very thing prohibited under penalty by the Act of 25, Hen. VIII, cap. 19. As it is by virtue of the series of statutes of which this is one, that you and I have for years claimed and exercised the rights and privileges which are peculiar to us as beneficed in the Established Church, I can hardly suppose that you think the Convocation of Prelates and clergy ought to have 'promulged and put in ure' their decision without the State's authority, in direct contravention of the statute. Yet it is difficult to understand your present scruples without supposing one of two things—either that you desiderate the sanction of the civil power to give force to the decision of Convocation, or that you think we ought to have broken the law by promulging our judgment, and 'putting it in ure' without such sanction.

I, of course, like most other people, hold that constitutionally the decisions of Convocation require the Royal assent and licence to give them binding force; but in my endeavour to put myself as fairly as possible in your position, and to give full weight to difficulties which had occurred to your kind, I have brought before you this resolution of both Houses of Convocation; and I still hope that when you weigh the matter fully you will come to the

H

conclusion that, according to your principle, it is an utterance to which you ought in consistency to bow.

There cannot surely be any doubt as to the meaning of this resolution of both Houses.

It is clear and explicit in forbidding any change from the usual ritual without the consent of the Bishop of the diocese. With reference, indeed, to what are called Eucharistic Vestments, you correctly point out that the resolution in both Houses may fairly be taken in connection with the Report of the Committee of the Lower House of Convocation, on the subject of Ritual, presented on June 26th, 1866. But you do not mention nor can I find, anything in that report inconsistent with the plain meaning of the resolution adopted by both Houses. Neither, as I understand, do you allege that by any subsequent act of the two Houses the decision then arrived at has been set aside. If you know of any such subsequent resolution or resolutions of the two Houses, I shall be obliged if you will call my attention to them as soon as possible.

In the close of your letter you refer, as I understand, to a judgment pronounced by Sir Robert Phillimore, late Judge of the Arches Court, laying down, as you state, the legality of what are called the Eucharistic Vestments. This judgment as you correctly state was reversed on appeal, and subsequent judgments have conformed to the decision of the Appeal Court. You seem to think that this judgment, which was afterwards thus reversed, has some ecclesiastical force peculiar to itself in the matter of vestments. You object to other subsequent judgments because, as you say, they were passed in mere obedience to the rulings of the Judicial Committee of the Privy Council. It has, I think, escaped your observation that the very judgment to which you seem to attach this peculiar binding force is itself distinctly based by Sir R. Phillimore on the construction which you supposed the words of the statute had received in two previous judgments of the Privy Council (*vide* Sir R. Phillimore's *Ecclesiastical Law*, vol. i, p. 918, quoting his judgment in the Purchas case).

To sum up what I have wished to bring before you, I consider that you are bound to express your readiness to abstain from the ritual observances which have caused so much contention in your parish.

First, because of the obedience which you owe to the law of the Church of England, as interpreted by the Archbishop's Court and the Supreme Court of Appeal.

Secondly, because you are formally called upon by me as your Bishop, in virtue of your oath of Canonical obedience, to conform to the order which as acting Bishop of Rochester I hereby lay upon you.

Thirdly, because, if through some scruple of conscience to me inexplicable you feel a difficulty in paying due obedience either to the law of this Church and Realm as interpreted by the Courts, or the Bishop set over you in the Lord, the decision of Convocation to which I have referred you seems to afford on your principles a solution of the difficulty in which you have involved yourself.

I should be sorry to believe that you desire to act in contravention alike of the law, the Bishop's order and the express decision of the two Houses of Convocation.

I remain, yours very faithfully,

A.C. CANTUAR.

The Vicarage,
Hatcham, New Cross.
July 7th.

My Lord Archbishop,

Your Grace has in some points misinterpreted my last letter.

What I said, in substance, was that I could not gather that the informal resolutions to which your Grace referred me either constituted a Canon, Constitution, or Ordinance Provincial, or other Synodical act, or had been promulged or put in use as such. I did not suggest that such an Ordinance Provincial or Synodical act should have been passed or promulged without the Royal licence or sanction; but I said that if it had been passed or promulged I should have obeyed it, whether it had or had not received such licence or sanction.

Your Grace must excuse me for reminding you that the statute prohibits equally passing without licence and promulging without sanction, any Ordinance Provincial or Synodical act. As, therefore, your Grace speaks of the Convocation of which your Grace was a principal member as bound in duty not to do what the statute prohibits, it is clear that the resolution to which you refer, did not, in the judgment of Convocation, constitute an Ordinance Provincial or Synodical act.

I am therefore in this position. The Church of England by the Synodical acts of her Convocations in 1661 adopted a particular order of ritual which I, at my ordination, pledged myself to obey, and your Grace does not show me, and I cannot discover, any Ordinance Provincial or Synodical act repealing that order of ritual, or dispensing with obedience to it.

I am, my Lord Archbishop, your obedient servant,

ARTHUR TOOTH

Lambeth Palace.
July 9th.

My Dear Sir,

I have to-day received your letter dated July 7th. I have endeavoured in our correspondence to put before you on every ground the solemn obligation which rests upon you to a dutiful submission.

If, against all the authorities I have advanced, you still assert your right to act in your public ministration on your own private interpretation of the law of this church and Realm, it is, I fear, needless for me to reason further with you. I can no longer hope that anything I can say will induce you to act as you ought.

I remain yours very faithfully,

A.C. CANTUAR.

The Revd. Arthur Tooth.

Lambeth Palace.
July 9th.

Revd. and Dear Sir,

I am desired by the Archbishop of Canterbury to forward to you the enclosed answer to your last letter, dated the 7th of July, and to inform you that his Grace considers it due to the Church that the arguments he has used with you should be generally known. His Grace therefore proposes to make public his letters to you, and desires to know whether you are willing that your letters should be published at the same time. His Grace hopes to hear from you on this point before Friday next, the 13th of July.

I remain, Revd. and Dear Sir, yours truly,

RANDALL T. DAVIDSON (Chaplain)

The Revd. Arthur Tooth.

The Vicarage,
Hatcham.
July 12th.

My Lord Archbishop,

I have nothing to recall in the statements I have made in various letters which I have lately had the honour of addressing to your Grace. They involve the question of the constitutional order of this Church and Realm, and may prove of interest to the public. I wish my letters to be published together with those written by your Grace.

Your Grace offers me what is not an act of Convocation, what is not a canonical decision of a Bishop, what is not an act of a Court received by this Church and Realm, and because from the nature of my obligations I am bound by a rule, and I am unable to exercise a choice and accept one of your Grace's alternatives, you think well to reproach me and say I 'still assert my right to act in my public ministrations on my own private interpretation of the law of this Church and Realm.' I must say that I do not care to attempt to defend myself from a charge of wilfulness which cannot be maintained by any authority beyond your Grace's statement.

I am, my Lord Archbishop, your obedient servant,

ARTHUR TOOTH

Kentish Mercury, July 21st, 1877.

This correspondence made every leader writer reach for his pen. *The Times* in a 2,000 word article in the issue in which the letters were published, set the tone and declared:

'Mr. Tooth is as impervious to argument as he has proved to be to persuasion. He has always expressed his willingness to obey what he has termed the living voice of the Church. . . . He still asserts his right to act on his own private interpretation of the law, whether of State or Church. . . . We question a little whether in his arguments with Mr. Tooth the Archbishop has shown his usual cautious wisdom. The letters on both sides are well written and Mr. Tooth gives as well as receives some exceedingly well-directed thrusts. That the Archbishop has the best of it is clear enough . . . his mistake has been in supposing that Mr. Tooth wished to be convinced.'

The Times then made the rather naïve suggestion that the Established Church of England is scarcely the proper place for a man with these singular gifts (that is, of not paying attention to laws he does not acknowledge), and concluded with an overt threat: 'It is Mr. Tooth's own fault if it is to compulsion that the next appeal must be made.'

The Daily Telegraph leader on the same day, July 17th, 1877, attacked Tooth in more personal terms:

'The Primate, we think, does right to enlist the feelings of all rational men on his side by proceeding gently with these wrong-headed persons. They are not intellectually formidable; the majority are gentlemen of rather mediocre attainments and but one or two possess anything like scholarship or literary powers.'

a gross understatement to say the least. It then commented on the incident of the destroyed confessional and rather surprisingly suggested that it might be

'sacrilege to remove or damage such an article even if it had been illegally set up. . . . As to Protestant prejudice against the "box" it seems to us not very shrewdly directed. The system itself is much worse without the mechanism. . . . Where the box is not used the priest hears the tale of sin in a vestry or in his own room, and the Church of Rome knowing much of human nature is aware of possible abuses under such circumstances. . . . The practice if allowed at all demands and requires such mechanical precautions against abuse. As it is now carried on in the Church of England it is open to objections ten times greater than those which attach to it in the Church of Rome, where its priests are trained, and are under strict control. . . . Our confessors are not trained, some of them are lawless like Mr. Tooth; in many cases there is no box, but dangerous interviews in private rooms; and the illegal practice is pursued stealthily against episcopal and parental authority, so that something clandestine taints it from first to last. We have in short the dangerous spectacle of rebellious priests using secret and illicit means to teach their congregations that obedience to the individual clergymen which they themselves refuse to the Church.'

The Daily News concentrated on a manifesto and appeal to the Queen on the Ridsdale decision. The manifesto appealed to the rubric of 1662 authorizing the use of all ornaments which had Parliamentary authority in the second year of the reign of Edward VI. As the alb and the chasuble were among the ornaments their lawfulness was considered to be established. This was Ridsdale's defence, and *The Daily News* leader declared the decision of the Privy Council to be an alteration of the written law of the Church. Forty-one thousand persons signed a petition to this effect and asked that Convocation should deal with matters of ceremonial. And the leader writer goes on to state that the Act of Submission:

prohibits Convocation from promulging without permission *(presumably Parliamentary permission)* a single canon or ordinance. . . . What the petitioners calmly ask, or rather assume to be their right, is a power which no Established Church possesses in these times.

It ended with an indication of Lord Penzance's position as Judge in the Court of Arches:

The petitioners will have no judge at all, that is, they will be their own judge, and this is a pretension which coming from members of the Established Church cannot be listened to.

The Scotsman took an unexpectedly detached point of view, considering its Presbyterian bias. 'Why should not confessing ritualists have a share in the Church, as well as non-confessing evangelicals? The only other alternative is the entire disestablishment of the Church.' It ends its article, 'Mr. Tooth, so far from being cowed by the experience of the past or the prospect of future imprisonment, indicates, by his recent correspondence with the Archbishop in which the latter has by no means the best argument, that he is not likely to abate a jot or tittle for those claims of spiritual independence which we have long ago learned in this part of the island to recognize inconsistent with the legal establishment of religion.' Within months Magee was to exclaim, when Gladstone became Prime Minister, that disestablishment was nearer. All the same, it never came.

The Church Review called the Archbishop's reference to the resolutions of the Canterbury Convocation of 1867 and the words *without the consent of the bishops* 'disingenuous and transparent,' for when the Convocations declared this it was on the assumption that the Ornaments Rubric was unassailable in a legal sense. It also hinted that the proceedings against Tooth might be quashed *ab initio*. The Archbishop's blundering, it added, did not take any one in except *The Times* newspaper.

The Rock published an analysis of ritualist churches from *Guide to the Churches of London and its Suburbs:*

> During the last year an addition of 46 has been made to the total number of churches *(that is having some ceremonial and weekday celebrations)*. Daily service is performed in 228 against 211. There is early, that is fasting, Communion in 440 churches against 393. There is choral celebration, which is really 'high Mass,' in 228 against 194; but as a set off to all this superstition 'evening communion' has advanced from 205 to 219. We are also glad to see that Gregorian tones have largely decreased; there is largely a falling-off in 'voluntary choirs' which seems to say that musical 'Rits' and 'Ritinas' are not so plentiful as they were.
>
> Turning to the millinery department, we greatly regret to find that there are 37 more 'surplices in the pulpit' than in the preceding account, too many by half. On the other hand 'Eucharistic vestments' have decreased by two, which we presume points to Hatcham and St. Vedast.
>
> The Pagan extravagance of 'Floral decorations' and the Romish observance of 'Dedication Festivals' have decidedly advanced, as also has the 'Eastward position' which is likely to become the battle ground of the future, and justly so, as it keeps alive the wholly unscriptural and blasphemous notion of the

'real Presence.' While *that* is maintained there can be neither peace nor blessing for the Church of England.

With this kind of polemic on one side it is not unreasonable to find retaliation from the other. There was the usual crop of meetings, and the Church of England Working Men's Society held its first anniversary with a corporate communion at St. Alban's, Holborn. The Hatcham E.C.U. sent a message of sympathy to the S.S.C. for the 'unjust treatment you have received at the hands of the Archbishop of Canterbury and others.' However, it was not all storm. At Hatcham there was a lively patronal festival in the grounds of the vicarage which lasted all day and included a Florentine exhibition obviously brought back from Italy by Tooth himself. They also had an enormous parish outing to Epping Forest, subscriptions for which Croom appealed in the national press with considerable success.

The name of the new Bishop of Rochester, Antony Thorold, had been announced. He was vicar of St. Pancras, an expert tract writer, and a confirmed evangelical. The appointment was hailed with delight by the Protestants and with strong courage by the Catholics. They already knew that his friend Canon Miller, the vicar of St. Alphege, Greenwich, would urge him to take all measures to put ritualism down. 'A colourless appointment,' said the *Church Times,* which had been malicious about Bishop Claughton's departure for the new see of St. Albans. When the clergy of the diocese of Rochester presented Claughton with an address of farewell it commented:

> We trust that the late Bishop of Rochester will not suppose that these eulogistic utterances express the sentiments of churchmen generally. . . . We can assure his lordship that not a few of the clergy and laity of his late diocese regard his departure with more than equanimity.

St. Pancras church was built on the lines of a classic temple before the Gothic revival. It was started in 1819 and cost £7,600. Most people considered that it looked more like a pagan temple than a place for Christian worship, having been designed on the lines of the Erectheum in Athens. The porticoes were supported by colossal Caryatides that flanked the sides. The figures bore a ewer in one hand, while the other one rested on an inverted torch, the emblem of death and considered most unsuitable by Tractarian ecclesiologists, who thought the interior undevotional. It probably was. Even in 1877 it looked old-fashioned, with its holy table crowded with communion plate, and the Commandments painted above. There was even an old Georgian box standing on the north side of the chancel from which the clerk read the responses, and in spite of possessing an organ there was almost no singing. The sermon was preached in a black gown. Thorold only held a communion service once a month.

So Hatcham Catholics were not exactly cheered when the identity of their next Bishop was disclosed. Almost immediately afterwards the news followed that he was to preach at Hatcham, though no one was willing to predict the outcome of such a visit. The curate, Browne, was about to move to a curacy at St. Columba's Church, Haggerston. No one can say with any certainty where Tooth was, since there are no registers. One wonders what his ministrations were. It is known that he did not celebrate in the church, but it would be extraordinary, if, having an altar in St. Michael's House, he did not take advantage of it, at any rate for the sake of the boys and the Sisters, if not for his parishioners.

The position of the school was most unsatisfactory. Tooth was in charge, yet unable to officiate in the church a stone's throw away. On Sundays the boys attended St. Peter's, London Docks, or St. Stephen's, Lewisham. Tooth came to the conclusion that he might transfer the establishment elsewhere, a policy he was able to carry out by a generous legacy of £10,000 given for the purpose. He bought Valentine Wright's magnificent house and estate, Woodside, at Croydon.

XVI

END OF A MINISTRY

MANY of the old congregation had left the church as E. F. Croom had done, for they could not accept any compromise on ritual that signified to them a compromise on doctrine. Corporate communions were arranged at St. Peter's and other churches. They felt that this was the right course for them to pursue, otherwise they would be making concessions which they had vowed they would never make. So they abdicated.

However, when it was announced that Bishop Thorold would preach on Sunday, August 7th, they all came to hear what he had to say. It was Croom's first appearance for months and perhaps Plimpton's too. Thorold preached from the text: 'God is a spirit, and they that worship him must worship him in spirit and in truth.' He denounced a too ornate service as a hindrance rather than a help to spiritual life, hardly a placatory contribution under the circumstances. The *Church Times* said it was a rash rather than a sagacious remark since he had no experience of his own to guide him. Thorold closed his sermon by saying that he hoped there were no persons in the congregation who were ashamed of being termed *Protestants*, 'for if the Church of England is not a Protestant Reformed Church she is a shameful schism and ought not to have an existence.' He thus showed that he took sides and that he was biased. The Catholics were deeply offended by such words; on the other hand these sentences were immediately seized upon gleefully by the Evangelicals as a catch phrase for the banner under which they fought. They later appeared on every copy of the Hatcham *Protestant* magazine and were quoted *ad nauseam* against the ritualists, although such a doubtful and unqualified statement brought Thorold into disrepute in moderate circles. The *Church Times* reminded its readers, *à propos* of Thorold, that it had once stated that no intelligent or right thinking churchman ever saw the Archbishop of Canterbury on his legs without a shudder. It now added that there were others on the episcopal bench to whom this could apply, implying that the cap evidently fitted the new Bishop of Rochester. 'An address suitable for Sunday school children by a superintendent who did not wish to go beyond his adolescent listeners' mental capacity' said a working man afterwards. (Could it have been a comment from Charles Powell?) Little was achieved. The members of the old congregation had hoped for some understanding of their position and some peaceful settlement; they laboured under a real sense of grievance that induced an aggressiveness which as individuals was not natural to them.

William Grant of the Hatcham Defence Committee took the matter up with a straightforward letter. He reminded the Bishop that he was not speaking to members of the clergy but to lay people. He said that he had been required all his life to profess faith in the 'Catholic Church' as in the Creeds, and to hold inviolate the *Catholic* faith. 'I have never been required to profess myself a *Protestant*, nor to acknowledge myself a member of the *Protestant Church*. My Prayer Book does not contain a single mention of the word Protestant.'

Bishop Thorold, like almost all nineteenth century bishops and perhaps many twentieth century ones too, firmly believed in his own infallibility. He was not going to retract a syllable or soften a word. He replied:

> I much regret to have pained you by the use of the word Protestant in my sermon on Sunday morning but I must honestly tell you that I used it with perfect deliberateness and that I inflexibly abide by it still.

He made the point that the word *Trinity* did not occur in Scripture, yet had never heard of the doctrine being repudiated on that account. He declared that the Church of England was Protestant in her attitude to the Roman Church and that seventeen of the Thirty-nine Articles were in controversy with Roman error. Of the Church of England he added that, 'If she does not still protest against the doctrinal errors of that Church her existence is an explicable and gratuitous schism.'

It was an unwise letter, and it is surprising that Thorold as a new diocesan dealing with a difficult and divided parish did not consult someone such as Bishop Moberly, or even the witty knowledgeable Magee, or Bishop Walsham How, who was known to desire peace and had written to the newspapers saying so. Thorold's reply drew a thousand word letter from Grant which would have gained by being crisper and shorter. Grant's main points were that the Church of England, though a Reformed Church, protested against the doctrines of Anabaptists as well as against Roman errors. The Protestantism of Luther denied doctrines which the Church of England retained such as a sacramental system, baptismal regeneration, the gift of the Holy Ghost in Confirmation, the Real Presence in the Sacrament of the Altar, the apostolic succession, the power of absolution. Every one of these the Church of England held as most necessary truths.

Some of Grant's points must have gone home for Thorold abruptly cut off the correspondence with a slightly patronizing letter:

> I am very pleased to see the deep interest you take in Church matters, though unfortunately we are not quite able to see everything in the same light. Love of the truth and charity to those who differ from us are gifts from on High which we all need in these anxious times.
>
> You will understand that I have not time to discuss the matter further but you will permit me with every kindly feeling to remain yours faithfully. . . .

Grant replied again:

> I regret that your lordship is unable to reply to the positions of my former letter but I may perhaps hope that the points which I have brought forward will—in the interests of that love of truth which your lordship so well describes as a gift from the Father of Lights—receive due consideration at your hands.

He expressed the 'deep interest' taken by members of the old congregation in 'Church matters,' the Bishop's phrase:

> There is not one of them who has not sifted to the bottom, the reasons for his churchmanship. . . . Your lordship must appreciate at least *the principle* upon which we resist the interference of the state with the *spiritual powers* of a minister given to us by the authority of our blessed Lord.

He ended by saying that he was forwarding the correspondence to the church newspapers.

Thorold made a strong and surprised protest, but Grant was adamant. The Bishop's visit had been widely advertised by posters and the visit was a 'matter of notoriety,' and 'any enquiry respecting the public utterances of our bishops is a legitimate matter for public correspondence. . . . I addressed you as my diocesan i.e. as a public official to whom the State had committed myself and others.' This was a sharp thrust for, of course, these erastian minded bishops prided themselves on being law-officers, and it was anyhow an incontrovertible fact.

Thorold reluctantly admitted:

> I do not apprehend that it is one of my functions to be a professor of theology in the diocese. It was this that made me

indisposed to argue the matter with you, not, permit me to say, that I had nothing on my side to reply.

The publication of the correspondence did nothing to restore the confidence in the new diocesan on the part of the old congregation. On the other hand it encouraged the opposition, and made a *rapprochement* much more difficult. In fact, divisions deepened as is evident from various meetings that took place at this time of the year. Each party had the brilliant idea of infiltrating the public meetings of the other. The Church Association held a public meeting in the Borough when a Mr. Dumphreys was to deliver a lecture on *Auricular Confession, Nuns, Prayers for the Dead and the Mass: Do they belong to the Reformed Church?* They invited the mission priest of All Hallows', Southwark (Mr. Berkeley), to attend as he was the priest in question, and he looked up a few supporters. If both parties had not been in such deadly earnest about matters that affected the deepest springs of their faith, the conduct of the meeting could have been described as ludicrous, and it is difficult not to be amused at it to-day. When Mr. Side, a local schoolmaster, took the chair he produced a memorial to be sent to the Bishop praying for Mr. Berkeley's removal. Realizing that there were those in the hall who were not prepared to support the petition, Mr. Dumphreys began his lecture with a hard glance round the room announcing that if any one interrupted his lecture he would be thrown out. At which there was loud and unkind laughter. He gave out the title of his talk, and as he posed the question on the handbill (Do they belong to the reformed church?) he was met with a shout of 'No.' He went on to make his Protestant hearers shudder by remarking that Ritualists prayed for the dead, which brought an audible comment from one of them that 'it shows they don't forget them'; and the statement of the speaker that 'They called themselves Protestants' was met with cries of 'No, No' from the other side. Dumphreys next produced from his pocket various Anglo-Catholic books of devotion, *The Altar Manual* and *The English Catholic's Vade-mecum,* and held them up to the audience who responded with tremendous cheers which lasted several minutes. The lecturer went on to quote in disparaging tones from an address in which Mr. Berkeley paid a tribute to the wonderful work done by the Sisters from the Convent of St. John the Baptist, Clewer. This was too much for one of the Catholic party who shouted 'Three cheers for them.' On which the whole of the dissident listeners rose to their feet and waved their hats, and gave three ringing cheers for the Sisters, and then sat down.

A scene of indescribable confusion followed as members of the Protestant League now tried to eject the Catholics. One of the most energetic was recognized as Elliott, the destroyer of the confessional. At length the uproar subsided temporarily and the speaker continued with passages from *The Priest in Absolution*. But as he read them he added his own comments of 'most filthy suggestions that could not be uttered in public' which drew shouts and cries and the taunt of 'Beast' from one of the ritualists. There was no hope of gaining support for the memorial to the Bishop, and the meeting broke up in disorder and confusion. But outside another demonstration of about four hundred had been organized by the local branch of the Church of England Working Men's Society in support of Mr. Berkeley. They carried their resolution with loud acclamation which drowned everything inside the hall. At the end the uninhibited local inhabitants who were mostly parishioners added three cheers for Mr. Berkeley and three groans for Mr. Side. When Mr. Dumphrey appeared with his supporters who were not local men, the rather rough indignation-meeting-supporters chased and hustled them, as they hooted with derision until they were 'driven out of the neighbourhood of Southwark.'

It must have been quite a fracas for a reporter says:

> Then and then only did the crowd feel satisfied and they left declaring that if they (the Protestant League) dared hold another meeting such as they had held that night, they (the Southwarkians) would serve them worse.

A cab followed Mr. Dumphreys and his friend for some distance and they were 'wild with fright' and ten policemen were 'powerless.' The Dumphreys' party were wise enough not to take a cab 'which would most certainly have been overturned by the mob.'

No one can say that such conduct was not reprehensible but there had been considerable aggravations on both sides, and these frequently reached boiling point. In some ways one regrets the calm apathy of to-day compared with the interest and rough enthusiasm of the last century. On the opposite side the Church of England Working Men's Society combined to campaign for the repeal of the Public Worship Resolution Act and gained substantial support for the proposal through its enthusiastic meetings. However, there was a political element in this radical point of view, and Bishop Magee was one of several bishops who disliked it and its 'violent' secretary as he called Charles Powell.

Meanwhile, at St. James's the remainder of the damaged confessional had been carted away. There was a mystery about its removal, since it was secretly done and without authority. The triptych had been removed and the unearthed stone slabs resembling tombstones stood beside the altar which was now divested of candles and flowers; the defaced notice with the names of the C.B.S. painted out also disappeared. Robert Webb, the churchwarden appointed by Tooth, was never allowed a key to the church. He made it clear in a letter to the *Church Times* that the verger's explanations were unsatisfactory as he was obviously in the pay of Fry. But remonstrances were useless. There was something of a scandal when it was known that a distant connection of Tooth's from Australia had been refused permission to see the church. Fry said that this was by order of the Bishop, and another lengthy correspondence followed in the church newspapers.

During September rumours began to circulate that Tooth was about to resign his cure. Browne was moving to a curacy at St. Columba's, Haggerston, a real grief to the congregation, for he had upheld them through much anxiety and difficulty. There was a presentation at a farewell party in St. James's House with the gift of a set of vessels for 'clinical' communions and baptisms. Tooth's personal contribution was a set of *The Library of the Fathers* in forty volumes. Tooth intended to farm Wright's great estate at Woodside, and continue there the school along with a newly constructed convent where the Sisters would take women alcoholics. Therefore, it was obvious that he would soon leave Hatcham, and he made it known that he intended to appoint Malcolm MacColl as curate-in-charge with a view to becoming vicar. There were, however, difficulties ahead, since it was possible that the Bishop would not license MacColl. MacColl was at present priest-in-charge of the temporary St. Augustine's, Bermondsey, where he had gone soon after his ordination in 1867 by the Bishop of Glasgow and Galloway. He had done a magnificent pastoral work in a very poor parish, but in trying to raise the permanent church he had incurred a large personal debt, a fact unknown to Tooth at the time he approached him. MacColl was credited with having personal means, an asset in view of the small stipend at St. James's, £150 a year. Malcolm MacColl, not to be confused with the unmarried Mr. Malcolm MacColl of the Bonn Conferences who was the friend of Gladstone, was a moderate-minded high churchman, a member of the Confraternity of the Blessed Sacrament, but not of the Society of the Holy Cross. He was also courageous, tough and determined.

Without the registers it is impossible to discover who was officiating at the church at this time. At least eleven different clergymen had taken the Sunday services between February and September. The old congregation never attended at all and were divided between three other churches, St. Peter's, London Docks, St. Paul's, Lorrimore Square, and St. Stephen's, Lewisham. Every one was now waiting for the verdict on Tooth's appeal against his sentence.

On November 5th, Guy Fawkes Day, Tooth's effigy was burnt at Brighton along with that of the Pope, Pio Nono. A mock bishop in full canonicals, so he was described, gave an address in support of Church and State. Ironically the appeal was allowed on the following day, and the former proceedings against Tooth quashed on the technical point that Lambeth was not in London, Westminster, nor in the diocese of Rochester. The comment of *The Times* was that the public is always glad to see a rat get out of a trap, a lightly infelicitous metaphor.

On November 21st, and without fixing a date, Tooth sent a letter of resignation to the Archbishop together with a long apologia:

My Lord Archbishop,

I am glad to avail myself of any early opportunity of stating to your Grace my intentions in reference to the decision which has recently been given in my favour by the Court of Queen's Bench. My personal interest in all this sad controversy is very trifling when compared with the real question at stake, and the habitual retirement of my life will be my defence against the charge of any desire on my part to raise a crisis on a difficult subject which is generally very little understood, and it was not until I was called upon to deny what I know to be true that I felt bound to vindicate within the limits of my own influence what I believe to be rights of the Church against a new jurisdiction imposed upon her without the consent of her synods, rights which are hers by virtue of her Divine origin, and which have been secured to her by the assent of the State. The Press has been emphatic in declaring that the Public Worship Regulation Act was nothing more than an easy mode of procedure, and persons in authority have assured us again and again that we should involve ourselves in no difficulty with our higher responsibilities if we would only obey it. The fact that the late legislation has involved the creation of a new jurisdiction is now beyond any doubt; the argument on which I rested my opposition to the Public Worship Regulation Act is now fully allowed; and if this is the only result of my painful experience in this matter, I shall feel amply rewarded. We have had it declared on authority which no one can now question that a new jurisdiction has been created in the Church of England. We must wait for the result. I feel that the first obligation that binds me is my duty to the Church. A question was raised, and

I offered my submission to my Bishop, pledging to free myself from the secular protection which my benefice affords me if he would judge me by the law of the Church. He did not assume the responsibility, and it was not until I was called upon to obey an alien jurisdiction that I refused to render obedience. My duty to the Church, as far as I have been able to perform it, is now, I trust, fulfilled, and I must turn my attention to the consideration of the claims of my congregation and to a parish, where I have spent the happiest days of my life. When it was right that my people should suffer with me I did not hesitate to throw myself on their patient endurance and to require them to take their part in this matter. Nothing now remains to be done, and I must relieve them from their difficult position. The patron, kindly acting under my advice, will make a new appointment. I resign the care of my parish in the hope that the severance of my personal interest may secure it from future litigation. I can never sufficiently thank my friends for their patient and loyal confidence in me. In reference to those who have caused the distress in my parish and are responsible for the legal proceedings, and are moreover for the moment liable to a series of actions for damages for false imprisonment, I would say that no compensation can ever atone for the wrongs they have inflicted on my parish; but it is not my intention to estimate them by reference to a jury. My health is broken, and I am content to resign my benefice and to devote myself for the immediate present to the extension of my orphanage work at Croydon, which I trust may not be allowed to exist without the good wishes and blessing of your Grace.

Believe me, my Lord Archbishop, to be your Grace's obedient servant,

ARTHUR TOOTH, M.A., Vicar of St. James', Hatcham.

He must have added the words following his signature with a measure of satisfaction.

The status quo had returned. He was not inhibited or suspended. He could demand the key of the church whose freehold he possessed by law. He could appoint whom he wished as curate-in-charge; and his brother, the patron, could nominate whom he liked as the next incumbent with every prospect of the man of his choice being inducted to the living. The vicarage was already empty so Tooth made arrangements for MacColl to move in and spoke of him as the next vicar.

However, there was a final farewell to be undertaken and for this Tooth chose the 8 a.m. celebration of Holy Communion on Advent Sunday. He resisted every attempt of his friends to make a formal presentation or to recognize his departure in any way. In

I

the weeks beforehand, as far as he possibly could, he had the church restored to some of its former glory. The cross was replaced on the chancel screen, one account says it was of oak and another that it was of deal. (This could be the missing Hatcham Cross were it not for an account of its destruction in 1886.) The triptych over the altar and another in the north aisle were both replaced. There was a large cross on the altar and six candles, as well as a handsome purple frontal and a pair of heavy new curtains. Described as a 'high' celebration the service was devout and orderly with over two hundred and fifty persons present, of which about one hundred did not communicate. He was himself the celebrant though assisted by MacColl, and was very obviously in poor health. When the service was over he left the church passing quickly through the ranks of the people outside and took the next train back to Croydon. Soon afterwards he left England for a long tour abroad, from which he did not return until the next August.

Now that he was known to be leaving, the Press displayed a new generosity towards him on the lines of *Let Byegones be Byegones*. MacColl, who looked on himself as vicar-designate, contemplated the future with confidence. He was far from inexperienced. The Hatcham Defence Committee headed by Walter Plimpton was ready to support him, and the old Croom-Hill party had returned to the church. There were many moderates who had settled in at other churches, but he hoped for their return. As for the trouble makers, Sanders, Fry, Thorman and Holloway, they kept a foot in two camps and were not particularly welcome in either. He hoped he could deal with them by a policy of moderation. Indubitably they were still bent on mischief, and it was disconcerting to compute the vast financial resources at their command through the Church Association, which had recently owned to having paid £40,000 on prosecutions. But there is every indication that MacColl, as he crossed from the vicarage to the church for the 11 o'clock service on Advent Sunday 1877, believed that he could establish peace in the parish.

Even without any personal letters of reminiscences to guide us there are strong indications that Tooth's outlook had changed in some way since his imprisonment. He had not altered his ideas on ecclesiastical politics, but he seems to have suffered some kind of painful disillusionment, almost a type of rejection. There must be some rationalization for his conduct. It is true that his health was precarious and no explanation for this has ever been given. That it was due to the nervous and physical strain of three weeks' imprisonment is unlikely. It could, however, be due to the long strain from the year 1871 onwards when he first clashed with Claughton, and the intense strain of the years 1875 and 76. Moreover, he must have undergone some tension on account of the consequences which his friends had to bear, Mackonochie, Lowder, Dykes and Purchas. He could have been depressed and disillusioned to a point which affected his outlook on his position as a parish priest. It does not seem that his illness impaired his intellectual ability for he made an excellent and restrained speech at the E.C.U. meeting in May 1877. His action in returning and breaking into the church holds something of his old attitude. Yet he never preached again to his congregation as far as we know after February 7th, the week before he went to prison, not even at the farewell celebration on Advent Sunday.

One possible line of argument is that the stripping and destruction of the ornaments in the church were a more painful blow than he admitted to any one, even to himself. But this was something he had always foreseen. Around 1874 or 75 he had drawn a witty set of cartoons, and circulated them to his friends to illustrate what would happen to the church if he were to be attacked by three aggrieved parishioners. The first showed the church as it was with a full congregation; the last as it would be bare and empty of worshippers. In between, it showed the Church Association informer dispatched with the connivance of the bishop to watch him from the back of the church.

The three aggrieved parishioners were Mr. Brown, who kept a chandler's shop (his business was at a low ebb and a little notoriety might help him) and Mrs. Brown, his wife, who said, 'I've no patience with them Papists, me and Brown 'as gone to Chapel for nigh thirty years come Christmas in the evening, though we goes to church in the morning. Brown and me is both true church people.' The second was 'poor Mr. Jones who kept a ham and beef shop. He was a sentimental man and wept tears at the thought of the gradual decay of our beloved Protestant religion.' The third was Mr. Robinson, a man 'of independent means who presided every Saturday night at eight punctually at a convivial.' Next follows the cartoon of the 'shepherd under whom the three aggrieved parishioners sat,' a lugubrious preacher in black gown, and a picture of them all spying from the back of the church and saying 'Look at that fellow in a yellow coat, I'm blest if he isn't worshipping in the middle of the altar, we can't have *that*.' After which they have to run hastily from the district for they had been recognized. Finally, the poor bishop waved the informer away with a 'we shall see the Church ruined and disestablished'; and a view of the church as it became after the case, bare as a barn.

This is almost precisely what happened, so Tooth was not unprepared, but was the reality more scarifying than he had ever
envisaged? There is a point where Tooth is defiant to the point of
exhibitionism, and then after his own experience he is almost the
reverse. Did he regret his fierce opposition to the 'intruding' clergyman, and his own autocratic instructions to his congregation; first
not to accept any other ministry than his own, and secondly to
absent themselves from the church after the riots began? It was
certainly this policy that lost the old congregation the church.
Perhaps Tooth realized it and could not afterwards face the painful situation of a worshipping community that was irreconcilable.
On the other hand there is every sympathy with him for giving
such advice; capitulation to the Bishop's nominees as curates-in-
charge would have been a tacit acceptance of the position into
which he had been forced.

He went abroad soon after his imprisonment; he returned in
May 'in excellent spirits.' He then suffered a relapse and went away
again. He was back in July for the sale in aid of the orphanage in
the vicarage garden, and in court in September to hear the evidence about the damaged confessional. Presumably, this is the
time when he made arrangements for the transfer of the Orphanage to Croydon as a different type of institution, for in October he
left the vicarage for Croydon. On Advent Sunday MacColl took
over as curate-in-charge with a view to being vicar. Tooth told
MacColl, 'If they (the people) have the doctrine of the Real Presence
and Confession, what more do they need?' This had not been his
view in 1875 and 1876, and up to the time of his imprisonment, for
then he considered ceremonial of considerable importance. A possible explanation of his attitude and apparent disinterest in his old
parish could be a changed attitude of his own to ceremonial and
ornaments. They may have become suddenly worthless and unimportant, rather as possessions destroyed in air raids seem a trivial
loss in face of physical survival. But if this is so, he could have
stayed on as incumbent acceding to the Bishop's demands. With
truncated ritual he could have carried on preserving the doctrines
that were so necessary to catholicism, while ignoring their outward
manifestations. This, however, is not a logical explanation in view
of Tooth's continued membership of S.S.C. with its insistence on
the Six Points.

He never contemplated seceding from the Church of England,
and Anglicanism was sufficient for his spiritual needs provided it
was of the catholic kind. As an unmarried priest he would have
soon been admitted to orders in the Roman Church, so there would

be no especially difficulty in crossing over as some of his friends had done. He did set a very high value on his work for the Orphanage, and it is possible that the clue to his severance from parish life lies here. Publicity that is relentless and unkind can wound and sicken. There is no refuge from it, and with the best will in the world it has an attritive effect on self-confidence for sensitive people. There is a passionate longing for anonymity and disinterested attention which can never be obtained. This is the kind of scorching daily publicity Tooth endured from 1876 onwards from almost every paper in the land and many overseas until 1878. It must have been a relief to enter the Orphanage with its bright happy boys and receive their limited concern and forbearance. Their youthful exuberance and untainted admiration may well have had a therapeutic effect on him; and because it made a contrast from the wrangles outside the walls of the Orphanage, he may have decided to devote his life to this side of his work. At any rate, it seems the most reasonable explanation. It did not cross his mind at the age of thirty-eight that he would never be offered even so much as an unpaid curacy, let alone a living or an honorary canonry by any diocesan bishop in the next fifty-three years of his life. Probably, on that Advent Sunday, it would not have made any difference. In one sense he was finished. He had made his contribution to the cause in which he believed so passionately, and others must now carry on. He had a path to pursue and his future choice was nobody else's business.

But in the parish of St. James's the outlook was cloudy. Already the word had gone round that Tooth had celebrated and the opposition alerted for the later service which MacColl would take singlehanded at 11 o'clock, Mattins with Litany and Sermon.

PART II

MALCOLM MacCOLL

Advent 1877 – Advent 1878

CONTENTS

ADVENT 1877 – EASTER 1878

AS MacColl entered the church, he observed that the building was full to the doors and supposed that it was in the expectation of seeing and hearing Tooth. The congregation at first glance seemed devout and quiet. His first misgivings arose when, on entering the pulpit, he saw a knot of men standing together at the back, some with their backs to him and whispering audibly. He tried to engage the congregation's complete attention by calling for silence in order to offer prayer on behalf of this 'distracted and troubled parish'; and he knelt down. This was met with an outburst of artificial coughing, which was taken up on all sides. As MacColl rose it stopped, and he delivered his sermon. But on leaving the church for the vestry with the choir, a torrent of hisses and groans broke out, with cries of 'No Popery.' MacColl saw a rush forward to the chancel gate. 'A fairly well dressed working man putting a white hat on his head shouted 'Now or Never,' rushed forward and grabbed hard at the solid oak chancel gates.' It was Evenden of the Protestant League, and he was followed by a crowd of others, some of whom were trying to pull him away while others restrained the first lot from assisting him. Meanwhile, defenders appeared in the chancel on the other side of the gate. By now a free fight had broken out; men were knocked down, their clothes torn off; women screamed and children huddled together. Inspector Rolfe and twenty police came in and took over. Webb, the churchwarden, hustled Evenden into the vestry, where he was charged and taken off to Peckham police station. The rest of the force set about restoring order and clearing the church, beginning with the north door and then continuing through the west. It took some time. MacColl consulted the churchwardens and an onlooker heard Webb say to Fry, 'I am satisfied that you had nothing to do with this disturbance.' Fry replied that he was only trying to restore order to the utmost of his power and added, 'My friends helped me most cheerfully.' To this MacColl made no reply. He may have thought that he would prefer to do without the assistance of Fry's friends. He moved forward and asked people to leave as soon as possible, although outside there was a good deal of shouting and shoving; but the police cleared a way and gradually broke up the noisy and obviously organized crowd. On the advice of Inspector Rolfe, MacColl cancelled the evening service. It was not a good start and once having experienced this sort of behaviour one can understand MacColl's rather timid and compromising future policy.

The gates were not severely damaged, the hinges simply having been wrenched away; but in court on Monday, the magistrate, Mr. Balguy, who had heard the previous case against John Elliott, took a severe view of it. He adjourned the case when it was clear that M'Clure, the Orangeman, was again at the bottom of the trouble. He was charged with aiding and abetting Evenden. M'Clure had been seen during the first lesson laughing and talking to Evenden. A woman gave evidence that she heard M'Clure say, 'We will wait until the service is over, we may see some dancing.' She also saw M'Clure put up his hand and begin to hiss, which was the signal for others to do the same.

At the next hearing counsel obviously from the Church Association, who appeared for Evenden, was stopped by the magistrate when he began to address the court on the subject of the restored crosses and ornaments. The magistrate also advised the malcontents not to visit the church, but M'Clure expressed every intention of continuing to worship there as he had for some time past, a statement which must have depressed MacColl. It was hoped that an adjournment would help the parties to cool down.

A fairly heated correspondence broke out in *The Standard*. A parishioner from Lewisham High Road, who sounds a bit of a Mr. Pooter, declared, 'I am not a ritualist and therefore no partisan; but I consider it the duty of all right-minded Churchmen to prevent the scene of yesterday and show those who appealed to the law, but finding that it is not one-sided enough for them are endeavouring to introduce mob law, that they cannot do as they please.' He described the scene:

> After the Benediction, at a given signal, a rush was made to the chancel for the purpose of destruction. A more shocking scene in the House of God cannot be imagined and it was only by the interference of the police that one of the ringleaders was arrested and order restored. On remonstrating with some of the most violent, I had my glasses knocked off and my eye grazed. I must say the people's warden, Mr. Fry, acted nobly and I should think he must be ashamed of his former supporters.

Webb, the vicar's churchwarden, wrote a little later saying that Fry's comment on the Protestant League was that 'he did not wonder at their rioting so long as there is Popery in the Church of England.' Therefore they can hardly be acquitted of connivance if not complicity. Fry's letter complained about non-parishioners attending the church. This was a situation which every ritualist church had to face since they were still fairly sparsely spread, though increasing in numbers, as *The Rock* pointed out. However, when the ritualists stopped attending the church during the interregnum there were almost no communicants, and local middle class people only supported it indifferently.

On the next Sunday, Advent II, for the 8 a.m. service of Holy Communion some outsiders arrived on the early train, having been notified 'by circular.' The number of communicants was variously given as forty (*Freeman's Journal*), and two hundred (*Camberwell and Peckham Times*). All was quiet and devotional, and no one was outside as the congregation left the church well before nine o'clock. But within an hour everything had changed and by ten o'clock the church was thronged and every seat inside taken. The candles were unlit on the altar, but the choir was robed and the service intoned, both grievances from the Protestant point of view. The space between the doors was packed with men standing, since there were no seats. Outside there were two hundred constables on duty. It seemed as though everything would be peaceful. MacColl finished the service and retired to the vestry, and the large congregation began to disperse, though there were a few idlers. Fortunately, a cordon of police had not budged from the north door, which had been considered the unprotected side since the previous January.

Suddenly, there was a cry from the surging mob, 'Let's see if there is anything on,' and within a second the cordon was broken and they poured into the church where fortunately there was additional police protection on each side of the chancel screen. Charles Powell's men had prudently taken their seats soon after 10 o'clock in the front rows, a great grievance to others. Shelves crashed to the ground, books were trampled into scrap paper, chairs were broken and damaged, while the Mr. Pooters retreated and tried to shelter behind them. M'Clure was in evidence, standing on a chair appealing for order. After all, the verdict of the magistrate's court had not yet been pronounced; he was on bail and a further charge would be serious. He was not given a chance of continuing for five policemen took him outside, while inside the shouting, shoving and screaming went on for some minutes. Gradually, the police restored order, making a way for the women and children first. MacColl cancelled the evening service, but in spite of this a great crowd collected and rival hymns were sung until at last the police again cleared the street. The next day the adjourned case was heard and M'Clure and Evenden were fined £5 and £7 respectively. MacColl appealed for Evenden's fine to be reduced. He took the view that he was an illiterate working man, a stooge in the miserable game of hunt the ritualists, and like so many others a subscriber to the unintelligent doctrine of 'What I don't like, you shan't have.' The following two Sundays all was quiet, but the police were on duty as usual, to the disgust of the Protestants.

The services of the dozen policemen on duty were dispensed with on the next Sunday, so MacColl began having the children in church again. The church was fairly well attended, being about three quarters full. It was the last Sunday in Advent, and many remembered the position a year ago and hoped that now this unhappy year was nearly over, some peace might be restored and a *modus vivendi* established between the factitious groups of churchmen.

In January it became known, however, that Tooth's resignation had to be postponed. Malcolm MacColl had incurred a personal liability to the builder in Bermondsey engaged on the church of St. Augustine. It is impossible to disentangle the rights and wrongs of the Bermondsey financial crisis; we know that rumours flew around thick and fast. MacColl may have been unbusinesslike or careless; or he may have given a guarantee for more money than he could safely apportion, rather as Augustus Granville had. There is one letter to Croom from a Mr. Gilborn of Bermondsey, who regarded MacColl's handling of the money as a 'misappropriation' of funds, which seems much too strong a term to use considering that MacColl afterwards produced a balance sheet; let us hope it allayed all the disaffection. There was a summons by the builder against MacColl and the Building Committee for payments due. However, had MacColl failed in his payment, it would have meant the sequestration of the stipend of St. James's, Hatcham, small though it was. So naturally Tooth had to consider his position again. He decided to retain MacColl as curate-in-charge but not present him to the living.

The other disappointing news was that Fry had started proceedings in the diocesan court for the removal of certain articles in the church and for alterations. The petition sought the removal of the remnants of the confessional box, the defaced panel on the wall with the names of the members of the C.B.S., music stands which were permanently fixed to the floor, the triptych affixed to the wall over the communion table which it was claimed excluded the light; the removal of the screen with gates separating the nave from the chancel, 'which interferes with the transit of sound,' and which now had the panels daubed; the removal of the screen between the chancel and side chapel, and also of three out of the five upper steps on which the communion table stood, and which made celebrating at the north end impossible; the removal of the wood beam, as we know the crucifix had been destroyed; the restoration of the stone tablets; and the re-erection of the screen across the north door to hide a gas meter. The case was defended by Tooth and others but they lost. They lodged an appeal but not a counter-application for a faculty. Eventually, the plaintiffs won on all points except the removal of the screen between the nave and chancel. Even the gates were condemned; one wonders why. In the evidence it transpired that the additions now to be removed had been the result of a bequest of jewels by Mrs. Robert Tooth for improvements to the church. The Chancellor said that many churches and cathedrals possessed screens to partition one section of the church from another, but the one dividing the chancel from the transept was finally condemned too.

As soon as the case was over, Tooth again left England, for apparently his health was still unsatisfactory. Accounts in the newspapers contradict each other but most agree that he was ill. Some say that he was postponing his resignation for the moment and that he would revert to a plain and unritualistic service on his return; and on the contrary that as a successor had been appointed at Bermondsey, MacColl would shortly be instituted as vicar of Hatcham. Even the *Church Times* declared that the daily services would be abolished and the church closed in the week.

Now Lent had begun again but it was not a peaceful one as every one had hoped. Each Sunday a batch of men and boys from the Protestant League filled the front rows of the church and tried to shout down the choir and congregation by saying the responses and psalms instead of singing them. It was painful and ludicrous, leading to a deafening accompaniment by the organ and an unmusical roar from the rest of the congregation. MacColl's appeals for peace in public and private fell on deaf ears. At St. Alban's, Holborn, Mackonochie was also in trouble. 'The cords of the law are tightening round Mr. Mackonochie's neck' wrote *The Rock* in its usual pungent style, for he had been ordered to remove a statue of the Infant Jesus with His mother. Mackonochie had pared down ritual to a minimum but his persecutors were unsatisfied, and there was a threat of an inhibition which was later served; after which he was suspended from his office as a priest and from the rights of his benefice. He obeyed the suspension. In fact, this was the end of his effective ministry and his physical decline began from then. Unlike Tooth, he was not in a position to travel frequently and recover, although the loss of stipend was subscribed by the English Church Union. There is just one happy occurrence to record and that is the birth of a fourth daughter to the younger Plimpton, Walter, who was still a worshipper at St. James's Church.

The Hatcham Defence Committee was also reconsidering its position and the use of St. James's House. It was MacColl's wish that a Parish Committee should be formed in place of the Defence Committee; there was nothing left now to defend. He wanted the house sold and a Mission established at the other end of the parish, but the committee refused to sell the house for the time being. It was obvious that a new policy was needed, and MacColl had the support of the congregation in his venture which was aimed at uniting the parish. The Defence Committee dissolved itself in favour of the Parish Committee and formed the house into a Churchmen's Club. MacColl spoke of 'new blood coming in,' so things were stirring. It was also hoped that the C.B.S., the Guild of All Souls, and the E.C.U. would meet there, thus preserving the devotional traditions of the pre-1877 era.

II

MR. CROOM'S DARKEST HOUR

HOWEVER, this Lent could be called Edmund Croom's darkest hour. Croom admired and venerated Tooth with a fervent and selfless intensity. He loved every inch of St. James's Church inside and out and he had given time, energy, money and his own deep spiritual devotion to serve it. He had been churchwarden from 1872–77 and associated with the earliest petitions to the Bishop to allow them to work out their own churchmanship unimpeded. Since then he had been closely involved in every move to defend Tooth and his policy. He passionately believed in the Catholic character of the Church of England and practised his faith with a warm and touching ardour. Both he and Joseph Plimpton were figures in the resistance movement at E.C.U. meetings; they were recognized and admired and applauded for their stand; they were the old unshakeables. But now he saw things moving, as he felt, from bad to worse. The foulest of all deeds to him was compromise. Suddenly it was proved to him unmistakeably that MacColl, to whom he had tried to give his unstinted loyalty as Tooth's nominee, was a compromiser. MacColl discontinued the use of vestments on weekdays; he had never used them on Sundays. It was a death blow to Croom's high hopes of maintaining Catholic doctrine and practice. An interview with MacColl only confirmed his fears. After reflection Croom resigned as secretary and treasurer of the C.B.S., and Hill resigned as sacristan. The correspondence is preserved in Croom's collection and it makes sad reading. Croom's draft letter contains many erasures and additions; it is worth quoting in full because it shows the stubborn attitude of the old guard, and the devotion they still held to Tooth's churchmanship.

> 265 Queens Road,
> Peckham, S.E.
> April 5th, 1878.

Revd. Sir,

In restoring to you as the superior of the St. James' Ward of the C.B.S. the various Books connected with that ward, I must take this opportunity of again expressing my deep grief that you should have found it necessary to discontinue the use of the Vestments at St. James' church as by so doing you have severed the last connecting link with the 'traditions of the past' for which our vicar endured so much, and which he informed us in a letter addressed to his churchwarden Mr. Webb you would respect. You informed me last night that some persons had stated that using the vestments on weekdays and not on Sundays was acting in a 'hole and corner way' and that this was the reason why you had determined to discontinue use of the vestments on weekdays. This hardly seems to me a sound reason for acting thus. I should have thought that having regard to the tradition of St. James' ritual under the vicar and to the known sorrow of the bulk of the communicants at the disuse of the vestments on Sundays, that you would have remedied the inconsistency of having different ritual on different days by adopting the use of vestments on all occasions—but doubtless in this matter you have done that which you think to be the best for the Catholic Church and for the greater Glory of God—this disuse of the vestments is however as you are aware a matter of principle with me, and necessitates my withdrawing from any prominent position which I may hitherto have held in connection with St. James', Hatcham. I could more easily have understood your not assuming the vestments when you first received charge of the parish but I cannot understand how having adopted them, you should now give them up, and especially that you should have done so at a time when such respected clergymen as Mr. Mackonochie and Mr. Edwards are exposing themselves to severe punishment, and Mr. Ward has actually had his licence withdrawn rather than render to Caesar the things that are God's.

I have written to the Revd. the Secretary of the Confraternity requesting him to forward the intercession papers to you for the future and shall be glad if you would meet the members of the Finance Committee to-morrow at St. James' House at 8.30 p.m. in order that I may submit a cash account and hand over the Balances of cash I hold as Treasurer.

And I remain, Dear Sir, your obedient servant,

E. F. CROOM

The Vicarage,
Hatcham, S.E.

Dear Mr. Croom,

Your own deep grief at the weekday discontinuance of the vestments for the present is not much greater than mine and such pain is only enhanced by the thought that I should seem to do anything painful to a Catholic such as you. You are mistaken when you say that the 'Hole and corner' remark was my reason. I asked you if you were one of those who had charged me with inconsistency while making such remarks and I was pleased to hear you were not. But you yourself had admitted the impossibility of my wearing vestments when I spoke to you at the H.D.

Meeting. Of course you may have changed your mind but you can at least understand me not changing mine. That impossibility was increased if one can use such a phrase. I think I might have been allowed to judge of that and still claim no action and prominent help. Your aim and mine must be the same to work for GOD not only in spreading the faith in the English Church but in keeping St. James', Hatcham at least on those lines which lead to our inheritance both in Ritual and Doctrine. You know that by reason of the Easter Vestry I am obliged to accept the Bishop's licence. The Vicar having left in case of need a nomination which is informal I was quite willing to go on without it but you surely would not wish to see two churchwardens Fry and Sanders. Again I do not think you make sufficient allowances for my difficulties, St. James' is not now like St. Alban's, St. Peter's or Prestbury. The Canaanite is in the land. You lost the church by your nine months' absence and there is now no united congregation while the faithful are banished from among the children of men. St. Peter's and St. Alban's and such are quite different now and their difference I do not think you take sufficient account of. Again you will remember that a parish priest has certain responsibilities not only to one but to feed the flock and you know that the flock which has weak ones and children were without food for well nigh a whole year. Are we ready to starve again? Doubtless when the time comes but I cannot take the fearful responsibility that now is the time. You care a great deal for the Vicar and his opinion and one day while he was speaking to us of the change in St. James', with me as compared with him, said 'If they (the people) have the doctrine of the Real Presence and Confession what more do they need?'

I hope that what I am saying will impress you with the need there is for every help in St. James'. We cannot afford any changes in the conduct of helping as much as in us lieth. I never did expect my line and judgment would command universal approval but I do venture to think that in this particular case no such resignation should be sent in until I declare the impossibility of ever wearing vestments or having lights. I admit the inconsistency of which I have been accused but it was a failing that leant to virtue's side and ought not to have been spoken of with sneers or shrugs but this does not apply to you. If anything I have said will get you to reconsider your resignation as treasurer I shall be more than thankful if not I must again express my intense regret that my conduct should be such as in your opinion necessitates such a mark of disapproval.

I remain, Yours very sincerely in our Blessed Lord,

MALCOLM MacCOLL

April 11th, 1878.

K

Queens Road, Peckham.
April 12th, 1878.

Dear Sir,

In reply to your letter of yesterday and after giving the subject contained in it my fullest consideration, I feel that I must still adhere to my determination to withdraw from my position at St. James'—upon this point I have referred myself to my spiritual adviser and have his full concurrence in my intended withdrawal from St. James' (I have also the same opinion from other priests) at this crisis. I need not reiterate the great pain this course of action causes me after my long connection with that church.

Your remark that before you had adopted the vestments at St. James' I had admitted the impossibility of your using them; but the fact that you have been able to use them from Advent to Easter in perfect peace shows that I was mistaken in my judgment and consequently I have changed my mind upon that point. The result shows that there is no impossibility in wearing the vestments or having lights—so I cannot admit that the impossibility has increased at all events from the cause we *then* feared— viz. riots from the mob—but if as I think I may deduce from your remark that you have been obliged to accept the Bishop's licence that the Bishop has put pressure upon you to give up vestments and lights, before he would grant you his licence—that is another reason altogether, and one I cannot admit so long as such pressure is the result of enforcing Privy Council Judgments—the Revd. Mr. Ward's position is similar, and I believe *you,* honour him for the action he has taken—I have no wish or right to interfere with your judgment as to the best way of conducting the service but I claim my freedom to withdraw when that way does not commend itself to my own judgment. It is no doubt very desirable to keep St. James' church in Catholic hands but I would a thousand times rather see that or any other Catholic church closed than that Catholic priests should even seem to deviate one iota from principle. If the vicar had thought of the ease of his communicants or the value of his personal teaching apart from or in preference to his determination to maintain Catholic rights: he could still be occupying his pulpit and vicarage but where would be the noble example that he set his brother priests (bravely followed at St. Alban's, Prestbury, and Bristol) and the inestimable lesson he taught the laity that England's church still has those within HER pale who would endure all things rather than barter away the Church's rights.

Again referring to my unwilling acquiescence in the impossibility of using the vestments at St. James' made last Advent I was so miserably impressed soon afterwards that I had done wrong in appearing to sanction a seeming dishonour to our Blessed Lord's presence in His Sacrament, that I referred my conduct to my spiritual adviser and he told me that I had committed a very grave indiscretion in so doing and I was urged never again to allow expediency to interfere with the broad line of principle—and it is now the same question of expediency, to give way a little in hopes of doing some good. You may be right in your line of action but I cannot concur in it; if I am wrong I hope I may be pardoned, do not think I am insensible of your difficult position. I have felt a great care in determining my own course which will affect but few—how much more onerous must be the anxiety of a priest, whose actions in a grave crisis as the present must and will affect not only the souls under his immediate charge but the faith of many of them whom he may not even know.

I remain, Revd. Sir, Yours respectfully,

E. F. CROOM

P.S.—I enclose you a cheque for the balance of cash in my hands belonging to the St. James' Ward C.B.S. which I hope you have safely received.

The Vicarage, Hatcham.
April 13th, 1878.

Dear Mr. Croom,

The kindness and tone of your letter make my regret still more keen that St. James' will lose your active help. I will not try to persuade you but let me assure you because it is important that the Bishop has put no pressure upon me. I have never even talked over the matter of vestments and lights with him. That I have been able to use vestments and lights in peace while others were unaware of their use is surely not a proof that they could be used in peace. Mr. Sanders' declaration that he is prepared to suffer three months is surely also a significant proof that the impossibility has increased. I would not bring anything of the nature of the accusation against you but I think if that resolution which was passed at the H.D.C. to support me and which I have relied upon, had been expressed in terms 'only so long as I use vestments and lights' I could have understood your action better though I would not have liked it any better. The picking up the broken threads of a scattered congregation and a ravaged parish is work that I still think every Catholic should help but then we are divided, only let us hope that you will not say nor believe that I have *abandoned* vestments without explaining that I have never used them on Sunday. The word can only be used by a special pleader and represents an action that I have never subscribed to. As to how far we may bow our heads in the storm must be entirely my responsibility but I may fairly ask you and such as you to add this consideration to the action 'for the present.'

Yours sincerely, MALCOLM MacCOLL

Croom consulted Father Biscoe of St. Peter's, London Docks, his confessor, who in turn consulted Lowder, who thought that on the whole his best course was to leave St. James's. 'As you are not strictly a parishioner your secession will be less marked,' he ended.

And, of course, Croom wrote to Tooth, who replied from Manila in June:

> I cannot blame you for the line you have taken. I cannot see that there was anything else for you to do. I very much hope that we shall, now that we are all in a better position to form an opinion on the state of things both in the parish and in the Church generally, adopt a definite policy which can be the only one to bring ultimate peace. I am very sorry for the continued disturbance in my parish. I think I can now look forward to some settlement on the old lines.
>
> The fresh outbreak in England will hasten my return home. I shall hope to arrive in July . . . my trip has been of the greatest benefit to me and I am much better.

So Croom took himself to St. Jude's, Peckham, where a Mr. Meade was slowly advancing the ritual. On high festivals he attended St. Peter's, London Docks, which had always been a home for the St. James's Catholics. After 1886 he attached himself to St. Katherine's, Rotherhithe.

But in the parish of St. James's, Protestant resistance to Mac-Coll was stiffening, and it is a pity that he had not the staunch Croom behind him. Fry had been heard to say that he was prepared to wait three months, which was taken to mean 'before the Church Association went into action.' He and his supporters now took a leaf out of the Catholics' book and formed a new committee for obtaining the services of the 'Protestant Episcopal Church,' and with the special object of winning their nominee's election at the coming Easter vestry. Fry rented the now empty house next to the church, formerly the Orphanage, and used it as a committee room. Both parties had leaflets printed and circulated to householders. Sanders was opposed by a man called Ballard, a moderate, who had never been associated with the old congregation, and denied that he was a ritualist, and who stood hoping to maintain peace. The vestry was fixed for Easter Tuesday at 7.45 a.m. On Easter Eve, there was a little hissing at the use of flowers which was far from a lavish display, but Easter Day passed quietly until the evening when disparaging remarks about the flowers, 'like a tea garden,' led to the words, 'It's a little better than a bear garden.' The police came in and moved every out to hisses and groans from the crowd outside. MacColl had held a high celebration at 8 a.m. followed by a low celebration at 10 o'clock and Mattins at 11.30. The collections came to £16 10s. and were given to MacColl.

But tempers were rising on both sides. On Sunday, April 7th, after the evening service, a young Sunday school teacher, Osmond Cole, who was also an ordinand, was walking away from the church with a Mrs. Fuller. Cole was a cripple and partly paralysed, walking slowly, when they were passed by the militant Protestant, Mrs. Fry, whereat Cole made the apparently harmless but audible remark, in what kind of tone we do not know, 'There goes the beautiful Mrs. Fry.' Almost certainly she was not beautiful, and this sarcastic statement was much resented, for it was later called 'an insolent comment' by the magistrate. It made Sanders angry, and he struck Cole on the back of the head so violently that his hat was knocked off and he staggered and fell. Sanders then pushed and ran Cole some twenty or thirty yards down the road. Sanders was summoned for assault, and after an adjournment he was bound over. Most of the congregation again took sides, and this division was further accentuated by the coming elections for the Easter vestry at which Sanders was to be put forward as the Protestant candidate.

III

AFTER EASTER

BOTH parties now campaigned for the Easter vestry and the election of the parish or people's churchwarden. The Protestant party had formed what they described as 'The Parish Committee.' The Catholics had dissolved the Hatcham Defence Committee in favour of the St. James's Church Society and Horace Plimpton was its secretary. Malcolm MacColl wanted to amalgamate these two committees in support of the St. James's House as a club for churchmen but without success for the old guard would not co-operate. With the coming elections each opposing party issued their own manifestos. Both employed sandwich men who paraded the streets in drenching rain.

Unfortunately, the Catholic leaflet was too wordy and too much on the defensive. The Protestant one said very little but impressed the name of their own candidate on the memory, declaring, *'Vote for Sanders, the candidate you can trust.'* On Easter Tuesday, a large and unruly mob pushed its way into the vestry of the church for the meeting called for 8 a.m. It was too late an hour for most working men, but then most working men were not ratepayers. It says much for the interest and enthusiasm of about one hundred and fifty men that they did attend at this most inconvenient hour. There was no opening prayer, and the meeting began badly with the reading of the minutes of the previous year. This disclosed that Tooth's letter proposing the previous vicar's warden, Robert Webb, had been written from Rome, and it was greeted with shouts of 'Let him stay there,' 'No Popery,' 'How much are candles?' and demands for the churchwarden's accounts and hisses and groans. These took on a more menacing tone towards MacColl, who remained impassive and unmoved, even at shouts of, 'Go back to Bermondsey,' and, 'We don't want you.'

Though it is difficult to believe it, the disturbance went on until half past eight, when according to one reporter, there was a pause for breath. Webb and Fry, the retiring wardens, then managed to present the financial accounts which were received with jeers and laughter. But somehow MacColl made his nomination of Nash as his own warden which was accepted with a bad grace. He put the name of Ballard, the non-party man, as people's warden, and it was seconded from the room. Fry forthwith began a speech calculated to arouse ill feeling and instead proposed Sanders. He attacked MacColl as a ritualist, a most unreasonable attitude, and he declared that if his nominee, Sanders, was elected he would promise to put down ritualism and uphold Protestantism. Sanders was elected by a majority of about 120 to 20, an overwhelming decision but scarcely one that represented the parish of ten thousand. At this point the unhappy Ballard, the middle man, crept away. When it was obvious that he was not there, there were jubilant shouts of 'He's sloped,' opinion being divided on the question of whether he 'quietly skedaddled by the cravings of the inner man for breakfast, or Citywards by the fact that time waits for no man.' There was more laughter and yelling, and Fry called out 'All, all' and upwards of 150 hands shot up with cheers, waving of sticks, hats and handkerchiefs, and the singing of the National Anthem. Fry now rushed out of the church to announce the news to a considerable crowd which had collected. It was as good as an entertainment when he and his supporters gleefully fired a salute of cannon to let the parish know that 'the Protestant cause had triumphed.'

Inside, however, the meeting had been closed, and Holloway and another Protestant proposed a vote of censure on MacColl. MacColl promptly vacated the chair and began to move away, when somehow, no one ever explained how, pandemonium broke out: 'a dreadful scrimmage . . . folks fought, shoved, shouted and seized one another by the collar.' MacColl was trying to reach the door, presumably the north one. There was another tussle while one party tried to push him outside and the other to prevent him. The door was not quite shut but could not be opened wide enough to let him or any one else through. MacColl contrived to send someone for the police, but by the time they arrived he was outside, hatless and collarless. The police promptly cleared the church and road; and, said one reporter, 'this was how Easter Tuesday was kept in Hatcham in the year of our Lord, 1878. An anonymous writer gave his own account of the Easter vestry meeting:

A large proportion of the majority consisted of habitual attenders at a neighbouring dissenting place of worship. The chairman was assailed from the outset and every effort was made to take the proceedings out of his hands. He was subjected to personal violence and had to be protected by a few of his friends until the arrival of the police. A few brave ladies who ventured to attend were subjected to a running fire of insults. Mr. MacColl is strictly within the law in the conduct of divine service but is not sufficient for some who . . . would simply carry out a work of demolition.

On the next day the adjourned case against Fry for assaulting
Cole was heard, and it is extraordinary that he was only bound
over to keep the peace considering his conduct at the vestry meeting; but so it was. There followed an inquest, which as usual was
conducted in the correspondence columns of the Press, and had the
inevitable effect of making local grievances a national debate.
Bullard began by disclaiming the label 'ritualist' given him by
The Times, and said he had been persuaded to stand in order to
'promote peace and quietness.' Webb, the retiring vicar's warden,
continued on the sore subject of the accounts, for part of the collections were still going back to Tooth, as vicar. Tooth was not at
that time in such affluent circumstances as he had been, partly
because of his new venture at Woodside and partly because, following the news of the legacy, subscribers evidently thought that
he was no longer in need; and also probably because other priests
were now suffering and money was being diverted to the new
victims of prosecution, Mackonochie and Pelham Dale. He does
seem to have treated MacColl rather stingily.

What was not sent to Tooth had been divided between the needs
of the parish, choir, assistant clergy, church expenses and the poor.
Webb stated that nothing had been spent on lights, incense or vestments, since they were no longer used. The offertory had increased
from £3 a week to £5 a week. The Easter communicants had risen
from twenty-five in 1877 to 200 in 1878 and the church was nearly
always full at the Sunday services.

The *Church Times* concluded that 'it would only need a little
firmness on the part of the bishops to repress the prosecution company, and the Church of England would present a united front to
her foes.' But there was plenty of unpalatable food for thought in
the next months. 'Things are very different to (*sic*) what they were
years ago at St. Alban's, Holborn,' wrote a correspondent to
The Rock. 'No incense, processions discontinued; on Sunday
morning only one "vested priest" is to be seen at a ceremony that
once vied with a Roman High Mass; and the little that remains is
now doomed.' For Mackonochie had been inhibited and suspended
for three years. 'St. Matthias, Stoke Newington,' it continued, 'is
an important outpost from which the enemy has just been driven.
At All Saints', Margaret Street, the vestments have disappeared. In
the other fashionable ritualistic churches they have never dared to
introduce the extremes, thanks to the Church Association prosecutions. At the following churches the ritualism has been simply
snuffed out: St. Ethelburga's (in the city), St. Vedast, St. Mary's,
Kilburn, and St. Mary's, Crown Street; St. Clement's, Whitechapel,

and St. Mary Magdalene's, Mortlake, and so—to a lesser extent—have St. Philip's, Clerkenwell, and Mr. Tooth's church at Hatcham. At Christ Church, Clapham, ritualism is still undaunted but the living is in safe hands. . . . There are only three churches in England where ritualism is quite what it was ten years ago . . . St. Peter's, London Docks, St. Paul's, Lorrimore Square, and St. Michael's, Shoreditch. Surely no time should be lost in marching against these positions.'

So the Church Association marched against Lowder at St. Peter's, London Docks, which produced such a fury of protest from his parishioners, whether churchgoers or not, that Bishop Jackson would not allow the case to proceed. But Mackonochie had been suspended from office for three years, and though an appeal was pending, every one was gloomy about the prospects. A sustentation fund was raised for him by the 17,000 members, 2,700 of them clergy of the English Church Union. All the same, looking at the review of prosecutions at the end of the year, the Church Association had not achieved much for the money it had expended. Technical faults in the law, the lack of support from some diocesan bishops, had disposed of several cases, although there was every hope by Protestants that the plaintiffs would fail in their appeal against the decision to remove certain ornaments at St. James's, Hatcham, as indeed they did.

There were two other occurrences in the news in the month of May, 1878. The first was the death of Crauford Tait, the Archbishop's chaplain and his only son. He had officiated at St. James's, Hatcham, in June 1877, together with Randall Davidson, the other chaplain. He was suddenly taken ill and died. To both parents it was a shattering blow and almost unendurable grief, and Mrs. Tait never recovered and died herself a year later. Crauford seems to have been a charming and devoted young man with more of a sense of humour than his father. On one of the letters in the Tooth correspondence about the imprisonment is a note in red ink concerning the Act of Parliament under which Tooth was condemned for contempt of court, which reads:

He was popped in under Geo. III cap. c. 27.

This seems to be a note by Crauford. Some sympathy must be given to Tait who bore these griefs with outward composure, but owned to having difficulty in controlling his emotion as he celebrated at the corporate communion for the Pan-Anglican synod in St. Paul's Cathedral. The other more relevant news was that Tooth was at Manila and on his way home.

As for Hatcham it was not for long out of the news. For weeks the Sunday congregations had been annoyed and harassed by gangs of local boys who gathered outside the doors at the time of the service and even came inside making derogatory remarks in audible tones about the choir and congregation. On one weekday, as a service was about to begin, MacColl was standing in the choir vestry ready to take the opening prayer and the door was open to the outside when he heard a loud howl and hiss and a cry, 'Look at that cross.'

MacColl decided he had had enough and making a dive through the open door grabbed one of four boys, brought him inside, the captive declaring 'It wasn't me that holed,' apparently meaning that it was his brother. The police were called, and eventually MacColl took out a summons against two boys, sons of an engine driver, who were aged fifteen and sixteen years respectively; one of them was a fireman on the railway. It is surely curious that when the case was heard they were represented by a barrister, and when a fine was imposed in lieu of fourteen days' imprisonment the money was forthcoming at once.

A good deal of sympathy is due to Malcolm MacColl for the way in which he was misrepresented by both extreme parties. Sanders, the leader of the anti-ritualistic party, hounded and execrated him. Croom and his party considered that he was a renegade unwilling to suffer for the faith that he professed, and for which Tooth had been a martyr. But the position in 1878 was completely different from January 1877 when Tooth was arraigned. Tooth had a united congregation; MacColl had a divided one, and with one half violently contentious. There is no doubt that he accepted the charge of St. James's with a view to succeeding Tooth as incumbent and yet he was still only curate-in-charge. He achieved a good deal at St. James's, built up a new congregation, retained a dignity and devotion in the services, and showed that he was working to unite the congregation. He tried to meet both parties such as they were. One of his offers was that of a monthly late communion service following Sunday Mattins, but it was very poorly attended; rather than appear to be unconciliatory he persevered with it in the interests of peace; the other was that of receiving the alms himself instead of, as in Tooth's day, delegating it to a server. He was also still convinced that he would eventually be offered the living by the patron and always spoke of himself as 'vicar-designate.'

After Easter Robert Webb wrote a reasonable and almost soothing letter to *The Woolwich Gazette,* thanking the congregation for their Easter offering to MacColl, and making certain points now that he had retired as churchwarden. He made it clear that the services at St. James's were far from ritualistic, that certain requests of Mr. Fry's supporters had been met and that it was useless to expect a church to draw only from parishioners as its congregation. He pointed out that at St. John's and All Saints' Church nearby the churchwardens were not even parishioners. Finally, he appealed for money for the schools, a curate's fund, and for kneelers and hymn books. It was a temperate letter and his appeal was necessary, for some of the militant Protestants never contributed to the funds. The schools were a great grievance, as they suspected that extreme teaching on religion was given there. However, no sooner had one pen been taken up by one man than another reached for his. This time it was from the other former churchwarden (Fry), and it was a long diatribe against MacColl and his practices, calling on him to abandon the dogmas of the Real Presence, Auricular Confession, Prayers for the Dead, Invocation of the Saints, and Mariolatry. This was most unfair, since Fry had never heard these doctrines taught in the church on Sundays. He accused MacColl of acting as the priest of a clique and not the minister of the parish, again an unfair charge. He asked for fewer services, of a more 'hearty nature,' without defining his wishes more closely. Having once started on this line of personal attack and false innuendo, a reaction was bound to come from the other side. MacColl had asked the vicar of St. Stephen's, Lewisham, R. Rhodes Bristow, to preach on behalf of the schools, with collections to be taken for that purpose. On the Saturday evening, Sanders told MacColl that he was going to demand Bristow's letter of orders. This led to another of those acrimonious and half ludicrous scenes so beloved of Sanders. On the Sunday evening Sanders demanded Bristow's letters of orders, and Bristow said he could not, or would not, produce them. So when the time came for the sermon Sanders and his henchman stood at the bottom of the pulpit steps to prevent Bristow mounting them. Sanders then addressed the congregation, and after a little excitement some people left. Bristow retaliated by preaching briefly from his stall. As MacColl and Bristow left the chancel for the vestry they were hissed. The police were called to escort them both to the vicarage, and what Sanders thought he had achieved it is hard to say.

We do not know what took place the next Sunday, but during the week Fry was successful in the suit against Tooth, for the appeal failed. The cross on top of the screen was to remain, as well as the screen between the chancel and nave, but not the gates. The side screen and altar steps were to be removed within three weeks. One can hardly accuse MacColl of retaliation, but on the eve of St. James's Day, the patronal festival, he took the choir round the church in procession headed by a cross and singing a hymn. However, on entering the side aisle, a body of staunch Protestants prevented the procession continuing. The procession therefore, still singing, wheeled round unconcernedly and returned into the chancel.

It must have been gratifying, at least for MacColl, to attend the consecration of St. Augustine's, Bermondsey, in the poor district where he had worked so hard. He may have been slightly ruffled by the strictures of *The Rock* on the 'box altar,' the 'Un-Protestant erection,' and on its statement that 'all these baldachinos shelter what is blasphemously called "The Body and Blood" of our Saviour and should be rigidly excluded or extruded from all Protestant places of worship.'

A first class row was, however, brewing at St. James's, concerning an 'ecclesiastical smell' defined as incense. MacColl opened the church one Sunday morning in August and recognized the tang of incense. There is no doubt that he was not responsible. It was one of those deceptions perpetrated by someone who had access to the church, undoubtedly one of the Protestants. Ritualists would never have burnt incense except in a service, and anyhow they would have considered the use of incense only a small triumph compared with, say, the use of vestments. At any rate local feeling was well inflamed; one local reporter managed to describe it as a cloud, a complete feat of imagination. After the morning service, Fry addressed the unyielding MacColl in his usual dictatorial terms alleging, after a fierce preamble, that 'should the illegal practice be repeated we are resolved to prevent its continuance and we desire to have your assurance that we shall not again be witnesses to such an offensive ceremony.' MacColl, who must have felt he had put up with enough contumely, said that he was not making any promise, and asked the Fry delegation to go. Fry's final words were that on Sunday next the parishioners would be present in hundreds to compel him to give up the practice. Meanwhile, Fry made arrangements for the alterations to the church following the Penzance judgement. Sanders then wrote to *The Daily Telegraph* alleging the use of incense, and MacColl replied in *The Times* denying ever having used it. He might perhaps have taken an extra day to consider his letter. All the same he had put up with an enormous amount from men far below his intellectual and spiritual level, and he let fly in no uncertain terms.

Mr. Editor,

It is not true as reported in some newspapers that incense was used immediately before the 10 o'clock a.m. service on Sunday in St. James's Church. It has never been used at any service since I have been placed in charge.

It is not true that it was used immediately before the service. . . . I found a certain ecclesiastical smell but I never saw, nor suggested, nor wished, nor ordered the use of incense. . . . But when I say that personally I do not object to the smell of incense and then am represented as saying I approve such a foolish freak, I see very good reasons for declining to say anything at all.

It is very satisfactory to have it recorded in *The Times* that there are such characters as 'men in orders' in Hatcham. I find it difficult to recognize this truth among the brawlers, iconoclasts, and mob spouters with whom I am surrounded and with whom this place is infested. When a churchwarden loses that pleasing equanimity which distinguishes the office, has to be bound over to keep the peace, he approaches more closely to a breach of the law than to a miserable evasion of it. When he orders his sidesmen in 'high-falutin' style' to go out and bring into the priest's vestry some 10 to 20 men no doubt to produce a sensible impression upon the 'man in orders' when this same mighty man of valour insults the popular vicar of a neighbouring parish . . . by demanding his letters of orders, and on refusal intimates his intention to offer a violent and forcible protest against his preaching, though for a charity, you will admit that it is difficult to imagine what such a one does 'expect from men in orders.' And when with the voice of Jacob, though with the hands of Esau, he comes to sniff the incense on the breeze of popular opinion I hope the always generous public will lend no countenance to that bullying and braggart system which dishonours this house of God. Parson-baiting is as debasing as badger-drawing or cock-fighting and surely every Englishman will pronounce it unmanly as well as ungentlemanly to insinuate that a man in holy orders would say five minutes before a service that there was not to be any procession and yet would there and then attempt it.

Malcolm MacColl was furious and did not mind showing it. He expected trouble on the next Sunday and arranged for the police to be in attendance. The church was full, but nothing happened except that Sanders refused to give the bag containing the collection to a 'chorister.' When MacColl stepped forward and took it there was some applause; Sanders had scored a point. The service lasted from ten till nearly one so presumably every one was ready to leave for home, and the 'keen demands of appetite' was the excuse for the large congregation dispersing quietly. Sanders threatened that hundreds would shortly attend the church to compel him to give up the ritualist practices.

Meanwhile, a reception committee from the old congregation met Arthur Tooth at Euston, then called Euston Square station, and a grand fête was held in the grounds of Woodside. There were special trains from Cannon Street running through the green fields between Lewisham and Croydon. The women alighted at Woodside station next to the grounds, but the men went to the next station and marched back in procession, an imposing sight. Tooth was in thoroughly good form and made some amusing speeches full of reminiscences of his travels. There was no reference to his parish or the position of such friends as Mackonochie. The Band of the 5th Kent and the 29th Middlesex played continuously, and there were games, exhibitions, a concert and food in an enormous marquee. In fact a good time was had by all, and it seemed as though Hatcham and its troubles were no more than a slight cloud on the horizon. Malcolm MacColl was not there. A Protestant inhabitant of St. Alban's, Holborn, wrote indignantly to *The Rock* commenting on the price of the excursion:

> I will engage to get Mr. Tooth twice 1,100 visitors next week, adults, who will be glad to get twenty miles outing, dinner and tea for one shilling and ninepence, provided that they are not expected to give Mr. Tooth an affectionate greeting as part of the bargain.

IV

AUTUMN – ADVENT

BY now St. James's Church presented a very different appearance from the days of Tooth. The remnants of the confessional had been cleared away, and a plain prie-dieu substituted. The beam across the church, which was an anomaly without the rood, was taken down. The altar in the side chapel, always described as the *Ladye* chapel, had been removed and replaced by a small ledge on which rested a little wooden cross; and the screen between the nave and side aisle was removed, probably to Woodside. The triptych behind the high altar had gone and one imagines the curtains as well. The gates of the chancel had been removed, and the panels which Tooth had painted and that had been daubed over in the previous year were planed out. On the high altar a cross and two candlesticks had been replaced on a ledge, all given by Walter Plimpton. So the church looked bare and large and unusual. The news of the incense controversy and renovations and removals brought a large and critical congregation long before ten o'clock in the morning.

MacColl arranged with the police that fifty of them with two Inspectors and the Superintendent should make the school their base. So with them at hand when MacColl entered the church from the vestry he must have contemplated with a measure of confidence the sixty or seventy tough-looking men who had obviously not come for the purpose of devotion. They were hefty dock labourers, easily recognizable as such in spite of their Sunday best, who sat 'sniggering and sneering' in hope of trouble. Evidently some of the women could hear their earthy remarks and were reduced to laughter, described pompously in one report as 'painful indecorum,' and there was a general buzz of voices throughout the service. At the end of the communion service about a hundred men walked up and down the church staring at the altar and looking up and down. Sanders asked them to leave, for the next congregation was trying to gain entrance for Mattins. By mid-day there was not a seat in the place, but unfortunately when some of the 'London dock gentry, weary of sitting so long, took their departure, their places were taken by men of the same class.' Outside there was a fair sized crowd which the police gently pushed towards the main road where they dispersed for good. MacColl may justifiably have felt that he had scored. All the same more than one newspaper gave the most minute details of the service, even noting that 'MacColl did not genuflect, nor did he sign himself and the people with the cross; neither did he elevate the sacramental elements, but simply knelt down before them in prayer after the congregation, the choir and some of the congregation had sung "O sacred Victim slain to save," which corresponds to the "O salutaris Hostia" of the Roman Catholic Church used at the most solemn moment in the Mass.' This reporting, though accurate, created a situation of tremendous delicacy. The reference to MacColl kneeling in prayer after the consecration was a reminder that this had been one of the charges against Mackonochie.

Outside the Protestants had been active, distributing leaflets, asking members of the congregation not to give to the offertory inside the church. 'The most English and constitutional method of redressing grievances is the refusal of supplies,' said the leaflets; the grounds being that MacColl had 'repeatedly advocated auricular confession.' This is very doubtful. If MacColl did so it was not at any of his services, for the fact would have been blazoned far and wide in the columns of the Press and would have been the subject of the usual long correspondence in their columns. The fact that neither Fry nor Sanders could ever specify chapter and verse makes it reasonable to suppose that MacColl, who would certainly hear confessions and probably did if asked, never used it as a subject in his preaching or gave notice of fixed times. To do so would have brought a storm around him not in keeping with his policy. But confession was the most sensitive point of high church doctrine for Protestants and Catholics alike, and induced on both sides an emotional reaction.

At this point MacColl took three weeks' holiday which he sorely needed. There was some trouble when ten–twenty men on one of the following Sundays made for the vestry declaring their intention of 'counting the collection,' but somehow they were dispersed. It must have been an organized disturbance for the vicar's warden cancelled the evening service.

With the usual result of adding fuel to the flames, Fry now published the correspondence between him and the vicar on the subject of the schools, in which MacColl had refused to call a public meeting in the schoolroom. Should this not be convenient, Fry suggested that his committee would cordially pay all expenses and join MacColl and his supporters in the New Cross Hall. This meant that the meeting would be packed with Church Associationites obviously. The position over the schools was serious. The schoolmistress was summoned for non-payment of rates, and it was then revealed that the boys' department had been closed. The Board schools were over full, and it was a real hardship to the poor not to be able to send their children to St. James's school. All the same, with the Education Act less than two years old, not all parents wanted schooling for their children. Some regarded it as a gross interference with their rights, and an attempt to deny the reasonable earned (or unearned) contributions of their offspring. Education had always been one of Tooth's chief concerns, and it was a first charge on the money and funds of the old congregation. Mr. Layman appeared in court for the schoolmistress sued for payment by the vestry of St. Paul's, Deptford, and due to them along with a similar debt from St. John's, Deptford. This location has an ominous ring, for it was the militantly evangelical church which the Protestants from Hatcham still attended officially. Mr. Layman said there was a difference between St. John's district and St. James's. St. John's congregation consisted of rich residents but St. James's did not.

The inquisitive and able reporter from the hostile *Kentish Mercury* was all agog, and the next week there was a long leading article, which was far from objective. Perhaps it was designed to keep the issue alive. The reporter certainly had his ear to the ground, for he claims that 'the religious instruction is such as no Protestant churchman could approve.' The sole justification for such a charge could only have come from Fry or Sanders. The editor called the parish rich and prosperous, which it was only in one or two roads (St. James, Laurie Grove, Amersham Road), but claimed that the Protestant churchwarden was right in collecting money outside the church and that anything was better than the inculcation of children in Romish principles. Mr. Croom must have laughed hollowly when he read the words.

There was a good deal of sheltering under pseudonyma in the next correspondence which ran on in several papers, notably *John Bull,* and certainly washed dirty linen in public. Rumours were abounding that MacColl would not be offered the living of St. James's since Tooth and the Church of England Men's Society refused to support his régime. This brought the supporters of MacColl to the fore declaring that MacColl had received sharp treatment from Tooth. It was publicly alleged that Tooth had had all the burial fees and had now applied for the marriage fees drawn by MacColl during the curacy. Meanwhile, it was widely rumoured that Arthur Stanton, Mackonochie's curate, had been offered the living, which had the effect of raising a petition in favour of Mac-Coll to Bishop Thorold, signed by 1,100 parishioners and communicants. The Sunday after this Fry, followed by a body of Pro-

L

testant supporters, removed the cross from the ledge where the side altar had been, calling it 'obnoxious,' and handed it to Sanders who took it into the vestry.

Croom entered the epistolary fray and disclosed that during MacColl's absence there had been a meeting between the extremes of both parties without reaching any conclusion, since the Protestants would concede nothing at all. The Catholics were willing to yield to the wishes of the Protestants at services other than the eight o'clock which the Protestants never attempted to attend. Croom's letter charged MacColl with leaving the parish without spiritual provision alleging that it was because Fry applied to Tooth as *vicar* to provide a new incumbent that the idea of a meeting was suggested. He attacked MacColl for implications against Tooth's good faith, and he also denied that the living had been offered to Arthur Stanton of St. Alban's, Holborn, who refused to leave Mackonochie and the parish. It had, in fact, been offered to another curate at St. Alban's, Holborn, Henry Aston Walker who accepted it. Meanwhile, the acrimonious and lengthy correspondence on the Tooth–MacColl situation moved from *John Bull* to the columns of *The Church Review* and the *Church Times*. Tooth's former sacristan, Hill, aired the most detailed financial arrangements and so did Croom, which drew a spirited defence from Mrs. Malcolm MacColl and really made her husband look underpaid and badly treated. MacColl's friends promptly raised a presentation fund for him and now sure that he had someone to succeed him, Tooth resigned on November 21st, 1878. His absence from his own parish seems to have been due to some differences between him and Mac-Coll. Tooth had been speaking at many churches in and around London at different types of meetings but never at Hatcham. Some diocesan bishops inhibited him from preaching; the Bishop of Ripon was one. So we can only conclude that there was some coolness between the two men and with such different temperaments it is not surprising. It was, however, a pity that the break came now with the difficulties of an interregnum again. MacColl had done an enormous amount for the parish during his year's ministry and except for the small Fry–Sanders faction peace could have come.

Rumours that high church practices would again be introduced at Hatcham now began to appear in the ever curious Press. There had been a fierce attack on Cuddesdon Theological College by Dr. Golightly and an attempt to censure it by the Oxford Diocesan Conference. Sir Robert Phillimore produced an amending motion which was carried. Cuddesdon College is 'always in hot water' and 'never clean,' said *The Rock* spitefully, but the publicity and mudslinging damaged the picture of ritualists, making them appear crypto-papists. In St. James's, Hatcham, it had its reverberations.

At this time the final appeals against the alteration to the altar steps were heard and lost. The churchwardens locked and closed the church so that the fairly extensive alterations could take place. MacColl, who was not told of the closure, removed the cross from the ledge behind the altar, and some ritualist put an unauthorized anonymous notice on the north door, 'This church is closed in order that Messrs. Sanders and Fry may finish their work of destruction.' MacColl's notice was fixed to the west door. On the Sunday before Christmas there was another of those painful scenes that every one hoped had finished. The church had been reopened and there was a visiting minister. After the evening service, there was a rush towards the diminished altar, or table, to remove the ledges or gradines behind it on which flowers and candlesticks had been placed. From the other side there was a move to prevent such action, and then a general fight followed until the police restored order.

There were no services on Christmas Day, for MacColl had already left to become curate of St. Mary Magdalene's, Paddington. The Bishop of Rochester is said to have asked him to resign a few weeks before. Rumours, often malicious and untrue, continued to circulate. *The Kentish Mercury* reported that one of the St. James's churchwardens, the Superintendent of the Sunday school and the secretary of the C.B.S. had 'gone over.' If this meant to Rome, it was not true. After Christmas, a series of local clergymen took duty, all in turn either too low or too high for some members of the congregation, who never concealed their displeasure whichever party it happened to be. The police were still on duty and cleared the gangs of roughs round the doors on several occasions, even taking names and addresses. It was finally announced that Robert Tooth had appointed Henry Aston Walker as the next incumbent.

As for Malcolm MacColl, to whom a well deserved presentation was made, he stayed two years at St. Mary Magdalene's, Paddington; after which he moved on to become vicar of All Saints', Kilburn Park, and then to St. Mark's, Jersey. His last cure was at St. Columba's, Clydebank, though he had a part time ministry as late as 1914, the year of his death. One of his daughters, Gertrude, who was a child of six years old at Hatcham, lived to the age of ninety-five, only dying in 1967.

PART III

HENRY ASTON WALKER

1878 – 1886

CONTENTS

I

INAUSPICIOUS BEGINNING

IF there are candidates for palms as a reward for martyrdom in the ritualist controversy, Henry Aston Walker's name should stand high on the list. Tooth's contribution was unique because he was the first to defy Lord Penzance's court and go to prison; but priests like Mackonochie and Walker were broken in the grinding daily round of petty persecutions in a way that he never was. The importance of Tooth's implacable stand for principles in which he believed should not be minimized. He made it impossible for those who followed him to do less. However, he soon removed himself from the arena of combat and lived inconspicuously and uncontroversially to reach a grand old age. It is true that he was afterwards ignored by the Church but his only loss was that of a parochial cure; and his work with boys and a spiritual ministry as retreat conductor was probably a sufficient solace for the restricted ministry he later exercised from Woodside.

Walker was Mackonochie's curate and experienced in the cat-and-mouse game of prosecution and appeal. Although he belonged to the Society of the Holy Cross and the Confraternity of the Blessed Sacrament, he was not an extremist. If any one could have brought about a settlement he would have done so, for he was well able to distinguish between what was essential and what was not. He was outwardly imperturbable but deeply sensitive, an expert on liturgical music, and the author of the *Missa de Angelis* and some popular hymns. He had left St. Alban's, Holborn, and was acting as chaplain to a sisterhood in the West End, probably the one in Osnaburgh Street. For his first few weeks he continued to serve both the convent and the parish. There must have been some reason on his side for accepting the unpromising cure of St. James's, Hatcham. It may be that it was from motives of friendship for Tooth. It may be that he believed he had an insight into the methods and grievances of the opposite faction and thought that he could bring about peace. It may be that he saw no prospect of a parochial ministry coming his way except through a friendly patron such as Tooth, and he decided to take the opportunity; or it may be that he conceived it his plain duty to accept a difficult cure. He was eventually broken in the process.

Three factors made Walker's position more difficult. The first was that MacColl was still living at the vicarage although taking

Sunday duty at St. Mary Magdalene's, Paddington, travelling from Hatcham to do so. The second was the judgement in the faculty suit which required the remaining ornaments in St. James's to be removed and alterations carried out to the altar, reducing the steps in front of it from five to two. These took place in the interval between MacColl's departure and Walker's arrival. Sanders locked the church while these alterations were carried out. On the Sunday before Christmas, after the evening service, Sanders advanced in his usual purposeful way, supported by some twenty men and the applause of a good many others who obviously knew what was intended. He proceeded to pull away the two gradines from behind the altar, and these exposed a patch of faded discoloured wall. But the opposite side must have been present too, for as the triumphant Fry was making for the vestry, there was a scuffle and a general disturbance which was followed by a free-for-all. The police once again cleared the church. The third factor was Walker's much lonelier state. MacColl had been upheld by a devoted wife and family. Tooth had a solid congregation behind him. Walker had none of these satisfactions.

There was no service on Christmas Day. After Christmas, a variety of local clergymen, organized by Sanders, and including his own vicar, Canon Money of St. John's, Deptford, took duty. This did not please the Croom–Plimpton supporters. When Canon Money said the Commandments instead of allowing the choir to sing the responses, the high church party got up from their knees and left, and the choir stumped out into the vestry. The consequence was that when the choir turned up in the afternoon they were refused admittance, and finally there was no service. There was no congregation either. This may have been because of the piercing cold; the gas for heating had been turned off as the bill had not been paid.

All the same one newspaper stated that there was a sizeable and devout congregation and that the collection was larger than usual. This must have been the morning service. The next week there was a good congregation in the expectation that Walker would arrive. The Protestant League turned out in full force, though one can hardly believe as a welcome to the new vicar. Canon Money again took the service. The choir, having been refused entry through the vestry door, came in by the west door and tried to take their seats in the chancel. When they were asked to withdraw they did so and remained for the service perversely and heartily singing the responses against the 'said' version of Canon Money.

Meanwhile, the 'old' congregation still kept the Sunday school going in the schools, a great grievance to the Fry–Sanders clique. Some thirty of the Protestant Leaguers headed by M'Clure forced their way in, as the children were leaving, collided with two of the Sunday school teachers, and tore down a crucifix, grinding the figure to powder beneath their feet. On the whole, local opinion, which deplored these tactics as horse play, was swinging towards the side of the 'old' congregation who had suffered for so long. Sanders, Fry and Holloway were not popular according to the local press, which recognized that MacColl's attempts at conciliating them had met with no success. The general conclusion was that the old congregation had been 'shamefully used and driven away and none has come to take their places.'

The parish was going downhill. There had been no baptisms for weeks, no weekday services and little parish visiting, although for needy cases the indefatigable Miss Vaughan kept some going and still had £81 in hand to disburse. It was Miss Vaughan who had written to Archbishop Tait complaining that those who disturbed the services only stayed to scoff and never contributed a farthing to the upkeep of the church or the schools. But by now the Protestant Committee had organized its own visiting by 'Bible women,' and were shortly to set up their own Mission. This may have been a beneficial move for it diverted the malcontents from the parish church as well as giving them something to do. *John Bull* commented on the miserable state of the once beautiful church, now with scarcely a window whole, the bell rope broken, the gas cut off, the altar stripped of cross and candlesticks, a layer of dust everywhere, and a general air of drabness and neglect.

The week before Walker's institution was preceded by one of those bursts of correspondence in the local press which were so familiar a method of directing the searchlight on the St. James's dark corners. Fry began it by attacking MacColl for reintroducing what he called 'Ritual and sacerdotal teaching,' and by the use of the capital, it was easy to see which he considered the more reprehensible. This produced a spirited defence of MacColl from John Fuller, a sidesman, and Miss Vaughan's letter. At the same time the well organized Protestant Committee met and thanked the Church Association for their 'valuable assistance' in connection with the faculty suit which had been brought, from their point of view, to a successful termination. It was a painful one for other people. All this was hardly a peaceful situation for the start of Walker's ministry.

It was an astute move of Walker's to be inducted to the living on a weekday. Canon Money, who had the archdeacon's mandate, admitted him to the rights of his benefice, and he rang the bell as a 'public notification,' watched by his two churchwardens and a few other parishioners who had been hastily gathered together; a reporter said he 'was very cordially received.' He did not know what was in store.

This friendly welcome doubtless influenced Walker in his action in replacing a small cross and two candlesticks on the super-altar, which Walter Plimpton supplied. He took the view that they had been declared legal in the Liddell-Westerton case at St. Paul's, Knightsbridge. The Bishop of Rochester had received a report following an inspection of the altar by Canon Miller, the vicar of St. Nicholas', Deptford Green, and he had not recommended their removal. Walker's case was that the ornaments were as legal as a font or kneeler or pulpit and required no faculty for their replacement since they had always been in use.

He was probably right in everything he said and wrote but it produced one of the most acrimonious Sunday scenes since the days of Tooth, as there had been a Church Association meeting during the week addressed by the fanatical Concannon which fired its local supporters to action once more, and they turned up in force. The bitterly cold church was almost empty when Walker entered at 11.30 a.m., half an hour later than the service had been under MacColl, but it filled up quickly from then on. This shows that the congregation was mostly local as every one seemed to know the 'unusual hour' of the service, and it was noted that hardly any sympathizers with a high ritual were present. In fact, they were all in the front, while several well-known members of the opposite party occupied seats at the back of the nave. Walker said the service, and only two hymns were sung. The Evangelicals repeated the General Thanksgiving with him. This was one of those contentious points that could rend a congregation, and apparently it was a Kent custom to do so, whereas in other places it was considered 'high' church. There was no ante-communion, and instead of a sermon the vicar read himself in, in a 'distinct and interesting manner.' At the end he gave the blessing or, as it was called in the local newspapers, the Benediction, 'holding up his hand in the simple way adopted by most of the bishops,' an attitude evidently accounted to him for righteousness. As he turned east for a final devotion on his knees Walker became aware of a noisy movement and upraised voices. Rising and facing his congregation he could see the stalwarts of the Protestant League advancing towards him with considerable support, Holloway, the churchwarden of St. John's, Deptford, at their head. Nash, the St. James's vicar's warden, stood at the entrance to the chancel, and Holloway called out to his Church Association colleague, Sanders, something like 'get rid of the things on there' (the cross and candlesticks). Someone hit out at Nash who was trying to bar the way, and Sanders began clearing the church, still filled with people; one account says more than a hundred and another one hundred and fifty. Sanders shouted to the vicar that he must remove the cross and candlesticks and obtain a faculty for them. The vicar and Sanders moved towards the vestry, and as Layman hurried forward to support Walker, he was recognized and followed by cries of 'Jesuit.' The church was not finally cleared till two o'clock, when those last to leave uttered threats as to what they would do at the evening service which was to take place in an hour's time.

Walker thanked his churchwarden for clearing the church. Sanders, for his part, made some statement about the need for a faculty as 'illegal' ornaments had been introduced. Walker, who was confident of their legality, concurred. Perhaps this was one of the early misunderstandings that led to so many recriminations later. Sanders offered to pay half the costs of the application for the faculty and Walker half assented. Sanders, however, knew that the Church Association would oppose the faculty and had every hope of success. Cross and candlesticks would then be banished for ever. The quick witted lawyer, Layman, realized this and therefore was forced to point out (and in hearing of the others) the probable result. This caused Walker to withdraw his agreement to an application for a faculty with consequent ill feeling on both sides. Walker's distrust and Sanders's animosity began to grow. One hopes that the Sunday dinner was unspoilt at whichever home Walker was the guest; and that somehow he managed to eat and enjoy what was set before him by a friendly family before he returned to the church for the service at 3 p.m. No doubt his heart sank as he looked at the full church from the pulpit that afternoon, unable to recognize one party from another but realizing that both were disputants and 'present in large numbers.' He intended his sermon to be objective and pacific, and he appealed to his own position as newly appointed priest and said he would not refer to past troubles. Perhaps he laid it on too thick when he used the words 'blasphemous' and 'profane' to describe scenes that had taken place because these were attributable chiefly to one side.

'If you desire peace,' he said wisely, 'you must do the things that make for peace, you must obey the Lord Jesus Christ, you must live better and more godly lives, you must put away from

you blasphemy, evil speaking, discord, slandering and drunkenness
which are the dreadful sins of to-day.'

The congregation rose and sang Ken's evening hymn, 'Glory to
thee, my God, this night, For all the blessings of the light,' eyeing
one another as they did so; but none in the church noticed the
irony of the choice. As soon as the vicar left for the vestry at the
end of the service, there was a 'scene of great excitement.' Blows
were exchanged, voices raised; one churchwarden, Nash, rushed
for the police, the other, Sanders, shouted after him that it was his
duty to clear the church. The Protestant League supporters were
yelling slogans, and Sanders tried to drown their voices by insisting
that the cross and candlesticks must go, and declaring that he was
about to remove them, which he did, carrying them into the vestry.

After this Henry Walker is said to have shaken hands with his
churchwarden at the end of the afternoon although he protested as
he did so about the removal of the offending ornaments, a statement which his churchwarden, Nash, supported. Outwardly, however, the decencies of social behaviour seem to have been maintained, but the church was not cleared until after five o'clock.

However, the next day reports were published in newspapers all
over the country and Hatcham was once more a boiling point of
controversy. On the whole, opinion supported Walker. It was exactly two years since the beginning of the riots, but this time no
one for one moment did other than condemn the doings of the
previous Sunday. 'They appeared to emanate solely from a persistent longing for hubbub,' said one witness, 'seeing that nothing
done or said by the minister was of a nature to afford other than
gratification to the mind of the staunchest opposer of Ritualism
that ever led the van of the Anti-ritualistic craze.'

Evidently, Walker had made up his mind to begin as he meant
to go on. He called a round table conference at which he offered
one service in accordance with their wishes to each party. Croom
was ready to accept but others on both sides could not agree. Years
before Keble had written to Gresley, 'Let us hope they steer clear
of church politics, fripperies and tittle tattle,' and this was what
Walker intended to do. He was an old-fashioned high churchman
in that respect.

Walker had not yet moved into the vicarage but was still living
in Lexham Gardens. The church was closed during the week, and
no services were held until the next Sunday at eleven o'clock, when
Mattins was followed by Holy Communion. But during the intervening days Sanders and the other Church Association members

were anything but idle, and circularized the parishioners with a notice delivered to every house:

> To the Protestant Parishioners of St. James's, Hatcham:
>
> You are requested to attend the services in your parish church on Sunday next at eleven and three o'clock and, if necessary, to protest against any attempt to reintroduce the illegal ornaments which were removed by your churchwarden.

Nothing indicated that the other churchwarden supported their retention, or that there was any other point of view in the parish. This inflammatory notice achieved its result. Walker saw it, and having consulted Layman and Plimpton arrived in church the following Sunday by 10.30 and waited. Within a short time Sanders bustled in, and announced to the half full church that he was removing the cross and candlesticks. 'They are illegal ornaments,' he told his hearers, 'and they ought not to remain to be the cause of disturbances among the congregation.'

Walker, who could hardly be expected to stand by in silence, then came forward, declaring that he regarded the removal of the cross and candlesticks as an insult and an unwarrantable interference with the performance of divine woship. 'I am not going to proceed with the service until they are replaced,' he declared. To replace them meant extracting them by force from the vestry where Sanders had placed them. Since this would plainly make matters worse, Walker's only course was to close the church which he proceeded to do. One 'lady' shouted, 'Better have no service if there cannot be one without candlesticks.' One is tempted to identify her as Mrs. Fry.

Meeting Sanders face to face as he was clearing the church Walker said there would be no evening service either unless the articles were restored. Walker and Nash then closed and locked the church and Walker pinned a notice to the door:

> There will be no service this morning in consequence of the interference of Mr. Churchwarden Sanders. Evening service at 3 p.m. if it can be held without molestation.
>
> HENRY ASTON WALKER
> January 26th, 1879.

It was promptly torn down though the one on the north door remained unnoticed and unmutilated. Sanders, quoting the Bishop of Rochester freely, then harangued the crowd which cheered and applauded him until it gradually dispersed. But by three o'clock they were all back again, and the space in front of the school was the spot from which Sanders addressed them on the subject of the crucifix. The police managed to restrain the crowd from entering and discovering whether another had replaced it.

Walker wrote to the Bishop with a full account of the incident, enclosing the handbill distributed by the Protestant faction. He ended:

> My lord, it must be obvious to you that this is no personal question of mine but one which ultimately concerns the whole Church, the interests of all the clergy and not one parish only. The treatment we have already endured is a system of bullying which is a shame and a disgrace, and makes the blood of just people boil.

He sent the letter to the Press, his only course since Sanders's action was reproduced far and wide along with the comments of editors.

Sanders sent a long defence to *The Standard*. He denied any knowledge of the circular and said it was 'the work of an independent parishioner' and denied using the Bishop's name in his demagogic oration to the crowd; he did not deny acting as speaker and inciter outside the church. Sanders ended with the revealing phrase:

> The sooner clergymen recognize that they are not above the law, the sooner they give lie to the line 'New presbyter is but old priest writ large' and the sooner we shall have peace in the Church of England and in our parish.

One of his beliefs was that the Church of England did not make priests, and what the Ordinal meant to him no one can guess. To him an incumbent was an ecclesiastic who functioned under civil and secular law in a local and national situation. Disloyalty to the law was equivalent to treason, so according to Church Association policy, ritualism was a form of treason to the State, and disloyalty to the Queen. Perhaps rather unwisely (but what other course could he have taken?) Walker summoned Sanders in the magistrate's court for brawling, not realizing that Balguy would never have passed a sentence that would have made a martyr of either plaintiff or defendant, whatever the evidence.

During the following week the Bishop of Rochester sent his reply and it was published in the Press. Thorold came down on Sanders's side as might have been expected from a man who was

the former vicar of St. Pancras Church and the personal friend of
Canon Miller of Deptford. He conceded that Sanders had no right
to remove the cross and candlesticks but chided Walker for aban-
doning the service. He dismissed the handbill as an irrelevancy and
supported Sanders for trying to enter the school when the children
were being taught. He then sat on the fence, stating that 'irregularities' had taken place on both sides.

> Ornaments in themselves legal, may be informally introduced
> and illegally removed. No doubt candlesticks on the Holy Table
> are legal; a cross is also legal if plainly separated from the table
> itself *(as this one was)*.
> The question in point is, how did these ornaments come to be
> there? *(This was hardly a fair question since they had been used for
> at least eleven years and had been declared legal by one Judicial
> Committee. They were also widely in use up and down the country,
> tolerated by bishops, even if not approved.)* You do not say who
> placed them there in the first instance, but you admit you replaced
> them on your own authority: and as even in a matter of such
> apparent insignificance, you do not possess the authority for so
> doing, you were hardly justified in exercising it.

In a purely legalistic frame Thorold next assessed the action of
Sanders and castigated him.

> But once there, they ought not to have been removed without
> legal direction, the faculty which was needed for introducing
> them being equally needed for removing them. The office of a
> churchwarden is held to be one of observation and complaint,
> not of control. Consequently Mr. Churchwarden Sanders even
> more exceeded his powers in removing these ornaments on his
> personal authority than you exceeded yours in replacing them
> there.

He also disclosed the fact that he had offered to visit the church
and preach in the morning or afternoon. Walker must have refused
to have him. His reasons may have been clear at the time since
Thorold's partisan attitude the previous August still rankled with
the Catholics. It was, however, at this stage a pity that he took this
attitude. The Bishop had said that no reasonable person would
dream of complaining that Walker was a high churchman. Had he
repeated this from the pulpit it would have given enormous kudos
to Walker, and probably commended him to many non-contentious
parishioners. But the end of the letter was on a different note and
even an encouraging one.

My brother in the faith of Christ and this English ministry, a great responsibility rests upon you, and you must face the alternative of being a blessed peacemaker, whom your flock will respect and love, or of earning the reproach of one who, refusing even for Christ's sake to surrender his own will, tempts his brethren to offend.

Ornaments may be reasonable and suggestive and decorous yet at the best they are but dumb symbols of our holy faith To preach Christ in the truth of His Gospel, and to set forth His life in the meek self-sacrifice of His example, is surely for all of us everywhere the most forcible method of recommending our religion. For you under your present embarrassments, it is quite the most excellent way.

And the Bishop signed himself as a 'faithful friend and well-wisher.' It may have been a one-sided appeal, but it was on a personal level, and did not include legalistic threats against him. Most unfortunately on the same day a private letter of Walker's was made public. This was in reply to one from a Roman Catholic sympathizer and well-wisher. Walker, who could never have dreamed that it would reach the Press, had written unguardedly:

I expect there will be a much more serious riot next Sunday. The ringleaders are all bad and immoral men, but the world does not mind that. It pets them because they boast themselves to be parishioners. I beg you will remember me at Mass.

It seems almost malicious to have communicated it to the Press; and it was used to the full by Sanders and Fry.

The Bishop then chided Walker for suspending the service:

Nothing but the gravest necessity can ever excuse an entire suspension of the ordinary services. While I am convinced that you really thought that you were acting for the best, I am quite as clear that you were mistaken.

Sanders and Walker corresponded with each other in the columns of *The Standard,* and their letters were reprinted in the local papers. Others took a hand; one Hugh Ryves Baker, a former member of St. James's in MacColl's time, asked Sanders to say who removed the cross and candlesticks which MacColl had replaced and which had never been traced. He obviously considered Sanders responsible.

One of the Sunday school teachers gave a vivid account of the entry of Sanders and Fry into the school followed by thirty or forty roughs, opening cupboards, demanding keys and hunting in every conceivable hiding place for the crucifix which they were certain had replaced the one they had destroyed. Baker also said that when the police wished to release the school children and teachers through a back door, Sanders explained to the mob what was happening, and closed the suggested exit. Those inside then had to leave by the front entrance followed by boos, hisses and insults.

The Standard, never before friendly to the High Church party, produced a surprisingly objective and informed letter taking a middle course almost supporting Walker. This was praise indeed.

> Candlesticks and a cross placed over the Communion table are part of the order of the Church. . . . The very simple and unobjectionable ornaments which moderate High Churchmen still desire to retain are all part of the order of the Church, and wholly distinct from the fantastic symbolism and tawdry perilities of the ultra-Ritualists. Yet the Hatcham churchwarden removed them instantaneously with as prompt a sense of duty as if they were confessionals or crucifixes. Does Mr. Sanders then belong to the great body of parishioners who are 'sick of division and conflict' and wish only for a clergyman who will minister according to the order of the Church, or does he belong to one of the extreme wings which put petroleum on dead ashes and then set them on fire?
>
> Mr. Walker, of course, ought to follow the Bishop's advice and take care to give no offence merely to gratify his own will. But he has others to think of besides himself. We have the Bishop's own testimony to the moderation of Mr. Walker's views. Nobody, he says, could call him a High Churchman. He is not complained of now as either a Low Churchman or a High Churchman. What, therefore, is the matter with him?

The 'matter' was that no compromise would satisfy Sanders and his followers. They supported another church as non-parishioners; they did not come to worship or communicate at St. James's, but they were determined to achieve the complete Protestantization of St. James's in accordance with Church Association principles. Sanders was rich, clever and indefatigable and single-minded in an almost megalomaniacal way. He was determined to succeed as we know he eventually did.

By now Hatcham again was red hot news as far as New York, and more than one heart must have been heavy as the first Sunday in Febraury, which was also the Feast of the Purification, approached. The police were in evidence once again. They ushered children and teachers into the school 'unmolested,' watched by a gathering crowd, which was quiet and orderly. Inside the building

M

was packed to the doors, and the conclave which Sanders and his friends were holding on the subject of the disputed ornaments was plainly audible to those around. Walker entered through the north door and went to the vestry. Sanders followed and handed him a 'notification':

> You have replaced or authorized the replacing of the illegally introduced cross and candlesticks into the Church of St. James's, Hatcham, in defiance of the order of the Bishop of Rochester. I now protest against you having so done and shall present you to the Bishop.

I am, sir, yours obediently,

W. H. SANDERS. Churchwarden

Walker, who always contrived to maintain an imperturbably calm manner, took it with a bow, and having robed went into the church for Morning Prayer. He could not help noticing the St. Alban's Working Men's Club in the front rows. There was an undertone of noise; and a few, but only a few, 'intentionally made the responses in a noisy and profane manner.' But after he had given the blessing with his upraised hand and left the church for the vestry, the congregation made no move to go. Suddenly, he realized that Sanders was addressing the congregation in the following words,

'Gentlemen, leave the church. The cross and candlesticks will remain as they are, Mr. Walker having thought fit to disobey the Bishop's orders, and will not even for Christ's sake forgo his own will.'

This produced an outburst of cheers and hisses. Sanders continued,

'If the gentlemen at the other end of the church will go out, the people at this end will be able to move.'

At this he was loudly applauded and the congregation slowly took themselves out to an even denser crowd, where an assiduous Associationite was distributing Canon Ryle's tracts, as he loudly called on his hearers to 'oppose ritualism.' It could hardly be a danger to any one who had been present at the service that morning. The crowd hooted and hissed Walker as he left but nothing worse happened. The police gradually edged the people away, but returned in time for the evening service at three o'clock 'in as sinister a way as in the morning.' It was, however, soon known that Walker had summoned Sanders under the Brawling Act for violent and disorderly conduct in interfering with him in the discharge of his duties. Walker was probably pressed to do this by his supporters, Layman, Nash and Plimpton, and he was entirely within his rights. But it was hardly wise or pacific, for it only gave Sanders more publicity and increased his self-assertion.

Nothing was achieved by the case which was heard the following Wednesday. Supporters of both parties attended, and after the preliminaries were over and the case stated for both sides, Balguy, who must have been heartily sick of these repeated hearings, retired with them to his private room in order to try to bring about a settlement. After an hour he announced that the case would be adjourned for the advice of the Bishop. *John Bull* described it:

> Two persons dressed as ladies, who were conspicuous by the amount of feeling which they manifested; the elder, a stout, somewhat ill-favoured elderly person, hissing at the vicar, whilst the younger female, whose delicately moulded features were suffused with excitement and passion, gave utterance to various derisive and satirical ejaculations.

These were the usual cries of 'Jesuit' and 'Go to Rome.' The crowd followed the vicar's friends a 'considerable way on their road home,' and they 'became the butt of much vulgar abuse at their hands.' The older woman was probably Mrs. Fry and the younger her daughter. A week later Balguy dismissed the summons, Walker asked for another summons, but was dissuaded from pressing it. A local paper commented:

> His Worship would really make a capital Bishop, for he has not gone in the isolation but has acted in a fatherly manner towards all concerned in this puny squabble, and has settled it into the bargain. In fact Mr. Balguy seems to have a clearer perception of the case in his little finger than my Lord Roffen in the whole compass of his rochet and chimere. Dr. Thorold has certainly not acted up to the mark in this affair, and has missed a splendid opportunity for Prelatial Statesmanship.

What the reporter intended by this phrase is not explained. *Punch* commented on the ritualist scene under a heading *The Agonies of 'Atcham:*

> Mr. Sanders 'e tried to restore Peace to us (not the convic' *Charlie*) by removin' of the Brazen Immages which the new parson put but it was no go. For in this new religion you can't get on no how without the Cymbals of devotion. But perhaps dear Sir

> you can recomind us an old-fashioned Parson who can pray
> without too Brass Candlesticks and a Golden Cross. . . .

This heavy ridicule was no help to any one. There were no
images in dispute, and the emphasis on *brazen* was undoubtedly
intended to arouse emotions on empty idols (as idolatry) which was
untrue.

Meanwhile, the cross and candlesticks remained on the super-
altar in spite of knowledge that the Bishop had issued a monition
for their removal, which Walker mentioned as 'legal difficulties' to
the two churchwardens. When the letter from the Bishop came it
was received with tepid satisfaction by both sides. In any case the
two churchwardens themselves held opposing views and we should
read the letter with this in mind.

> I write to you about certain legal ornaments lately introduced
> into St. James's Church and which were twice removed by
> Mr. Churchwarden Sanders. . . .
> When the vicar appealed to me against the churchwarden's
> action I explained that though the ornaments had been irregu-
> larly introduced, they had been illegally removed. . . .

The Bishop then referred to the monition which Walker had
ignored and after saying that 'no steps have been taken to procure
a faculty' he continued:

> No doubt it is open to me to instruct you to remove the orna-
> ments but after full consideration of the case, it is not my inten-
> tion to do so. In the possible event of your being unable to act
> together, an awkward conflict would ensue.

Nash had obviously stated his case well. His last section was dip-
lomatic and it is sad to know that it fell on deaf ears:

> There can be no advantage in stirring a passing dispute about
> a matter in itself of utter insignificance into another burning
> controversy. Nor do I feel it incumbent on me, in vindication of
> an authority about which in the present case I cannot pretend to
> feel much sensitiveness, to risk a harassing and tedious litigation,
> the charges of which I could not with propriety suffer others to
> share with me, and which must either end a failure far more
> mortifying than a prudent inaction now or in a judgment which
> it might be undesirable to enforce.

We know he consulted Tait asking whether he should issue a
monition and saying that he did not want the expense of prosecuting 'Moreover, victory in an ecclesiastical court now seems to

be a very real kind of defeat.' He also mentions Walker's own letters to him complaining unreasonably that they are of a 'somewhat insiduous courtesy.'

Tait's reply was in character. He advised Thorold to ask Walker to obey his instructions to remove the offending articles. If he did not comply, the churchwardens could apply for a faculty, not realizing that the churchwardens were divided on this. Thorold could then leave the legal process to take its course. Thorold wrote almost indignantly to Tait saying he would not dream of instructing the churchwardens though he would tell them what advice he gave to Walker.

It sounds as though Bishop Thorold, however, had consulted his brother bishops informally for in his friend Bishop Magee's biography there is more than a hint of attempted unanimity. Magee, who supported the Public Worship Regulation Act in 1874, detested the Holy Cross type of priest as well as the Church of England Working Men's Society which he regarded as its lay equivalent. He wrote:

> Heaven knows I came to this diocese no High Churchman and willing enough to co-operate with the Evangelicals; but they are driving me more and more in spite of myself into the arms of the High Churchmen who, I suspect, know very well I do not thoroughly belong to them.

All the same Tait advised Thorold that no good would come of any more court orders, quite an admission.

From the time of the imprisonment of Tooth there had been some shifting of opinion among the bishops and even some transigence on the part of Archbishop Tait. What never seemed to occur to Thorold, or to any other bishop, was the idea of attempting to solve the problem by ordinary human contact and simple pastoral care. Thorold never appears to have interviewed Sanders or to have visited Walker. A little charitable interest such as Ernest Wilberforce used when he was Bishop of Chichester might have helped a great deal.

At any rate the *Church Times* applauded Thorold's letter. *The Rock* described it as unusually vague, 'with phrases to balance each other as though the writer was to counteract every effort for extracting its significance. A bishop is bound like any other officer to administer the law of the country and not like the Bishop of Oxford (Mackarness) to remain inactive . . .'

The Rock was still more unhappy about the possible attitude of bishops when in the same month Lightfoot was appointed Bishop of Durham. It was well known that, as a scholar, he believed that the 'harlot' of the Book of Revelation was Pagan Rome and not Papal Rome; he did not therefore secure a welcome from Church Associationites. However, the Protestants in Hatcham gathered momentum for their opposition. They had held a successful meeting in New Cross at which all the so called aggrieved parishioners of St. James's attended and two resolutions were passed. One condemned 'endeavours to reinstate the ceremonial of the apostate Church of Rome into conformity with the tenets of the Church of England.' The other called upon 'all members of the Church of England to use their influence in supporting the Church Association to enable it to disseminate Protestant truth.'

II

GUERRILLA WARFARE – 1879

THERE was no English Church Union meeting in New Cross during March, but the old Hatcham Defence Committee assembled and reinstated itself as 'The Saint James's Church Society.' This had the effect of bringing into prominence its opposite number, 'The Saint James's Protestant Committee.' Strong rumours that the Protestants were to set up a 'Free' church must have heartened the ritualists. However, it transpired that they were only trying to form their own Mission, charities and Sunday school. This local schism was extremely successful, supported as it was from the useful financial resources of the Church Association, which made their benevolence so attractive.

The Church Review in an article headed *Is Bishop Thorold Quite Fair?* remarked:

> One of the most trying features of the present distress is the determined unfairness and persistent want of candour with which those in authority treat any one charged with what people call Ritualism. Even by bishops who sympathize with them far more than Bishop Thorold does, real or suspected ritualists are dealt with as no other person ever would be. The justice meted out to them is very scant in its proportions and kindness and indulgence are treated as things entirely reserved for the use of other sections of churchmen.

It ended with a prophecy which the writer may not have lived to see fulfilled:

> It is a long lane that has no turning, and our day will come sooner or later. We are rather tired of waiting for it, but for all that we mean to wait till it does come.

Lent could have been a refreshing spiritual season for Henry Aston Walker but it must also have been full of anxieties. The reorganization of the St. James's Church Society was more than justified in view of the meeting called by Mr. Churchwarden Sanders at New Cross Public Hall to which all parishioners were invited to attend. There were many present who were not parishioners, or who, if they were, communicated at other churches and held office there, such as Soliague of St. John's, Deptford, and Bradshaw of St. John's, Nottingham. The object of the meeting was to whip up support for Sanders's successor as churchwarden at St. James's at the coming vestry meeting. Sanders urged the ratepayers among the audience to come and vote for Ernest Collard. Church attendance was no qualification and non-residents and the poor were excluded. Collard made a speech in which he vowed to put down ritualism, though where he expected to find any such practices at St. James's was a mystery, since Walker did not even wear the now almost respectable stole. Bradley, a Church Association member, gave his account of methods in Nottingham which had counteracted ritualistic tendencies, and Sanders announced the opening of a Protestant St. James's Sunday School; money rolled in for this purpose.

On the other side the St. James's Church Society had an application for membership from William Grant who had been such a prominent defender of Tooth. Grant had been one of MacColl's supporters and Arthur Tooth's critics at the end of the previous year. He approved of the policy of MacColl, and opposed Croom when he left the church. It would have been sensible to forget this action. But any criticism of 'our heroic vicar, Father Tooth' (as he was coming to be called), touched the Plimpton–Croom–Layman crowd where it hurt most. They refused his application and once more the whole correspondence was forwarded to *The Greenwich and Deptford Chronicle,* probably by Grant. By this time Grant had become an extreme churchman, and was secretary of the Order for Corporate Reunion, which had as its object reunion with the Holy See. If he held that post at the time of his application to join the St. James's Church Society the committee may well have had to think twice about admitting him. On the other hand the objects were simply 'to uphold the rights and liberties of the congregation, and to preserve reverence and order in St. James's Church.' But Grant dragged the old MacColl–Tooth controversy into the open and did the new Society and Walker renewed harm. He later seceded from the Established Church to Rome.

Meanwhile, Walker nailed one notice calling the Easter vestry on the door of the church and Sanders nailed another. This last one, besides calling a meeting for the election of the churchwardens and passing the accounts, also said that it would 'consider the desirability of passing a resolution on the appointment of the action of the vicar in the matter of the cross and candlesticks.' To make things more controversial the Protestant Parish Committee issued a circular to all parishioners urging them to attend the vestry meeting and support the candidate, Ernest Collard. 'Will no one stop this scandal?' commented one local paper. 'Cannot the sensible men in the congregation do something?'

The meetings were called concurrently for Easter Tuesday at the not very convenient hour of nine o'clock in the morning, and it usual unconcerned and even urbane, and somehow was allowed to act as chairman which he did by standing on the steps between the vestry and the church. Around him was a milling mob most of whom he had never seen before. Sanders then read out his notice which received hearty applause. Walker began reading the previous year's minutes held in 'the sacristy,' a word which produced a howl of protest as a 'Romish word,' but somehow he managed to continue. Sanders described the end of the previous year's minutes which had produced a resolution censuring the moderate MacColl in that 'he has rendered the establishment of peace in the parish more difficult than ever.' Sanders said that this resolution had been carried unanimously in MacColl's absence and had a right to be included in the minutes. He castigated his fellow churchwarden for not being present to propose the accounts, and a vote of censure was passed on the unfortunate Nash who probably had gone to work. At this point Walker nominated his own churchwarden, Mr. Walters, as was customary. This produced a storm of groans, hisses and cries of 'He's a Catholic,' 'Let him go to St. Joseph's' (the Roman Church), all of which Walker ignored. He waited until he could be heard and then asked for nominations for parish (or people's) warden. Sanders began a long harangue. He attacked Walters as not a fit person to hold office. 'Birds of a feather,' shouted someone. He then attacked sacerdotalism, ritualism and men who belonged to the Society of the Holy Cross. All this was aimed at Walker. He ended by saying that the vestry must appoint a man who would uphold the true principles of Protestantism and he nominated Ernest Collard.

Collard's election was carried by a large majority, and he replied saying that he was at variance with the vicar, a statement which was greeted with 'Turn him (Walker) out,' 'We mean to,' 'We'll support you' and 'Mrs. Fry for ever.' There was another disturbance over the choice of sidesmen which was left to the churchwardens to decide. One member from another church spoke of boys in church and 'tomfoolery,' but at this point Walker got up to leave, not without protests; some of his own supporters left with him.

In a fighting speech a man called Morton condemned the patron's appointment of Walker who was in the 'ritualistic conspiracy,' a member of the S.S.C., and the C.B.S.:

A minister belonging to these societies is not worthy of the confidence of his parishioners, as these societies are almost if not quite Roman Catholic. We want Protestants not Roman Catholics, a minister not a priest, a table not an altar. We will confess to God not to man. The Church is the Church of England. We have put on our armour and we intend to fight till victory.

Next followed a vote of thanks to Sanders for 'his indefatigable efforts on behalf of Protestantism,' who 'have no piracy (*sic*), priesthood or confessional.' A resolution was proposed complaining against the action of the police in coming down to St. James's on Sunday 'to guard Ritualistic practices.' Apparently there had been forty-five on one Sunday and seventy-five on another and this caused great displeasure. No wonder there had been no disturbances on the Sundays in Lent.

Two letters appeared next week in *The Greenwich and Deptford Chronicle* both from eye witnesses, giving their own versions and opinion. One was from E. Montague Cavenaugh of Shardiloes Road, quite a young man:

> After the three cheers for our noble selves and three groans for all who don't think as we do, the climax of effrontery exhibited by the so-called Protestant party was reached. The party which for two or three years has behaved itself in such a manner as to disgust every one above the highly respectable vendors or turnip-tops, or butter, or cats' meat who compose it, proceeded solemnly to denounce the presence of the police.

The writer then recalled some of the actions of the Protestant group, such as breaking into the schools, destroying its furniture, and removing hangings in the church, and ended:

> If the Protestants do not want the police, let them show that the police are not wanted but it is only common sense to keep a watch on one who has 'shet' [*sic*] at you once, and still presents a weapon.

The next letter was signed with the initials F.H., and after describing the vestry meeting as a disgrace to Englishmen, and mentioning the theft of 'black hangings' on Palm Sunday, he continued:

> Is it the Vicar's party that molest their opponents in the streets and call them most vulgar names? Is it the Vicar's party that go into the chancel after the service with the intention of making others follow and make a disturbance? I must say the behaviour of these Protestants both in and out of church is something disgraceful, they appear to be in charge of an elderly woman, who,

I suppose, is the same to them as Mrs. Girling to the Shakers. Those assembled at the vestry meeting seemed to have made a great fuss about the money collected considering they never put one farthing to the offertory. Sunday after Sunday do these Protestants allow the bag to pass them without putting anything in it.

As Walker was about to move into the vicarage which had been set in order by Tooth, the St. James's Church Society held a meeting to make plans and he took the chair. He agreed to begin again the 8 a.m. Sunday service of Holy Communion which had been in abeyance. Thomas Layman appears to have pressed for choral services and a mid-day sung celebration. Evidently, there were two opinions about this, and news of the disagreement leaked through *John Bull's* columns. It was even rumoured that 'one of the chief supporters of Tooth during the troubles will continue his support of the present régime'; evidently an allusion to Croom. The committee set about plans for a curate, and Walter Plimpton began a fund. There could then be two celebrations each Sunday and they decided to revive the choir and Gregorian music. Layman's idea was to try for a curate whose views were not known, but Croom, if it was Croom, protested against 'moderate' men. Walker asked the meeting not to give to the offertory at the celebrations of Holy Communion, but to make donations and to subscribe in another way. Since these alms were at the disposal of the churchwardens they would not be available for Walker's necessary work if Sanders could prevent it. From then on there were two sets of parish accounts and this perhaps aroused the deepest and most bitter resentment of all. The meeting was well aware that Sanders had applied for a faculty to remove the cross and candlesticks and it was evidently agreed to let this go by default.

The meeting may have been slightly heartened by an extremely stiff letter from the Bishop of Rochester to Mr. Churchwarden Sanders, which had suddenly been published two weeks after he received it. One can only suppose that the Bishop had allowed this course. After saying that he had compared Sanders's letter with that of the vicar's the Bishop wrote that differences would not prevent him from doing justice and protecting Walker if necessary. He ended:

> As to the rudeness, I really hope that some of it may be unintentional, and while it sometimes happens that persons are ill-mannered from want of knowing better, it is so unusual for a clergyman of character and education to be ill-treated by one of

his own churchwardens that I hope to find myself right in the feeling that if there has been roughness on your side, there has been oversensitiveness on his. . . . With respect to the alleged irreverence (and which, from intelligence that has reached me for months past, and from quite unprejudiced sources, I have only too much cause for fearing to have occurred) it is my duty to remind you and all whom it may concern that such conduct is a grievous dishonour to Almighty God, and a kind of outrage on his house of prayer. The Lord Jesus does not care to be served by the weapons of irreverence and uncharitableness, and those who by such means think to promote the cause of truth and order, only succeed in inflicting on it a vital and permanent injury.

Sanders, enraged to find this letter published in *John Bull* and copied in the local Press, obviously made a careful reply. He ignored the charges which he said were still under dispute and the subject of further correspondence with the Bishop. The charges of irreverence he dismissed as vague, saying he had not seen anything except acts of superstition forbidden by the rubrics. He denied the charge of unbearable rudeness adding:

I told Mr. Walker the first time I saw him that I detested his principles, and that I should oppose them to the best of my power in a right and proper way. From that position I have not swerved. I am not the officer of the vicar as the Bishop seems to think, but the representative of the parishioners and the part of the character of Mr. Walker which affects me is his public one, and in that he presents the extreme ritualistic wing. Is it possible to expect that the relations between a warden elected solely on the ground of Protestantism and a vicar who has been curate of St. Alban's, Holborn, chaplain to a Sisterhood, and is a member of the Society of the Holy Cross and of the Confraternity of the Blessed Sacrament, and who chooses his advisers solely from the supporters of Mr. Tooth, can be of the pleasant nature they would be had we for vicar a minister of the Church of England and nothing more?

This letter made clear that it was war to the knife, and bitter war at that.

The faculty for the removal of the cross and candlesticks reached Sanders on May 7th. The next Sunday he was there as soon as the church opened for the eight o'clock service when he informed Walker that he was about to remove the articles in question. Walker said he had no notice of the faculty sent to him, but Sanders swept the ornaments off the ledge under the eyes of a small congregation who were discussing what they ought to do. They had not anticipated that Sanders could carry away the ornaments from the church. One wanted to stop him by force, since strictly speaking they were the property of Walter Plimpton, who was reluctant to intervene and cause a fight. So he tried to persuade Sanders to return the cross and candlesticks to him as he had provided them. Sanders refused to do this without a statutory declaration of ownership and an explanation of how his property came to be there. This undertaking Plimpton considered it an indignity to have to give, as though his word was in doubt. Six letters followed on each side and Sanders retained the offending articles. Plimpton sent the correspondence to the Church newspapers, so it was reproduced in other journals. During this time *The Greenwich and Deptford Chronicle* had correspondence on ritual from the indefatigable 'Unity' still trying to uphold 'said' prayers as against 'sung.'

But so far as Sunday services went at St. James's Church, Hatcham faded out of the national news. One concludes that Walker carried on with his policy of moderation with the addition of a sung celebration following choral Mattins at 11 a.m. on Sundays. He had now been in the parish for six months and perhaps he wondered what he had achieved. He advertised and obtained a curate, J. A. Pearson, whose stipend was covered by Walter Plimpton's fund raising committee. He also reintroduced Sisters to the parish.

Evidently, there were a number of St. James's confirmation candidates who were presented to the Bishop at other churches. Thorold never visited Hatcham during Walker's incumbency. However, the work of the schools was carried on with teaching by Walker, Pearson and the Sisters, helped by various members of the parish, who also undertook parochial visits. There were various successful organizations, regular weekday services, and about two hundred members who formed the Sunday congregation. Some of these were deliberate disturbers. *The Greenwich and Deptford Chronicle* sent a reporter following one of those intentionally aggravating letters meant to arouse feeling and signed with the anonymity of the single letter 'X':

> who can consider the present condition of Church affairs in Hatcham, and we may add, in a less degree in St. Paul's, Deptford, without feeling that an awful responsibility rests upon someone? . . . ecclesiastical law is in a sad and disgraceful muddle.

For St. Paul's, Deptford, was running into trouble over 'the Ritualistic sliding scale of innovations' as the Protestants called it, because there was a little more music; and the vicar, greatly daring, had asked his brother priest, Charles Lowder, of St. Peter's, London Docks, to preach in the church.

One petty aggravation of Collard's was to tear down the list of services posted each week at St. James's. Eventually the St. James's Church Society provided a frame; but Collard removed it and put it on his seat, and afterwards it disappeared. The Society, or some supporter, tried again with a second frame. One Sunday in October Walker spoke about this from the pulpit. In the hymn following the taking of the collection, Fuller, a sidesman, picked up the frame and was making his way to the vestry with it when Sanders rushed forward, snatched it out of his hands and smashed it to the ground. This was the same Sunday on which there was a hand to hand struggle between Walter Plimpton and Collard for the offertory bag, which was torn in the process. It was noted that Collard replaced the sum that was lost. Fry meanwhile held open the vestry door to allow onlookers who had not attended the service to come in; some of M'Clure's supporters it seems. The police were evidently present for when Collard asked them to take Plimpton and Hornewood, another sidesman, into custody they refused. It was reported:

> These parties make a great fuss about the money collected at St. James's yet they never, the Vicar's party allege, give one farthing to the offertory. They come to a church they do not support, and want to interfere with money to which they do not contribute.

At the evening service there was a rough lot at the church, who had gone with the intention of making a disturbance, and were with great trouble ejected. They waited outside till the vicar came out, when they hissed him.

Consternation was aroused when the Protestants of Hatcham observed a fence and wall being set up around the school. This was apparently in order to fulfil a Government regulation for which a grant had been made, and had nothing to do with parish politics. All the same the police were again present as there was a strong rumour that the Protestants would destroy it. Inside the church the nuisance tactics continued. For example, one Sunday a man stood in front of the altar facing the west door. As devout parishioners bowed to the non-existent cross on the altar, he returned the courtesy 'in a mocking way.' The Sisters too had a good deal to put up with. The four of them sat in the same seats each week behind the pulpit. A young man, who was supposed to be a wealthy contributor to the Protestant Committee, 'carrying a profusion of wrist band and collar and wiping his mouth incessantly with his pocket handkerchief,' began to lead in some local boys, who took these seats and 'repeated the responses in a discordant tone, turning round and staring behind them, and other disgraceful conduct, to annoy these ladies' (the nuns).

The correspondence between 'Truth' (the Ritualist) and 'Unity' (the Protestant) continued with an occasional diatribe from Sanders and probably encouraged by the newspapers concerned because it assured an increased circulation. Every Sunday from May onwards the Protestant committee had taken a collection outside the church. Leaflets explaining this were widely distributed through the parish, a new provocation, and H. Plimpton has one of them in his collection. Although the struggle now appeared local so far as St. James's was concerned, Mackonochie, and notice of his suspension from officiating at St. Alban's, was national news. Following the last Penzance Judgment it was widely expected that he would go to prison, for this battle had been waged against him for thirteen years. Meanwhile, both Tooth and Sidney Faithhorn Green were inhibited by the Bishop of Ripon from preaching in his diocese.

In spite of this distress a small but united congregation gathered Sunday by Sunday, and there was a certain unity in parochial life as the year drew to a close at Hatcham. Walker had appealed for funds to restore the church roof, heating apparatus and the school house, while his curate wanted supplies of magazines for the Boys' Club, and to which generous donors made regular subscriptions week by week. It was probably this measure of success that prompted a further protest from the dissidents of the Church Association, who handed a statement through Collard, the churchwarden, to the vicar before one Sunday service, and which was already in the hands of the Press for publication the following day. The protest ran:

> We the undersigned being your parishioners and debarred from partaking of the Holy Communion in our parish church by reason of the evident intention on your part and on the part of your choir who are under your control, to turn the administration of the Lord's Supper into the celebration of a sacrifice and into a Mass—a thing unknown in the Church of England—and which is evidenced still further by school children being brought in to assist; by the prostrations of your server; by a veiled attempt to introduce an *Agnus Dei* though declared illegal; by the unlawful position you persistently take up *(presumably eastward)* and by the whole tenor of the Service, do hereby protest most strongly

against being deprived of our just rights as members of the
Protestant Church of England, against this attempt to introduce
a Service which is repugnant to the word of God, alien to the
teaching of the Church of which you are a member, and obnoxious
to nearly all your parishioners. We are compelled to protest
formally, representations having proved ineffectual, against this
attempt to teach an objective Presence, independent of the communicants, in the Lord's Supper.

This was signed by Collard, Fry and Sanders, and a 'large number'
of parishioners, some of whom never entered the church. It was
this document which caused the reporter of *The Greenwich and
Deptford Chronicle* to attend the service the following Sunday and
found nothing 'ultra-ritualistic.' He said that when the bell tolled
between Morning Prayer and the Communion service that followed,
it caused much perturbation to a middle-aged bald-headed gentleman (Sanders presumably), who hurried from one of the front seats
to the vestry in a rather excited manner, and presently the bell was
no more heard. He also noted that after the exhortation ('Ye that
do truly . . . '),

'as if by pre-consent, about thirty men and women sitting in the
front seats rose, and hurriedly, not to say noisily, came down the
church and went out by the west door . . . perhaps they were all
conscience stricken at not being in love and charity with their
neighbours. . . . Half a dozen or so remained at the end of the
church, and for the remainder of the service continued to pass
remarks apparently of a laughable nature on the conduct of the
service. The remainder of the service was very quiet. . . . We came
away thinking that as far as outward ritual goes there is but
little to be seen at St. James' that is at all unusual and as far
as we are able to judge at all illegal, but that the doctrines
inculcated in the sermon were of a real objective Presence in the
Holy Communion. The hymns too were decidedly Catholic. But
what surprised us was that the malcontents or Protestants seemed
to join in the singing and listen attentively to the sermon but to
find a *casus belli* in the method of *performing* the service. . . .
Cannot the Hatcham people and their clergy turn their attention
to filling their church and carrying out their duty laid down in
the sermon of last Sunday. . . .'

Feeling was running high again on the subject of the prosecution
of Dale of St. Vedast's, Foster Lane, as well as Enraght and Green.
Even low churchmen were appalled when a consecrated wafer was
discovered to have been filed in Lord Penzance's office as evidence

against Enraght of Holy Trinity, Bordesley, Birmingham, who was later put in prison for contempt of court. It is to the credit of Archbishop Tait that he demanded the wafer, and after some difficulty obtained it and consumed it in Lambeth Palace chapel. The Protestants had not the slightest compunction in doing this. In an article printed in the *Hatcham Review* (the Protestant threepenny magazine) a writer on the *Bordesley Wafer* stated 'The priest confesses to bring Christ down from Heaven and make Him incarnate in a bit of altar bread.'

> Altar bread is not dear, you may buy half-a-hundred wafer gods for sixpence. The East Grinstead Sisters are said to have the best recipe. Some go so far as to say that unless the utmost care is taken in the fabrication of these wafers, the Sacrament itself may lose its validity. This is a sorry prospect for the wretched votaries of this abominable superstition.

With statements like these, which were intended to shock and divide one half of the congregation from another, reconciliation was an impossibility.

The uncertainty of Mackonochie's future at St. Alban's brought this church again to the fore. Meanwhile, wild rumours were circulating to the effect that the Bishop of London, the indecisive Jackson, was about to withdraw the St. Alban's curates' licences. It was then supposed that the benefice would become vacant and a new incumbent be appointed. The prosecution of the vicar of Miles Platting, Sidney Faithhorn Green, if successful, would certainly end in a prison sentence. The Church of England Working Men's Society, the English Church Union and the Liberation Society were holding packed meetings and passing resolutions framed in the strongest terms. Public indignation was therefore diverted into different channels. In face of this the fracas at Hatcham seemed very small beer, and by the end of the summer when Thorold was due to preach, it was no longer front page news even in the local Press.

N

III

ANOTHER NEW YEAR – 1880

IT was now three years (Christmas 1879) since the devout and elaborate celebration that in effect marked the end of the Tooth era. In the previous year, 1878, there had been no Christmas celebration at all. Without any record to guide us we can only suppose that the services at St. James's produced a quiet, pious congregation absorbed in the spiritual truths underlying their outward observance. We can also assume that Croom was back in the congregation since he was a subscriber and supporter of the St. James's Church Society. We have to imagine the difficult position Sunday by Sunday as collection bags were passed round to which almost no one contributed; the Walker supporters because they subscribed to a series of funds in weekly sums which were collected by one of the members of the St. James's Society; the anti-Walkerites because they had their own Protestant Fund for which bags were offered outside the church and then carried away by Collard. On the previous Hospital Sunday the congregation inside the church contributed £2 6s. 8½d, and the one outside the sum of £6 12s. 6d, which Plimpton noted on the church accounts, and which he had printed and distributed in the seats of the church on Sunday, January 18th, exactly a year after Walker's arrival. The total sum of less than £173 represented what was taken in church. It did not include the sum raised by subscription for the curate, or for the schools for which subscribers were asked to promise sums from 1s. a year to 5s. a quarter. The Protestant Committee was enraged to see the printed accounts and on the next Sunday produced two leaflets. The first disclaimed any responsibility for the statement and requesting 'you' (presumably the man occupying the particular seat) 'to abstain from contributing to any collections in the church until the churchwardens are able to render a properly authenticated statement of Expenses and accounts.' It bore the name Ernest Collard. The other half of the same sheet was unsigned. It began by quoting Article XXV and continued:

> Remaining during the Communion Service without communicating, is contrary to the teaching of Scripture and the Article quoted above. The attempt of Ritualists to encourage this custom is a degradation of the Lord's Supper to the Romish Mass— Articles XXVIII and XXXI. You are therefore requested to leave

the Church *immediately* after the Prayer for the Church Militant and thus show you have no sympathy with the party which wishes to assimilate our Services to those of the erring Church of Rome—Article XIX.

It was a clever move which would show Sunday by Sunday to which party every single worshipper belonged. It also had the effect of hardening resistance in the two parties since it defined them so easily and regularly.

The Walker party claimed in accordance with Tractarian belief and practice that the Liturgy was the worship of the church in which all baptized persons were to participate. Any one baptized was entitled to offer the sacrifice of praise and thanksgiving so that whole families could attend. Among them would be those not yet confirmed. But all could share in the hearing of the Word and the eucharistic offering. They supported this argument by pointing to the rubrics. The words 'Draw near' at one time in Laudian days had been the signal for communicants to gather round the altar 'conveniently placed,' leaving behind those who were only attenders; the rubric about giving notice the day before of an intention to communicate from a much larger congregation; and similarly the one which demanded a convenient number to communicate with the priest from a full church according to his discretion. And perhaps not expressed, but no less present in their mind, was the fact that custom supported attenders who were not communicants and always had done. Moreover, it could be expected that at this service where provision was expressly made for a sermon, that some who were not confirmed would be present. And since part of the service could be said or sung, this postulated the 'high' celebration which people who had already communicated might wish to attend as a second service. The provision of a large number of special collects, epistles and gospels for holy days was considered to imply that there would be those present for the whole service who might not wish to 'take the sacrament' but would use the service as a means of corporate worship. The other side pointed to the provisions for ante-communion and the rubrics which were relevant when there were not any communicants. However, they did not only use this argument but quoted the article which was intended to prevent processions of the sacrament.

Looked at in any light, however, the division on a subject so fundamental to Anglican belief and practice was intensely wounding. Walker published his own broadsheet which was issued early in February and widely distributed and placed on every seat in the church warning the parishioners of attempts to deprive them of their vested right 'as Englishmen and Churchmen to worship in your Parish Church during the *whole* time that Divine Service is going on. . . . As the law of the land now is (*and this was better than appealing to rubrics*) Parochial clergymen *cannot* perform Services with closed doors. He may not refuse admittance or exit to any decently conducted person who desires to attend, and he has no power whatever to compel any one to withdraw who is not misbehaving to the annoyance of others. (*An oblique warning to those who were doing so.*) This is your right.'

He next drew a parallel between those who were onlookers at Calvary and those who remained when others had forsaken Him, and denied that such participation was idle gazing. He then compared the witnesses of the Sacrament of Baptism where the rubric commands that this be 'publicly administered in the presence of the congregation.' This was an ingenious and slightly casuistical illustration since there never had been any intention of adoration in baptism. It was, however, a wise reminder that the 'custom of all the leading Nonconformist sects in this country permit, nay, encourage, the presence of non-communicants when the full members are partaking of the ordinance, that they may become familiar with it, and in their turn apply for admission to a fuller share in it.' Lastly, he reminded his readers that there was no break in the Communion Office from the first Lord's Prayer to the Blessing when the people are 'let depart,' words which imply they are not to dismiss themselves earlier.

The reply drove Sanders and his party to complain to the Bishop again. They made three points; that Walker had removed Collard's printed sheet inviting the congregation to contribute to the collections outside the church; that the number of communicants on weekdays was less than the statutory three: and that the Sunday school children were brought into the church after Mattins as attenders at the Holy Communion. Walker must have known that a letter was on the way and sent his own version.

At the beginning of March the Bishop's reply to Walker was published in the Press, and it is interesting to see that Sanders and Collard did not make theirs public as Walker did. The Bishop supported Walker's retention of monies collected outside the communion service. 'Of course I sustain Mr. Walker in his claim of controlling such collections.' Walker in his letter had complained about the behaviour of Collard and of Sanders, first of all their notices without his permission, and for muttering under their breath and making audible remarks during the curate's sermon.

Pearson had drawn on one of Isaac Williams's hymns for his sermon. Sanders described it as mariolatrous, 'with sundry exclamations of vexation.' Both these actions the Bishop condemned in no uncertain terms, which must have been balm to Walker and the St. James's Church Society.

> If the minister introduced any irregularity into the service they *(the churchwardens)* have no authority to interfere. I hold that the action of distributing papers in the church both about this matter (the *offertory)* and another *(Non-communicating attendance)* was unauthorized. Should such papers again be distributed without the vicar's authority he will be at liberty to give orders that they are to be taken away.

The Bishop then went on to the 'audible dissent from the curate's sermon' and said 'a sense of duty compels me seriously to censure his conduct. A clergyman standing up to teach in God's name is not to be publicly contradicted as if he were merely taking part in a debating society. Nor is the house of prayer to be treated as if it were a vestry room. . . . The remedy for such conduct is with the police and magistrates and not with the churchwardens and he went on to quote the relevant Act of Parliament. As to the complaint of less than three communicants Walker had replied saying that out of 122 occasions there had been two Sundays at mid-day and eight weekdays when this had happened, and on neither of these occasions had he any reasonable doubt that there would have been three persons to communicate with the priest. The reply enraged Sanders and led to a profane scene between him and Walker; a climax in all this unhappy contest. The Bishop accepted Walker's explanation. However, he did object to the attendance of the Sunday school children at the mid-day celebration.

> Against this practice I most emphatically protest . . . the almost certain result will be that, through fatiguing them with what they can neither share nor understand, it will fatally alienate them from it perhaps for the rest of their lives. It is my distinct and emphatic desire that this practice be at once discontinued.

Walker was doubtless assisted by Layman in his reply. He thanked the Bishop for his 'substantial support' and said he realized he could have had recourse to the secular law. But he felt it 'undesirable to follow an example set too often in these days of making disputes on church questions, matters of litigation in the public courts instead of having them settled in a more spiritual fashion.'

He was too astute to refuse to accede to the Bishop's ruling on the subject of the Sunday school children and asked for 'some further explanation.' He added that 'this portion of the memorandum is worded differently from all the preceding clauses' in which the Bishop had stated the 'law of the case.' He continues that instead this seems to be only 'an expression of private opinion as to the expediency of the practice.'

> I am quite open to conviction on the question in issue and if your lordship will be good enough to point out to me the enactments whether by rubric, canon, or statute, which enjoin or necessarily imply the exclusion of children from the Communion Office, I will at once comply. . . . But if your lordship has been merely expressing your personal belief that the result of such a practice must needs be unwholesome, I should be glad to learn if you are speaking from practical experience, or merely offering what appears to you a reasonable conjecture.

Walker added that his own experience, not inconsiderable, did not lead him to justify changing the arrangement. It drew a long reply. Pearson, the curate, had submitted the sermon of which Sanders complained, and Bishop Thorold stated that he was bound in candour to say that there was no teaching of Mariolatry in it, and he told Sanders that 'there was nothing he could lay hold of.'

By this time Lent was drawing to a close, for Easter Day fell on the last day of March and there was the awaited ordeal of another vestry meeting, with this time some solid support from the parish and the achievements of the past year to rely upon. It is worth noting that the *Church Times* acknowledged a contribution on March 25th of £6 for 'St. James's Hatcham' from three anonymous contributors. There had been 2,683 Communions Easter 1878 to Easter 1879, 200 Baptisms from February to December 1878.

The meeting was held early on Easter Tuesday morning and it does not seem that the police were present, which sounds as though it was less rowdy than in the previous year. The outwardly unemotional Walker presided and had his curate beside him. Fortunately, Pearson had paid two quarters' rates and so was eligible. The minutes were read, but evidently the additional resolutions for the previous year, censuring Walker for being what he was and not for anything he did, had not been included in the minutes. Walker assented to these being a public record as, of course, he had to. Following this, Walker refused to produce an account of the monies collected during the preceding year. An uproar broke out. Sanders moved a resolution of protest, and a Captain Worth proposed that the parish warden take charge of all monies. The Walkerites stuck this out solidly, as the Bishop's sanction was good enough for them. There was then a question about the church doors being locked the previous Sunday, presumably Easter Day. All Walker could say was that it had not been done by his orders and he did not know who the man was with a heavy stick who was said to have kept the ratepayers out. Walker then proposed his churchwarden, Walters, who nominated his own sidesmen as was customary, and chose Walter Plimpton and John Forbes. Sanders then proposed alternative sidesmen, and in his role of unofficial chairman had the motion carried in spite of Walker's protest, since it was illegal to pass a resolution not put by the chairman. The names of Plimpton and Forbes were not accepted. After an attack on the vicar for overruling the law of the land Sanders was elected parish warden, and chose his sidesmen. A vote of thanks was passed for Collard's work as churchwarden. A vote of thanks to Walker for presiding was proposed, probably by Walters, but it was so obviously opposed that it was not put to the meeting. On this note the rather stormy and excited but not unmanageable meeting was dissolved.

The Plimpton–Walters–Croom party thought it could have been worse. But heartened by the increased number of communicants and the progress made during the year, they met later in the day at the meeting of the St. James's Church Society, and passed a vote of confidence in Walker from the communicants at St. James's. They probably also made their own plans. The Protestants had produced a rather superior type of monthly magazine, *The Hatcham Review*, at the high price of threepence per copy. This had produced a counterblast from the Catholics in the form of a St. James's magazine at one penny, which was a more acceptable price. *The Hatcham Review* only lasted about a year. It was followed by 'The St. James's Hatcham Parish Protestant Magazine.' The Mission must have been working; in *The History of Deptford*, it is given as having thirty sittings in 1882. A 'Bible Woman' was visiting the parish. There are accounts of visits to Tooth at Woodside and of concerts and entertainments at the schools. All the same, the undercurrent continued. Layman addressed a rather involved letter to the Bishop of Rochester on the subject of the Sunday school children in church. The Archdeacon of Rochester, Mr. Grant, visited St. James's and afterwards dismissed as 'simple fiction' the *Church Times*' report that he had publicly expressed his disapproval of the strife engendered by the Hatcham Ritualists.

The Protestant Parish Committee issued a circular for Hospital

Sunday inviting contributions outside the church and reminding their friends to leave the church immediately after the prayer for the Church Militant. Matters blew up at the Patronal Festival held on Sunday, July 25th. The altar was full of flowers. This had been the custom since the cross and candlesticks had been removed and they covered the damaged wall with a curtain as background. In front of the pulpit a small cross of fresh flowers was hung. The preacher was Mr. Jackson of St. Thomas's, Regent Street. He preached extempore, but he is supposed to have made derogatory remarks about the opponents of Ritualism who belonged to a 'rotten, decaying, and lying heresy.' That was the version in *The Rock* but no one else confirmed it. Whatever he did say it was something to enrage the anti-Walkerites. Sanders rushed into the vestry when the service was over complaining bitterly to Walker about the sermon, and opening the door to the outside admitted about forty men, evidently M'Clure's men, who were waiting to make trouble. Walker told Sanders to clear the vestry, saying it was his private room. Sanders retorted that it was nothing of the sort and belonged to the parish, but was edged out. He mounted the pulpit and ripped off the small cross of flowers and then turned his attention to removing the curtain behind the communion table. When he came back, he harangued the people outside from the vestry door while inside the church blows were being exchanged. Feeling ran high, insults were exchanged and epithets bandied. A large crowd listened attentively, and Walker had no alternative than to take the advice offered in the Bishop's last letter but one and apply for a summons against Sanders. As before it was granted by the presiding magistrate, Mr. Balguy. At the same time Morton, a member of the congregation who may have been a conjuror for he worked at the Egyptian Hall on 'business affairs,' also summoned the organist and an extremely pugilistic choirman for assault.

Morton was one of the rare worshippers but a yearly troubler at the vestry meeting, and he had undoubtedly received more than he gave in an unequal and undignified struggle between the organist and a choirman. He was represented by a barrister, and the ritualists by a local solicitor whose sarcastic interpolations did not do his clients much good. Fines were imposed on the choirman and organ blower and the case against Sanders dismissed. Sanders was, of course, represented by the indefatigable Le Jeune, instructed by the then famous Hyram Corsedge. The learned counsel defended Sanders on a technical point of law, namely that the service had been completed, and therefore his client was not guilty in the legal sense. The presiding magistrate evidently realized, however, that Sanders was the instigator of the uproar, and that the case against him was not altogether disputed. He said that he wished to prevent these matters at St. James's from coming before him again. He wanted Mr. Sanders to say something to bring about peace. Sanders's reply came through the urbane speech of his counsel expressing regret, and saying that there might have been an error of judgment, an understatement indeed. Le Jeune appealed to Walker to terminate the case, a difficult decision for him to make. If Walker terminated the case and did not apply for a fresh summons it looked as though he conceded the case. On the contrary to apply for a new summons meant a continuation of the unhappy and notorious public proceedings. Moss, the vicar's solicitor, said that if there were a pledge from Sanders that such scenes and conduct would not be repeated he would ask the vicar to 'stay' his hand, that is, not renew the summons. Mr. Balguy again appealed to Sanders to promote a better feeling in the parish towards the vicar, for he knew about the repeated circulars, the scenes at the vestry meeting, and the expensive subsidized counsels engaged by the Church Association. Le Jeune, for Sanders, then offered to refer the case to the Bishop. This was another clever move because the Bishop was out of the country for three months. If Walker agreed to this course it looked as though he conceded the case, and was asking the Bishop to adjudicate instead. On the other hand if he refused, it looked as though he wished to continue the warfare. However, at that point the case was adjourned for fresh summonses.

Meanwhile, Sanders had conceived a new idea for annoying the congregation and venting his animosity on Walker. On the next Sunday the preacher was to be a Mr. Davidson, the chaplain of the House of Mercy, Fulham, one of those Tractarian houses of care and reclamation which gave women a fresh start in life. It does seem as though the new annoyance was Sanders's own idea because there is no parallel, so far as one can tell, in any other Tractarian church.

Following the summonses and the unpleasant notoriety and bad feeling that had been rekindled, the church of St. James's was more than usually full. The altar was covered with flowers and a cross of fresh flowers hung suspended over the pulpit out of reach of the arm of a casual destroyer. Above the altar or communion table were the words *Holy Holy Holy,* and below it a cross painted on the wall and flanked by two tiger lilies, evidently to replace the curtain which Sanders had removed. At the close of Morning

Prayer the vicar went into the vestry and the children were ushered in from the school by the Sisters; the congregation waited for the service of Holy Communion to begin. They waited for another twenty minutes. Walker left the vestry, walked down the nave and out of the church. No one stirred, there was an air of crisis. Sanders had objected to Davidson preaching because he was not in possession of a bishop's licence. In a few minutes that seemed much longer than it actually was, Walker returned with a book in his hand, Prideaux's *Churchwarden's Guide*, almost a Bible for incumbents as hard pressed as Walker was. Walker referred Sanders to the section which declared that letters of orders annul any licence, so Davidson was legally able to preach. But Sanders pointed to Canon 50 which declared that:

> Neither the minister, churchwardens nor any other officers of the church shall suffer any man to preach within their churches or chapels but such as, by showing their licence to preach, shall appear unto them sufficiently authorized thereunto. . . .

Sanders was adamant; no licence, no preacher. Walker then entered the pulpit, read the banns, and announced there would be no sermon on account of Sanders's interference which was an absurdly legalistic interpretation of a canon. The protest was intended to embarrass a Tractarian preacher and, of course, his continuous butt, the vicar.

Walker suggested that Davidson should preach from the chancel steps, but Sanders refused, and there must have been some threat of a disturbance or Walker would not have submitted to this treatment. Sanders also made a long and bitter complaint against the omission of the prayer for the Queen in Morning Prayer. This was doubtless due to the custom of omitting at Morning Prayer what would be doubled in the service of Holy Communion.

As a member of the Confraternity of the Blessed Sacrament, Walker did not break his fast until after the service of Holy Communion and perhaps for once nettled, though outwardly indifferent, he told Sanders that the service would in future begin half an hour earlier, that is at 10.30 a.m., in order to provide for extra prayers. He would not be so uncharitable, one imagines, as to have hoped that this would inconvenience Sanders. He announced this from the pulpit together with reasons for the omission of the sermon.

Considerably delayed, the service then continued, and the offertory for the repair of the roof of the church was collected by Sanders and Hallett in bags at the end of sticks. A clergyman, the curate perhaps, stood at the chancel steps with a gilt salver to receive the alms, and seeing the collectors were about to by-pass him remarked that it was the 'decent bason' of the rubric; but Sanders, audibly no doubt since the reporter heard it, remarked that it was *not* according to the rubric. With Hallett he passed into the chancel, and placed the offertory in the hands of the vicar who was waiting at the communion table.

At the end of the Prayer for the Church Militant Sanders's supporters got up from their seats and left the church. Of those who remained about half a dozen received the sacrament. At the west end a crowd of some twenty or thirty strolled about and made remarks about the decoration, particularly the pendant cross of fresh flowers. Sanders at last asked them to sit down quietly or leave, but as soon as the service was over they again wandered up and down the aisles until told to go. Outside the church a lively discussion about the sermonless service was going on, but with two constables of 'P' division standing stolidly by and moving on obvious loiterers, there was no disturbance.

As for Sanders, his name was a byword from end to end of England. *Fun,* an independent journal, published a cartoon where a farmer's wife answered a complaint of the local curate over her eggs: 'The fact is, sir, y'ought ter go ter hatch'em yourself' to be met with a horrified reply from the clergyman 'Go to Hatcham with Churchwarden Sanders there, Heaven forbid.'

In September 1880 Charles Lowder, the vicar of St. Peter's, London Docks, died. Tait, as Bishop of London, had paid him grudging admiration, and though there had been an abortive attempt at prosecuting him, nothing had come of it. He had the whole of his slum dockside parish solidly behind him, including those who did not come to church. His funeral rallied Catholics and showed to outsiders a strength and power which many had not believed possible. Before the funeral the church was open all night. There was a constant stream of penitents and the first Mass was said at 3.30 a.m. At 8 a.m. it was announced that the body had arrived at Holborn Viaduct station, at which news a procession was formed up to meet the hearse and bring it to St. Peter's. Every house emptied and the people lined the streets three or four deep. At the bridge, the Wapping boundary of the parish, the Church of England Men's Society was lined up with hundreds of representatives of other parishes and societies and nearly a hundred priests. So, singing psalms and sentences, the huge procession moved into the church where parishioners, poor and humble, stood in tears. When the service was over an even greater procession followed the cortège through a completely silent crowd, with traffic suspended, to the special train which carried them to Chislehurst. The train held six hundred but eight hundred contrived to travel by it, and those who could not afford the shilling for the fare had gone ahead on foot. Others went by alternative trains so that at Chislehurst Common it was reckoned that there were 'ten thousand people and ten hundred priests.'

'It was more like a triumphal procession,' said one onlooker. 'And to think that in these streets around St. George's *(St. George-in-East)* he had been pelted and ill-treated. England has never seen such a funeral.'

The Rock needless to say charged the Ritualists with making religious capital out of his death, and complained bitterly of 'Jesuitism.' Even that journal said it did not want to depreciate Lowder's zealous and self-denying labours, and spoke of the respectful gaze of the depressed parishioners lining the streets.

Meanwhile, the Sanders–Walker guerrilla warfare continued undiminished. Sanders tried to force Walker to settle the 'ecclesiastical' dispute which had resulted in the last summons for brawling. But it was too late though the scene became slightly less tense. There was no point in starting it all over again. The correspondence at Sanders's request was published in *The Observer*, and Thomas Layman added his comments. A clergyman described how he had mistakenly received semi-confidential documents on the policy of what he called 'The Church Ass.' These described some of the harrying and organized tactics that were to be pursued in order to combat the 'Romish proclivities' of individuals and societies such as the S.P.G. and A.C.S. It also disclosed the unpopularity of Church Association policy among former supporters, not all of whom agreed with the prosecutions of Dale, Enraght and Green.

Thomas Pelham Dale had been charged with ritual offences by his churchwardens and a sidesman, one was a bootmaker of Gutter Lane, a resident but not a worshipper; the other two were a warehouseman and an auctioneer, both non-communicants, and the former a dissenter. He refused to give up his keys to the Bishop of London and he was imprisoned in Holloway Gaol from October to December. Aged seventy he was suffering from a painful abscess in his right hand. By December Richard William Enraght of Holy Trinity, Bordesley (the case of the consecrated wafer), was also in prison; and it was only a technical hitch that kept Sydney Faithhorn Green of Miles Platting from joining them as he later did. Green went into Lancaster Castle where he remained for twenty months until November 1882, during which time all his possessions were sold to defray the costs of the case.

IV

ATTACK AND COUNTER-ATTACK – 1881

YET as far as parish life can be assessed at St. James's, Hatcham, there was steady growth. Christmas Day 1880 was quiet and orderly. The number of communicants increased by thirty-three, and there was a congregation of between two and three hundred at the Choral Eucharist but only twenty–thirty at Mattins which preceded it. The Sunday school was flourishing, an Institute for evening classes had been opened in Angus Street and an additional Mission in Dixon Street. There were three different Bible Classes, a Mother's Meeting, a Boys' Club and a Temperance Society, as well as the benevolent clubs for providing coal and clothing, boots and shoes to needy families.

Dale had been released on bail before Christmas but Enraght was still in prison, and next March Sydney Faithhorn Green shared the same fate. All over England meetings took place to arouse sympathy with them and to condemn the law which put clergymen in such a position. The Church of England Working Men's Society organized a huge meeting at Birmingham Town Hall at which Charles Powell and Tooth were among the speakers. Another under the same auspices was held at the Cannon Street Hotel. The E.C.U., in branch after branch far and wide, made the position abundantly clear to their supporters. After all, the year 1881 was dawning, and it was nearly fifty years since Keble's Assize sermon and thirty years since the days of the riots in St. George's-in-the-East and St. Barnabas's, Pimlico. Ideas had developed, a new generation of clergy had been born, and among many there was a sense of tolerance, if not agreement. Even Bishop Magee now wore a cope in his cathedral.

In January the St. James's Church Society published a statement of accounts signed by the vicar. It showed a much improved financial position, even allowing for the fact that sums had come in directly through public appeals which had been devoted to the relief of the sick and poor and did not appear on the parish account, and disclosed through the Sisters, now re-established in Laurie Grove. The treasurer remitted the debt of £28 on the schools so that the year could begin unencumbered. Nearly £65 had been spent on church repairs still leaving a debt of £91 from the deficit of £107 in the previous year. Another £27 had been paid privately through a few local subscriptions and private donations received by the vicar, including over £7 from Walter Plimpton who evidently collected it from his friends, as he did another £40 towards the assistant priest. The church expense account only amounted to £51. Gas, insurance and cleaning came to over £30, and we hope that the gas account was partly for heating, and that the appeal for heating was likely to be successful. The organist was unpaid and the balance of £59 was in hand for the next year's insurance. The windows in the church had been mended, the vicarage garden replanted. Given bare courtesy and toleration the church could have found its feet. Sums of money still came in from outside as we can tell by acknowledgements in the *Church Times*. The St. James's Church Society kept its own parish accounts in a separate fund, and Sanders and his supporters continued their policy of collecting outside the church. Their Bible woman, Mission hall and rival Sunday school were all at work. As the numbers in the parish were given as over 15,000 in 1882, there was scope for this enterprise had it not included the harrying tactics which damaged their cause in the eyes of the world.

All this time Bishop Thorold did nothing in the way of pastoral intervention or even ordinary social contact with the clergy of Hatcham. Towards the end of the year he made a new appointment in the parish of St. Paul's, Lorrimore Square, a flourishing church run on Tractarian lines which had supported the St. James's congregation in 1877 and given them hospitality. For some reason the vicar, Baden Powell, had given up, and the Bishop had appointed the Reverend E. F. Alexander in his place. This had not been done without strong protests and representations by both churchwardens who stayed away from the induction.

St. Paul's had been opened twenty-four years ago, 1866, two years before Arthur Tooth came to Hatcham. It was at that time in a state of 'parochial paralysis,' and there were the 'black gown, pew rents, droned out services few and far between' and a 'sparse congregation.' When Baden Powell came he built a vicarage and schools, abolished pew rents which opened the church to the poor and started up various organizations and educational projects.

After Baden Powell left, on hearing of the Bishop's new appointment, the congregation departed *en masse* for St. Agnes's, Kennington, the patronage of which was in Catholic hands. Many of the Hatcham disturbers assembled at St. Paul's and processed to St. Agnes's to demonstrate there but were prevented by a strong force of police who were 'excellent tractarians.' Before the induction of the new vicar, E. F. Alexander, the Bishop of Rochester's apparitor visited St. Paul's Church and, without a faculty, gave orders for the removal of two side altars, the reredos of St. Mary's altar, and the crucifix from the rood loft. Mr. Alexander agreed to keep the seven lamps in front of the altar and the pictures of the saints on the pillars. St. Paul's was then opened for Mattins (said), the reading of banns and nothing else. The new vicar made it known at once that Sunday school children would not be allowed to attend the Holy Communion service even occasionally. The teachers met him after taking Sunday school on his first Sunday when they then resigned in a body. One newspaper noted that the early communion service now consisted of ten people, five men and five women, instead of the customary average of one hundred and sixty. He also noted that at eleven o'clock a great many Hatcham Protestants were present, and one can only hope that this was some relief for the hard pressed Walker, whose Christmas services may thus have been less of a strain for himself and his flock.

The St. James's Protestant Parish Committee published their accounts at the back of a manifesto in the same cover as *The Hatcham Review* and with the rather brash words of Dr. Thorold on the front:

> I hope there is not a person here who is ashamed of the word *Protestant:* for if the Church of England is not a Protestant Church she is in shameful schism.

The 'Appeal,' which was for Protestant support in cash, recapitulated the events under Tooth. The complaint listed by the Protestant Committee was the introduction of 'outward forms and ceremonies,' 'the teaching of false doctrine,' the introduction of a branch of the Confraternity of the Blessed Sacrament with a list of the members fixed up in the church, the removal of a very

> handsome pulpit of white stone and dark marble pillars in favour of a mere platform with an ordinary iron railing; profuse costly and illegal vestments for the Priest.

Another of its injunctions followed:

> At what is blasphemously called 'High Celebration' a procession round the church took place to the Chancel. . . . You may be surprised, Protestant friends, all this actually took place, and wives and daughters of Englishmen, professed members of the Church of England, encouraged by her professed minister confessed their sins to a man.

After describing the ritual the pamphlet went on:

> Those things positively took place in our Parish Church and ought to call a blush of shame to those who took part in such idolatrous services.

It passed over rather hastily the proceedings against Tooth, merely saying that 'though the parishioners succeeded in all vital points through a miserable technicality the judgment was quashed by the Court of the Queen's Bench.' The writer next described conditions under Walker, 'who was a curate of the notorious Mr. Mackonochie and is according to the "ritualistic Conspiracy" (*an earlier Protestant tract*), a member of the same societies as Mr. Tooth.' The next complaint is against the Sisters of Mercy; 'installed as teachers in the Sunday school, these children are brought into the church to attend—not Morning Prayer—but "Celebration" during which they are kept on their knees . . . the children are further taught to say their prayers with crosses and crucifixes as supposed helps. A colourable imitation of the illegal *Agnus Dei* is sung during the communion Service at which a man assists called a server, an office not known in our church.'

The writer had to admit that there were many young people attending St. James's, for he regretted that 'so many of the young are caught by the specious and sensuous aspects of Ritualism.'

With sweeping condemnation of Rome whither, he claimed, Ritualism leads, he continued:

> What is the outcome? Atheism and Infidelity; this is proved by all Roman Catholic countries, the men of which are nearly all Atheists and Infidels.

The manifesto concluded with an appeal for £1,000 to build permanent Sunday schools or £300 to erect a 'temporary iron room where, in addition to the morning and afternoon schools, we hold two services for the children.'

They evidently had an active organization working already, district visiting, a weekly mothers' meeting, and a clothing club supported by 155 subscribers. The appeal was signed by Sanders and Thorman, and the names of another twenty-two members of the powerful committee. The accounts showed an expenditure of over £100 of which legal expenses took £40, the Bible Woman £14 and printing £12. The Sunday school cost £35 of which £23 was rent and the rest included £2 5s. 8d. for a banner (which one would have thought would be anathema to the committee). There is also

O

an item of ten shillings and ten pence for 'children's fares to Lambeth Palace,' for what purpose is undisclosed.

On the one side the general impression is one of implacable hostility to Walker's policy of moderation, and on the other hand a slow growth with a new congregation, who would be too young and too poor to influence the election of a churchwarden at the vestry meeting the next April. It also appears that in spite of the imposing list of committee members in the Protestant 'Appeal' as though their militancy was weakening except for Sanders. It was well known that Sanders no longer wished to continue as churchwarden for he was seeking ordination, but none of his party would come forward to take his place. This is an interesting sidelight on the position, for it makes one wonder whether any successor would feel committed to the Sanders policy and was having second thoughts about some of his tactics.

As for Walker and his curate, Pearson, who was even more disliked than Walker by the Sanders party and their supporters, the vestry meeting was now an annual unpleasant mortification to be endured which had little relation to the daily grind of parochial work.

The vestry meeting on Tuesday, April 19th, 1881, followed the usual pattern. The Sanders party, 'including many Dissenters mustered in force,' took possession of the vestry. They then bolted the door to keep out any who did not hold their views. Walker took the chair and refused to begin until the door was opened to allow any one who wished to come in, but there does not seem to have been any violent rush to do so. After managing to have the last year's minutes confirmed Sanders brought up a motion on the question of the church accounts and protested against Walker's 'usurpation.' Walker put the motion which was carried by 28 to 6, which gives us an idea of the size of the meeting. Turner, a member of the Protestant Committee, then asked if Walker had consented to the curate's offering of prayers for Sydney Faithhorn Green, now a prisoner in Lancaster Castle, and compared it with praying for a burglar. He also asked whether it was by the vicar's consent that Pearson had given out that there would be a 'three hours' agony service' on Good Friday. This devotional service was now customary at St. Paul's Cathedral, and as a preaching and teaching service was widely accepted. Walker declined to answer either of these points and continued by nominating his warden, Mr. Bridges of St. Donatt's Road. Sanders then made a long speech condemning the curate, ending with a resolution which called on the vicar to resign. Walker could hardly put this motion himself and naturally declined to do so, and Sanders took over the role of chairman. The motion was, of course, carried 'by a large majority.' Walker turned to Pearson who appears to have been boiling, and advised him not to reply to Sanders's charges, adding for the benefit of the meeting that he entirely approved of everything Pearson had done. This brought the cries of 'You ought to be ashamed of yourself,' and 'Go to Rome,' which Walker took without a flicker of expression. Another of Sanders's party, Mr. Hallett, then proposed a resolution asking the Bishop of Rochester to revoke the curate's licence, a motion which Walker as chairman refused to put to the meeting but it was carried by acclamation. Sanders was then re-elected as parish warden and chose Hallett and Thorman, of whom we shall hear more, as his sidesmen. There were the customary laudatory votes of thanks to the retiring churchwardens; one to Walker for presiding was defeated. The noisy but not unmanageable meeting broke up after an hour. It was widely reported in the local Press.

There was a sequel to the meeting on Visitation Day at St. Alphege's Church, Greenwich, when Sanders raised a presentment against Walker for irregularities in the church. He also raised the question of sidesmen which the vicar refused to admit. This was due to the fact that Sanders had first protested against the vicar's warden appointing his sidesmen. Walker had now done the same, in order to avoid four Protestant sidesmen and no Catholic instead of two of each. The reply was, as it had been the previous year, that the only remedy was an appeal to the Queen's Bench. It seems likely that Sanders took counsel's opinion, and it was probably this that suggested his later course of objecting to the vicar's custom of nominating one warden. Hatcham was in the news again when Inspector Rolfe visited Hatcham in connection with some other investigation he was engaged upon. With another inspector and a constable and in Walker's presence, the church was searched with great thoroughness. After a 'considerable' time they discovered under one of the seats a bulky bundle wrapped in filthy and half rotten material which came to pieces as it was handled. This was the old altar cloth packed around two candlesticks, altar cross and cruets which had been missing from the church since Gardiner's time.

Feeling was running high in the long golden summer of 1881 over the continued imprisonment of Green which dismayed many moderates. To a question in Convocation put by Archbishop Tait the bishops vouchsafed no reply, nor any expression of sympathy. And the fact that there was soon to be a Royal Commission on the

Ecclesiastical Courts brought no suggestion as to how one of the victims could be released, since Green, like Tooth, refused to make his own application to a court whose jurisdiction he did not recognize. He was to remain in prison for more than another year.

Partly on Green's account, since the Hatchamites were particularly sympathetic to 'sufferers for conscience sake,' there was another incident in church which led to a case in the Greenwich Police Court. Layman brought the case against Sanders for indecent behaviour but was challenged as to his *locus standi*, so Walker substituted his own name. Past experience should have taught them that they could never win against Sanders and Balguy. A boy, according to one witness who saw the whole scene, was sitting quietly by himself in a 'pew,' which seems to have been a seat Sanders appropriated to himself for there were not at the time any pews, only chairs, in the church. She said Sanders took hold of the boy by the neck saying that he (the boy) had insulted his wife (who was not in the church). And though the vicar said the boy could sit where he liked, if he did so again, he (Sanders) would sit in the chancel, as in fact he did in future. By this time the rest of the congregation was hissing Sanders, and a man called Helling said 'he saw Mr. Sanders take hold of the boy and he was pale with anger at the time.' Layman heard the commotion outside the church, came in and saw the boy crying.

Balguy dismissed the case, saying Sanders might have been too zealous, but was not guilty of 'indecent behaviour.' The case aroused the parish, however, and confirmed the belief that legal victories were to the strong and rich, and not to the weak and poor. This may be the reason the summons was never taken out. Feeling must have run high against Sanders or he would not have been driven to increased retaliatory actions which he saved up for the patronal festival, always a great time in the parish, and this time falling on a Monday. The chancel was gay with flowers, and there was a cross of flowers over the pulpit and a wreath hanging from the desk as usual. This time some of the banners introduced by Tooth, and banished since his day, had been restored and placed against the wall, a fact which was conveyed to Sanders who was not in church on the Sunday. At the festival Evensong when a Mr. Begbie was preaching, Sanders challenged him, as he was about to mount the pulpit, to produce his licence. The preacher refused and returned to the chancel steps where he delivered the sermon without further interruption. It was clear that every one's temper was roused, and as the choir left the church the verger rushed in and put out all the gas burners but one which had the effect of making the congregation leave. By eight thirty it was almost dark (this was before the Daylight Saving Act). Outside every one was discussing the removal of the banners and the renewed animosity, when Sanders appeared from the vestry passing a group of which Croom was the centre. With what degree of audibility we do not know, Croom uttered the one word 'Thief! ', at which the enraged Sanders dealt him a heavy blow on the side of the head' with a stick or umbrella. A free fight followed down the road and Sanders lost his hat, which was later recovered battered beyond repair. He retreated into a friend's house and gradually the contestants dispersed. The following Sunday two constables were on duty but nothing happened. Sanders and his friends left as was their custom after the Prayer for the Church Militant.

After this the usual correspondence followed in the local newspapers. There was one letter from Sanders to Walker:

> I have considered it my duty to remove the banners illegally introduced into the church so as to prevent any unseemly expression of opinion on the part of the parishioners at these Romish symbols.

Walker replied requiring Sanders to return them to the church, 'as you have no right to retain them in your possession.' The banners, he said, were 'strictly Biblical, viz., a dove, a cup, a small picture of the Blessed Virgin and her divine Child: but Biblical symbols, together with quiet order, decency and reverence in the House of God would seem to be of little worth in the eyes of Mr. Sanders.' *The Law Times* published an article in which it declared that churchwardens had no business to remove ornaments even if they were illegal, and this was the view taken by Bishop Thorold.

> The banners so imprudently brought into the church and so hastily removed from it must be restored to their owners. I wonder equally at the eagerness evinced for displaying them and at the indignation wasted on them. The churchwarden should have been content with reporting them to the Ordinary. He exceeded his powers in removing them until instructed to do so.

A statement like this was not entirely acceptable to the Walkerites but it did censure Sanders's actions. The Bishop also said of Walker that 'a lay patron is responsible for his appointment . . . and his parishioners must make the best of him.' The Bishop here conveniently ignored the consequences of his own patronage of

St. Paul's, Walworth, now so unhappy and divided a parish. He continued, 'Like all of us he (Walker) makes mistakes now and then, but I am satisfied that he has the welfare of the parish at heart . . . ' And this was damning with faint praise.

On the question of Sanders's behaviour he fell back on his election by the vestry: 'he is presumably the representative of the parishioners. They knew his opinion before electing him.' The Bishop can hardly have been so naïve as not to know of the propaganda, the packed vestry, and the yawning gulf between the ratepaying rich and the non-ratepaying poor.

However, he did conclude with words that must have soothed ruffled ritualists:

> But is it not time that these miserable feuds should cease? They make the parish a byword; they shock the faithful; they harass the quiet churchpeople who belong to no party, but simply wish to be let to worship in peace; they justify the taunt of our enemies that ours is only a cure-state-unity; with our Roman adversary they stir a bitter but pleased scorn,

and he begged the two parties 'to invoke the law of love . . .'

So far as the Hatcham Protestants were concerned their reaction was to call a public meeting of Protestant churchmen 'to discuss efficient checks to the increasing practice of Ritualism and to memorialize the Diocesan on the subject.' The Bishop's words went unheeded and in fact aroused a fiercer resentment than ever.

It was the day after the publication of the Bishop's letter that Sanders took his seat in the chancel, saying that he had a perfect right to claim a seat for himself, and turn any one else out of it, but that instead of doing so, as he knew that the children had been put there to annoy him, he should sit in the chancel. In fact the bench he mentioned was not full and there was plenty of room had he wanted to sit there, but in the chancel he had a good view of the vicar's manual actions and hoped to make a charge on the point of cleansing the vessels, as he afterwards did. These tactics certainly had a lowering effect on Walker, and led to his final breakdown.

The memorialists supporting Walker were on the whole gratified by the Bishop's reply and wrote again and told him so, expressing their 'wish for the cessation of strife and eventual unity.' They also made it plain that due to the vicar's hard work and unselfishness in the face of opposition and misrepresentation the church was going ahead with increased congregations and communicants.

The vicar's warden, wise in his own generation, cashed in on the not altogether unwelcome publicity and appealed for contributions towards the heating system before the winter set in. The first anniversary of Sydney Faithhorn Green's imprisonment would occur soon after Christmas, and meetings of protest were beginning all over again. Nine-tenths of his parishioners had signed a petition for his release. The Royal Commission on Ecclesiastical Courts had now been set up and these two events may have been the subject in an oblique way of the sermon preached by a Mr. Skinner at St. James's at the end of November. Sanders was sitting in the chancel as usual. As the preacher announced the text, which unfortunately we do not know, he said some words reported to be that the clergy had no right to obey the law in matters ecclesiastical, and as Mr. Green had been in prison for over nine months it was quite time to speak out. Sanders jumped up from his place in the chancel and rushed into the vestry. He returned with a handful of papers saying in loud and angry tones, 'That is not true, you have no right to say that; I protest against you saying that in a pulpit of the Church of England.' Sanders claimed that he would have been justified in turning the preacher out of the church. Whether Mr. Skinner finished what he had to say we do not know, but the next day there was another application for two summonses against Sanders by Pearson, one for indecent behaviour during the divine service and the other for disturbing the duly authorized preacher. This time and perhaps with the Bishop's appeal in his mind, Balguy addressed Sanders more severely than he ever had before, saying he was wrong from a common sense point of view, but added that he was guilty of indecent conduct in its 'most minor form.' He did not mention the other charge and Sanders gave an undertaking not to interfere again. The summonses were held over for a month for the parties to meet.

Rather surprisingly, and perhaps because there was not much news at the time, *The Daily Telegraph,* devoting a twelve hundred word article to the subject, took up the cause of the churchwardens and made Sanders look rather silly. Perhaps after this Sanders stayed away from St. James's. At any rate the year ended peacefully, but did not long remain so when 1882 came in.

Eventually the summons was heard again. It then transpired that Sanders had introduced a new form of annoyance. The psalms at St. James's were sung antiphonally by vicar and congregation. Sanders joined in with the vicar and induced a few others to do the same. Perhaps they were singing to the best of their ability, said Balguy drily. It sounded ugly and was a great hindrance to devotion. Balguy deprecated the situation and readjourned the summons, so no one had gained anything, and Sanders returned to St. James's for Morning Prayer and his persecuting tactics. Fortunately, there were never many there until the end of the service when they arrived for the Choral Communion which followed. But when the assistant priest of St. Peter's, London Docks, came to preach, Sanders again stopped him on the way to the pulpit and demanded his letters of orders. Perhaps he had been forewarned for they were instantly produced. On the same day in the evening Walker preached and expressed his opinion on the continued imprisonment of Green, now for over a year. Sanders was furious and showed it, but could not interrupt.

The Easter vestry was regarded as an annual parochial hazard, and there was an expectedly large noisy crowd. The vicar appointed his own churchwarden, a man called Bridges. Sanders continued as parish warden. Sanders commented on the teaching at the church and Walker did not react outwardly when Sanders asked him whether St. James's was a Protestant or Roman Catholic Church. After the usual complaint from Sanders about the parish accounts Fuller replied for the opposition. He said that the persons who contributed to the offertories formed nine-tenths of the congregation and were perfectly satisfied with the method of disposal. He asked the vicar not to be influenced by a few people who rarely attended the church and never contributed to its upkeep (*uproar*). Thorman then proposed the re-election of Sanders as churchwarden and made a fierce speech against confession, saying with more truth than he realized that they had got rid of the confessional but not of confession. There were then the stereotyped resolutions condemning the vicar, and wild statements attached to the speeches about the service of Holy Communion being a copy of the Romish Mass, and the music being no better than two bluebottles could produce. Pearson, the curate, made a defensive speech over his sermons, the contents of which Sanders had complained of to the Bishop who, Pearson said, upheld him. Finally, the meeting closed. The customary vote of thanks to the vicar for taking the chair was lost.

This time Sanders appeared in the role of plaintiff at Greenwich Police Court before the indefatigable and unhostile Balguy. He had two complaints, the one undisputed against Helling, a member of the congregation, who (tit for tat) tore down the Sanders's opposition notice of the vestry meeting with the resolutions condemning the vicar written thereon. Helling claimed that the notice was illegal because it was signed by only one churchwarden, and secondly a notice had already been posted by the vicar. Sanders withdrew this summons. The other summons concerned a disturbance on Palm Sunday when children were evidently processing from the schools with branches of palm and Sanders said he could not allow large bunches to be carried in. One of the teachers had a bough claimed to be as large as an umbrella, and Fuller evidently called Sanders an 'ass' and 'stupid,' epithets which stung, so Fuller was summoned for an 'indecent' word. Balguy said that the one word to which an Englishman objected was 'stupid' because so often the word fitted. When the defendant agreed to retract the word which he admitted hearing used, Sanders then withdrew the summons and paid the costs. What did he think he had gained?

V

SUCCESS AND FAILURE 1882–1886

THE next discomfiting incident happened in June (1882). It took place at a weekday celebration at 7.15 a.m., a service which was never attended except by loyal parishioners. The Protestant party rarely made their communions at St. James's, preferring All Saints' Hatcham Park, or St. John's, Deptford. On this particular Friday Sanders turned up; the vicar's churchwarden was present and also the curate and three ladies. Following the priest's communion, Bridges went up to the altar and knelt at the rail (in those days it was customary for men to go first and women second). As none of the ladies seemed about to move, Sanders went to each in turn and asked whether they were going to 'partake.' He then bustled forward to the chancel where Walker had already begun to administer the sacrament to Bridges. As Walker returned to the altar for the chalice, Sanders interposed himself between the vicar and Bridges and said in a loud voice, 'Mr. Walker, there cannot be any communion with only one communicant.' Walker took no notice and lifted the chalice whereat Sanders went on to the communion step and said in a quieter voice,

'On a previous occasion, Mr. Walker, when complaint had been made to the Bishop of you holding a Communion Service with less than three communicants, you informed him that you did not know so few would come to the table. I have now informed you that having asked each person, no more are coming up; therefore, there is no Communion service, and it is your duty immediately to give notice to that effect and stop the service. I most solemnly ask you if in what to you of all people is the most sacred service, you intend to be guilty of an illegal act and of disobedience to your Bishop?'

And all this time Bridges continued to kneel at the rail, and Walker to stand with the cup in his hands. This is the account in *The Rock* which Sanders himself must have contributed. Sanders then held his open hand between Walker and Bridges and continued, 'I must ask you for an answer, or I shall object to the service proceeding.'

There was an interval of tense silence. With the idea of supporting his vicar, Pearson came forward and said something to Walker. Sanders broke in, 'Let Mr. Pearson partake and I will ask one of the ladies present to do the same and then everything will be in order.' He did not offer to do so himself. Walker then whispered to Bridges and Pearson to withdraw, and he finished the service.

The next morning Walker must have flinched inwardly when Sanders again was present in his usual place in the chancel. This time Pearson was officiating and it was perfectly clear that he was using wafers. After the service, at which there were evidently three communicants, Sanders followed Pearson into the vestry and asked him to show him bread similar to that which he had used at communion. On a ledge in the vestry was a small silver box in which the pressed bread (or wafers) was always kept and which Sanders considered should not be used, but he could not see it. Outside the vestry door Thorman was waiting and Sanders let him in. On returning to the priest's vestry, the box was discovered there and on being opened was found to be full and unused. Sanders then accused Pearson of not using it but of having provided wafers from some other source. To all this Pearson made no reply. Sanders made a longish speech ending with a threat to provide the bread in accordance with his rights, and to take what steps he thought fit to prevent the use of wafers.

On Sunday, therefore, Sanders brought the bread with him 'in case of necessity' and placed it on the credence table. It looks very much as though Walker used some of the bread provided, for, commented *The Rock,* Sanders 'was obliged to walk right up to the table to see that no wafers were being used' though almost certainly the officiant, a Mr. Fawcett, used a priest's wafer.

On Monday Walker again took out a summons against Sanders for brawling on Friday. This very distressing case, reported in the national and local newspapers, described how Walker three times tried to pass the chalice to Bridges but was prevented by Sanders, who interposed his body by placing himself in front. Balguy said that Mr. Sanders appeared to have waited until he caught the vicar in a trap, that is, until he saw him actually performing an illegal act and service. Through his counsel, Le Jeune, Sanders hotly denied this. His action was in fact aimed at preventing the vicar acting illegally and so not rendering him liable to criminal prosecution. For once Balguy affirmed that Sanders had conducted himself improperly; he had mistaken his duty and there would have to be a conviction. He fined him two pounds. A brawler in the north for a lesser offence had been fined five pounds. Sanders's stock was beginning to diminish in the popular press.

Sanders did not lessen his efforts to discomfit Walker, however. On the following Tuesday, the patronal festival, the vicar of St. Paul's, Knightsbridge, H. Montagu Villiers, was preaching at

the evening service and the church was full. As Villiers left his stall
for the pulpit during the hymn, Sanders came forward from his seat
opposite and demanded to see his licence before he could preach.
Villiers spoke to Walker, and then remained till the singing had
stopped when he announced from the chancel steps,

'I have been asked for my letters of orders by the churchwarden.
I was not asked for them before the service. As I have left them
in the vestry I must go and fetch them.'

Villiers brought them from the vestry, showed them to Sanders,
who then allowed him to pass up the steps into the pulpit where he
preached an 'eloquent sermon.' When the service was over Villiers
was clapped and Sanders booed.

Newspapers far and wide took up the tale and the correspondence columns were full again. One letter came from *A Parishioner*
who was not a regular worshipper, saying:

> such a disgraceful scene I never before witnessed in a church.
> If that was Mr. Sanders who caused the scene, I say the sooner
> he is removed from the office of churchwarden the sooner peace
> will be restored. . . . I have never sympathized with Ritualists.
> Since I have paid a visit to St. James', my sympathies are all for
> Mr. Walker.

Not all the letters were favourable to the Ritualists. *A Parishioner
for Over Twenty Years* thought that Sanders's request to the
preacher was reasonable 'owing to the very extreme men who are
asked to preach in this church.' The writer went on to describe the
hissing that followed the sermon and the scene outside afterwards:

> When the Revd. Mr. Villiers left the vestry he was received
> with hurrahing and clapping of hands, but Mr. Churchwarden
> Sanders came in for groans and hisses. Such was the conduct of
> the Ritualistic part of the congregation, several of whom had no
> doubt received the Communion that morning. There were many
> strangers who, if they cannot behave better, had much better
> remain away.

And, of course, there was the inevitable one from Thomas Layman
commenting on Sanders's conviction.

Another from *A Ratepaying Parishioner* described Sanders as a
'jack in office' who claimed that he was acting for the Parish Committee of which six did not live in the parish. The writer denied
that Sanders was acting for the parish and the parishioners. This
correspondent also disclosed that Sanders had hawked round an

address to the Bishop stating that the parish approved of his behaviour, but apparently he was not successful in getting signatures as no more was heard about it. Letters like this invite replies and a sturdy newcomer, J. Ballard, then conducted a wordy battle with *Parishioner*, taking the view that both Walker and Sanders were equally culpable. This brought an answer from another Protestant, who wrote under the pseudonym, *Protestant But Not a Bigot*. He pointed out that 'Sanders is not compelled to go to St. James's Church, nor ought he to get his acquaintances to go round to beg of the ratepayers to attend to vote for his re-election to office of churchwarden. . . . I have seen quite enough of that gentleman to lead me to the conclusion that it is rather his thirst for applause at certain meetings which he values rather than a *pure* regard for the house of God or what he calls his Protestant Principles. Mr. Walker on the other hand ought, whilst in receipt of Protestant bread and a so-called Protestant living, to avoid all those extreme points, or be honest enough to go over to the Romish Church.'

This writer blamed the bishops. 'Where lays the blame but with those who are dressed in clothes of purple and fine linen or lawn sleeves, faring sumptuously every day, while the hard working curates hardly have bread enough for their families, much less to spare.'

This letter is interesting as it shows the temper of the ordinary pious parishioner and his ideas of the episcopate. Had there not been the bitterness stored up by Sanders, such a man would probably have accepted Walker.

An article written by *The Peripatetic Pagan* described Hatcham and its worship as the

> scene of more disorder and un-Christianlike conduct than any other church in England, not even excepting St. George's-in-the-East. It would be difficult to find a man other than a Protestant churchwarden who would desecrate the church and turn the services into ridicule and obloquy . . . and the Bishop does not intervene to end it. An unwarrantable feeling prevails that Sanders' position is stronger than it looks and the past conduct of the Bishop favours this assumption unfortunately, but this is an error.

And he predicted an eventual triumph for Walker.

In September 1882 Pusey died at the age of eighty-two. His life covered the beginnings of the Oxford Movement and the Tractarian era that followed, whose adherents became Puseyites and eventually Ritualists. In a slightly back-handed obituary one writer declared that the 'Ritualists have persevered, threatening to involve in one common ruin both themselves and the more sensible Anglicans who represent the first authors of the Tracts.' Gladstone attended Pusey's funeral at Christ Church, Oxford; and Newman, who was prevented from going, was represented by the Superior of the Birmingham Oratory. Gladstone was not in favour with High churchmen and Ritualists because of S. F. Green, who looked like staying in prison indefinitely. No one believed that Gladstone with his egalitarian and liberationist views could not have done more than he did. Green was released in November after an intervention by Archbishop Tait. The Bishop of Manchester, Fraser, made an application to the Lord Penzance's court for his release, on the ground that he had purged his contempt. The well-known counsel, Le Jeune, who defended all the Protestant Hatchamites, also defended those who had been instrumental in putting Green in prison. Though Green had been deprived of his living he had only just resigned. The Hatcham case was freely quoted by Le Jeune as one of the successful ones from his point of view.

At Miles Platting another curate-in-charge, Mr. Pym, had been appointed by the Bishop and accepted reluctantly following Green's resignation to the patron of the living, Sir Percival Heywood. Heywood associated himself with the protest of his fellow parishioners for 'we cannot forget you (Pym, the curate-in-charge) were willing to have intruded yourself in this case, and therefore most distinctly state that your presence here is distasteful to us and are unable to welcome you or to hold out the right hand of fellowship.' There was, however, one difference between them and the Hatchamites. They remained with the church and never gave it up to the malcontents who, it must be said, did not show the persistence or vicious tactics of Sanders's crowd.

The year closed at Hatcham with an increase in the number of communicants at Christmas. The church was well though not profusely decorated, and there were no disturbances. This was the time when St. Alban's, Holborn was in the news again and the dying Tait was weary of the struggle. He suggested that Lowder's new successor, Suckling, at St. Peter's, London Docks, should exchange benefices with Mackonochie at St. Alban's. It would be almost impossible to find a ratepayer in that dense slumland to proceed against the vicar, and it was expected that Mackonochie would find peace. The move was welcomed by the Catholics and condemned by the Protestants. They ought to have thought again; Tait deserves no praise at all from Catholics. In any case it was not a success from Mackonochie's point of view; his health was suffering, he was nearly broken by the struggle. Within a year's time he resigned, with prosecutions and deprivation as the likely outcome. His physical powers declined rapidly and he died alone in a snowstorm on a Scottish moor in 1887. He was sixty-two years old.

VI

VICTORY AND DEFEAT

AT Hatcham a new curate, W. F. J. Hanbury, replaced J. A. Pearson. The struggle continued over visiting preachers who now showed their letters in the vestry. Sanders kept his place in the chancel where Walker's every action was closely scrutinized, and must have been a constant source of strain. Sanders was suffering a decline owing to a good deal of miserable persecution from some of the rougher elements in the congregation. People threw dirt at his front door, spattered his gate with mud, shouted offensive epithets at him and his family and even insulted him through anonymous letters, some of them very unpleasant. With roughnecks on both sides there was no monopoly of gentlemanly behaviour.

However, one of the Walkerite Sunday school teachers, slightly dotty no doubt, went too far. He was soon traced, and made a handsome public apology, but not until more indignation had been aroused on both sides, the one ready to execrate and the other to disavow responsibility.

This mistaken man, Smeaton, signed Sanders's name as William Henry Sanders (H. W. Sanders) and wrote a letter to the Princess of Wales threatening her life. When a detective visited Henry William Sanders, the latter was able to show other anonymous letters in the same hand which he had received. A little acumen soon revealed the identity of the hoaxing writer. Sanders replied by saying that he and Thorman, who was tipped as next church-warden, and their families had been subjected to abuse and worse from the Ritualists. This drew a kindly reply from Mr. Knollys, the Prince's Private Secretary, perhaps kinder than he intended had he known it was to be made public later on, for he said that he had shown Thorman's letter to the Prince of Wales who had shown it to the Princess. He added that 'immediately they learned the circumstances of the case from the police authorities, they thought no more of the matter; and they only regret that you and Mr. Thorman should be subjected to such disgraceful and cowardly persecution as that which they understand you have been undergoing for some months.'

Sanders regarded this as good electioneering material in the campaign about to be fought at the next vestry meeting which would take place after Easter. With a fair-sized congregation, and good will among the ratepayers of the parish, the Walker party had hope of defeating Thorman's nomination as parish warden and were prepared to demand a poll for the parish warden. Though more subdued than the Sanders's's crowd their conduct at this meeting was not exemplary. So when the preliminaries of the vestry meeting were over Walker nominated his new warden, Bridges. A member of the St. James's Church Society then nominated another member, Mr. I. Forbes. This led to an outbreak of jeers and cross questions. 'Are you a Ritualist?' was one to which Forbes replied, 'I should like to know what you mean by Ritualist?' Another shouted 'Are you a member of the Confraternity of the Blessed Sacrament?' and when Walters, who was standing near said, 'Don't answer,' his words were overheard. There were cries of 'He's ashamed,' and 'Go to Rome.'

Sanders then made a speech saying that the choice for the parish was between Protestantism and Rome and produced Knollys's letter which he read aloud. It created a sensation. Although Thorman was elected parish warden it was only by twenty votes, so that in demanding a parish poll the following day in the school, the Walker party had a chance to oust him.

Each side had distributed leaflets; the Protestants on behalf of Thorman and anti-ritualism; the Catholics on behalf of Forbes and peace in the parish. At the declaration of the poll that evening, Thorman had 622 votes and Forbes 261. *The Greenwich Observer* remarked that at the morning vestry the disputants were pretty evenly matched in numbers but that 'some of the ratepayers present were not churchmen; one told me he never attended a place of worship but simply came there to uphold Protestant principles; another of those who clamoured most loudly is known as an atheist.'

More than one account in the Press mentioned the 'calm and dignified silence maintained by the vicar amidst the storm of insults.' Walker evidently apologized to Knollys for the publicity given to a letter which he ought to have treated as private. And Walker also made public a part of the reply which made it clear that Sanders had committed a severe breach of confidence and good taste; for Knollys wrote that his communication was one of 'essentially a private nature having nothing whatever to do with the affairs of Hatcham and certainly not intended for publication. It was read without my authority . . .' Reading the letter as expressive of sympathy with Sanders, Walker commented, had as much to do with the vestry as the religious riots in Colombo.

John Fuller, who had been the one to call Sanders 'stupid' and so paid two shillings costs, recapitulated the whole events of the

P

last few years and begged for an end to 'paltry disturbances and attempts at mob law.' There was also the usual spate of letters, one from *Disgusted* in which he recommended Sanders and his friends to 'wash their dirty hides.' *Inquirer* pointed out that Disestablishment was the solution; and this was proposed as the subject for a local debating society.

The St. James's Protestant Committee began laying plans for their next offensive. A four page circular recapitulated past events inveighing against the continued 'idolatrous' services at the church, 'frequent and illegal signs of the cross, kneeling at the Incarnatus,' and praising Sanders for his 'untiring zeal in exposing the errors of Ritualism.' It ended by asking for support not for the parish church of St. James but for the outside activities, clothing club, roll of visitors, mothers' meetings, Sunday schools, organized by their committee.

Thorman soon made a complaint to the Bishop of Rochester about Walker, namely that on Sunday, April 22nd, he committed seven illegal acts. These were that he assumed the eastward position and his manual acts were obscured; the bowing and kneeling at the time of the Prayer of Consecration; the elevation of the paten and chalice; the ceremonial washing of these; the use of pressed bread (wafers); wearing a stole; and employing a layman as server. Thorman followed this up with another complaint relating to Sunday, April 30th, when Walker 'communicated only one person, although others were present.'

The Bishop replied through his secretary and apparitor informing Walker of the charges, and Walker sent his explanation. He admitted bowing at the Lord's name but denied kneeling during the Prayer of Consecration, or genuflecting, or elevating the paten and chalice. He admitted cleansing the vessels in church but with no intention of giving a ceremonial character to the act. He did not use pressed bread; he did employ a server.

As to the charge that he had communicated only one person when others were present, Walker answered that others were present in the church; he was therefore uncertain how many would receive. He had reason to believe that there would have been more, but the sudden intrusion of a number of men known to him as trouble makers unnerved several people who would otherwise have come forward. The Bishop completely accepted this excuse as valid and dictated a long letter through his apparitor. He said that Thorman's allegation that the manual acts could not be seen was not proved; neither was the one concerning 'pressed bread' to which he added, that were it used he could not interfere. He said that he accepted Walker's denial of elevating the chalice and paten, kneeling during the Consecration Prayer and genuflecting. He thought that the employment of a server, analogous to the obsolete office of parish clerk, was unnecessary where there was a curate, but that he was not in a position to forbid such 'employment.' The explanation given by Walker for only communicating one person, the Bishop said 'with profound regret' he accepted as valid. He then proceeded to castigate Thorman in the plainest and most severe terms, and in a tone which he had never previously used:

> From private letters which I am constantly receiving both from parishioners and members of the congregation, I am reluctantly compelled to believe that the liberty of worship and personal devotions of the congregation are systematically and deliberately outraged by the gross misconduct of certain persons who come to the church at the time of the celebration of Holy Communion, not to worship, nor to communicate, but rudely to scrutinize the communicants as they pass; in a word utterly to repudiate the sanctity of God's House and the respect due to his people at a most solemn moment. While one duty of your responsible office is that of observation, it was never meant to be one of intolerable and offensive espionage.

He went on to state his disapproval of 'an almost incredible practice, the like of which is not conceivable in any other church in the diocese' and which he described as 'cruel, odious, exasperating, and in the highest degree insulting to the majesty of the Lord,' and 'which must inevitably provoke a strong and stern reaction against the principles and doctrine you profess to uphold and thereby neutralize suitable methods for maintaining the law of the church.'

The Bishop's reply was widely reported and on the whole, with the exception of *The Rock,* widely acclaimed. Walker put a copy in his parish leaflet and complied with the Bishop's desire that he should cleanse the holy vessels in the vestry, which as the Bishop had said was part of the chancel and the church. Thorman immediately wrote to the Bishop an indignant, fighting letter describing himself and his friends as 'earnest and true-minded Protestant gentlemen making sacrifices in time and money for the sake of defending their religion from gross error.' He also invited the Bishop to visit the church and see things for himself, and it is a pity the Bishop did not do so. But of course Protestant ire was aroused, and so their next step was to charge the hard working and loyal Horace Plimpton. Thorman applied for a summons at Greenwich Police Court against him for illegally acting as server in the administration of the Holy Communion. This time Balguy refused to grant it.

Sanders by now was studying for the ministry at the London College of Divinity. He was ordained in 1884 to a curacy in Nottingham and died in 1889. His obituary must be the record in this book.

By this time the summer had come and with it the eagerly awaited Report of the Royal Commission on Ecclesiastical Courts on which Croom led a discussion in Hatcham. This Report recommended the repeal of the Public Worship Regulation Act, a move which would have been gratefully received if it could be accomplished. At St. James's there was a most successful sale of work, both parties held summer outings, and the church was fuller than it had been for a long time. Perhaps it was not without good reason that *The South Eastern Herald* printed Walker's sermon of July 1st on the text of Matthew 5: 22, because it had a double edged blade which cut both ways: 'What we regard as a cause (of anger) is very different from what God regards as such.'

But peace was still far away, although Sunday by Sunday Thorman no longer continued the Sanders's habit of demanding letters of orders or a licence from visiting preachers. The finances of St. James's were in a healthier condition and a Penny Association begun to help the poor and needy; the organist was now paid, and a system of heating had been in use throughout the previous winter. Many repairs had been carried out to the church, the schools and the vicarage. The morale of those who were attending had been high since the time of the Bishop's letter to Thorman. On the wider horizon, Archbishop Benson was a wise and moderate Primate, and there were no priests in prison. The Church Association had come in for some heavy criticism for the methods disclosed by the evidence of its secretary, Valpy, to the Royal Commission on Courts; and it was now fairly widely agreed that the Public Worship Regulation Act had failed in its purpose.

The vestry meeting held on Easter Tuesday, 1884, was as noisy and strong as ever with the usual row over accounts. Croom was present, as he had moved back into the parish, and so qualified as a ratepayer. In spite of the uproar there were moments of near amicability. There was a move to oppose the re-election of Thorman as parish warden by a candidate named Helling. Sanders reappeared for the occasion and proposed Thorman, and made his usual contentious speech, saying that Helling was 'in the habit of attending that notorious church St. Peter's, London Docks, because the ritual at St. James's is not high enough.' Sanders then produced some devotional picture as an example of decadent ritualism which had been given to a child. When someone pointed out that it was a Christmas card his answer was that 'it might lead to something higher,' which produced smiles all round. 'Let the parishioners show they value the Protestantism handed down by their fathers.' (*Cheers and uproar.*)

Croom now proposed Helling and in doing so made a good and pacific speech generously praising Thorman for no longer demanding the licence of a visiting preacher, and making it clear that those who supported the church, supported Helling as a parish warden. There were taunts that the congregation consisted of young people and children; many clergy would rejoice in such a situation to-day. Needless to say Helling was not elected.

The vote of thanks to the chairman, Walker, was not defeated this year since it had no seconder. Perhaps this was a more dignified way of censure and Walker never showed any embarrassment or resentment. Someone said that if they wanted to see mountebankism they had only to watch the performances in the church. Thorman made a violent attack on Walker at the end of the meeting declaring that the plain service of the Church of England was what he meant to have. Croom considered that Thorman had it already. The usual correspondence followed, first on one side then on another but *The South Eastern Herald,* tired of this useless publicity, closed it down.

Presumably parish life continued, and the congregation seemed to accept the situation on both sides. But the strain of the last years with the necessity for iron self control had told on Walker. Unexpectedly and suddenly his health gave way and he suffered a complete breakdown. It must have been severe for he himself wrote that he did not ever expect to work again. He was in his forties. It was a crisis of the first order for the parish.

Croom wrote at once to Tooth whose brother was the patron. All Tooth said was that he greatly deplored the unexpected condition of things at Hatcham, that 'every one would regret Mr. Walker's resignation' and that he had 'no influence in a future appointment.' Perhaps he knew the advowson was already bartered. Croom also wrote to Kirkland, the successful curate of Tooth's early days, who said he could do nothing till he heard officially of Walker's resignation, though he was obviously interested in the possibility of succeeding Walker as vicar. Croom next wrote again to the patron, as he thought Robert Tooth was, suggesting Kirkland.

Robert Tooth replied with an evasive and irrelevant letter. It was with considerable misgiving that in October, two months after Walker's resignation, Layman discovered the truth about the patronage of the living. Robert Tooth disclosed that he had disposed of the advowson, and that it had passed out of his hands; he did not know to whom. This was because he had been declared bankrupt and the advowson was one of his assets which had been sold. Why Arthur Tooth did not buy it one cannot explain, but presumably it was because of the expense of Woodside. £600 was all he would offer but it was sold for £800. All the same, a hint to the 'old' congregation would surely have raised the money.

Walker was horrified when he learned of the position in which the benefice was placed, as he thought his successor had already been named. It was therefore with a sense of relief that Miss Vaughan, who had written to the Bishop asking whether the resignation could be postponed, was told that the benefice had not been resigned, as the 'law is cognizant of acts, not intentions.' This at any rate gave a breathing space, and Walker considered either asking for leave of absence or finding a parish for an exchange, although both these solutions would be temporary ones.

Letters passed thick and fast between Charles Brooke, the vicar of St. John the Divine, Kennington, and Walker, Croom and Layman. Meanwhile, by November the Bishop was pressing Walker to resign, for the curate's position was anomalous. For whatever reason, either the hope of buying the advowson, or staving off the evil hour, Walker did not resign until after the next vestry meeting in April 1885.

This was the usual fractious affair, with shouts for the accounts and enquiries when the vicar would resign. The two churchwardens were re-elected and with mutual recriminations by one party and the other the meeting eventually closed with Thorman's threat, soon to be consummated, that they would 'drive out that filthy Ritualism' from the parish.

As Hanbury refused to put the resolution calling for Walker's resignation, Thorman took over control of the meeting and put the resolution which was sent to the Bishop of Rochester. There was no more that any one could do to preserve the Tooth, MacColl, Walker tradition.

It appeared that the last purchaser had sold the advowson to the highest bidder. Since £1,100 had been dismissed as too low a price, the sum of £1,400 was eventually agreed upon. The purchasers were a low church Trust, the Church Patronage Society, whose chairman at the time was the Bishop of Norwich.

Walker resigned in June and by August the patrons appointed

S. A. Selwyn of Holy Trinity, Sheerness. Robert Tooth contested the nomination which only delayed the appointment. The curate, Hanbury, carried on in the parish until the Sunday before Selwyn's induction and took his last service on Sunday, January 17th, 1886. It was a poignant farewell at the altar on that morning for every one knew that changes must come as they speedily did.

Three weeks later, February 7th, Selwyn read himself in at St. James's, and he and his wife received a royal welcome from the anti-ritualists at a tea and conversazione. A circular was sent out by Thorman stating that the tickets would be one shilling each and ladies could apply for tea trays, which presumably they gave and served, at five shillings each. Very few of the Walker congregation would have had money to spend like that. In his opening address at the conversazione, Selwyn mentioned particularly the people in the parish in 'terrible distress' from poverty and undoubtedly he set out to relieve it; but he gave them little encouragement to come to church with the high pew-rents he initiated, costing from two guineas to eight guineas a pew from some two hundred sittings. Before his first Sunday Selwyn and the churchwardens cleared away everything reminiscent of the old régime; no broom could have swept more clean. Crosses, candlesticks, communion table frontals, vestments were put at the disposal of the churchwardens. (The registers probably went too.) Hanbury wrote and asked whether he could purchase them, and eventually was allowed to do so for the sum of £20 plus carriage.

The cross on the screen had to have a faculty for its removal but a better idea occurred to someone. It could not have been Selwyn's, who would never have been party to deceit. He said that it was an eyesore but he would surely have gone about removing it in a very different way. The idea was that the screen should be 'strenuously cleaned.' During the process the workman knocked the cross in the centre of the screen and it fell to the ground in five pieces. The speaker who reported it at the vestry meeting said 'It was pure accident,' to which another member added that it was one of those fortunate accidents that sometimes occur. This produced loud laughter, whereupon Forbes, the other warden, suggested that if it was an accident it should be repaired and restored. This received no support. The meeting closed with a vote of thanks to the chairman, the new vicar, which Croom seconded, an action not in the Sanders–Fry tradition.

Changes followed thick and fast. A new choir replaced the old one, which had refused to come to the already introduced evening communion. All the seats were removed and the pews reinstated, rents from which made a handsome addition of £450 per annum to the vicar's stipend of £150 a year.

It is only fair to close by saying that from now on St. James's Church progressed from strength to strength. It was a comfortable living and soon two curates were engaged. The congregation grew, and with Mrs. Selwyn and her tenuous royal connections through a German princess who was her godmother, the church established a social status which attracted the new suburbia. Whereas the poor parishioners, now firmly excluded from the church, called Arthur Tooth, 'Father,' they all to a man entitled Selwyn, 'Sir.'

As for Walker, he recovered and became vicar of Chattisham, Ipswich. He died in 1906, and there is a memorial in the church which indicates that he was honoured and loved by his parishioners.

PART IV

VERDICT ON HATCHAM

CONTENTS

I

OBITUARY OF ARTHUR TOOTH
1878 – 1931

ARTHUR TOOTH remains an enigmatic personality. There are one or two incontrovertible conclusions; he loved the Church of England and was a loyal son to the day of his death; and he was willing to sacrifice money and ease to continue his educational and social work. The Schools, St. Michael's for boys, St. Gabriel's for girls, the Convent and the Home for inebriates, St. Raphael's, were his life's work. It eventually crystallized into the one school, Woodside, which must have cost a fortune to buy and equip and furnish. To him it was well worth the cost of sinking it in the venture. In 1878 in spite of his financial assets, he found ready money a problem, and this was when he claimed the burial fees from MacColl and took two of the collections a month for himself, small contributions it seems in view of his enormous commitments. By the May of 1878 he had furnished a chapel which Mr. Hodgson, the vicar of Croydon, inspected on behalf of the Archbishop of Canterbury, and reported back that there was a 'movable crucifix on a ledge at the back of the Holy Table,' and that he felt obliged to submit this to his Grace's judgement. Evidently Tait was indifferent.

Tooth was making plans for a convent where six Sisters would have their own accommodation and rooms for the women alcoholics and occasional visitors and retreatants. It was completed in 1882 and a wing of it still stands in Ashburton Park as the Library, with the cloister which joined it to the house now covered in. The estate originally extended as far as Woodside Green and across the road that is now Addiscombe Road with considerable outbuildings and stables. It was a pity that Valentine Wright's classical porticoed house was demolished when the grounds were compulsorily purchased by the Croydon Corporation in 1924.

Tooth wrote to Archbishop Tait, who was his diocesan, asking for his good wishes in seeking a licence from the Bishop of Chichester, which Tait readily gave. This was an astute move, for Tooth, who made frequent visits to his brother, Robert, at Brighton, could now ask Bishop Durnford of Chichester for a licence adding that, in seeking it, he had the good wishes of the Archbishop. Thus it was unlikely that Durnford would refuse and a way into parochial life might open up and perhaps, he hoped, later lead to a cure, full or part-time. In this he was disappointed.

He also tried to buy a disused Nonconformist chapel which Tait refused to license, fearing, doubtless, the founding of a 'Tooth Mission,' even schism, a project which Tooth never contemplated. As Tooth was trying at the time to borrow the use of the gymnasium at Addiscombe College for his boys, it is more likely that he had quite different plans which were not religious. The school was growing. There is an account of an Army officer's three children, one of six, sent by the courts following a matrimonial tangle to 'Mr. Tooth's School for the sons of destitute gentlemen.' It may be that to accommodate a whole family of children the girls' wing was opened, but did not last for long owing to the shortage of Sisters and the development of the work among women alcoholics. The number of boys increased to seventy and an inspector reported that they looked the picture of health. Tooth, who loved an outdoor life, encouraged them to swim, shoot and ride and learn about farming and camping with a view to emigrating. The school featured in Cook's *Guide to London* and there was an open day for visitors once a week. The concerts and sales of work attracted tremendous crowds from all over the country as well as London. Hatcham was still news and Tooth was famous as having been its vicar.

In 1882, Archbishop Tait died, thankful that he was avoiding the humiliation of being pushed about in a bathchair. In these last days he tried to bring about the settlement at St. Alban's, Holborn, and imagined mistakenly that he had. Archbishop Tait's successor was the reserved and scholarly Edward White Benson, the first Bishop of Truro, a theologian and liturgiologist. The Church Association, which had a dwindling membership and low prestige, was looking round for new victims and lighted on James Bell Cox, the vicar of St. Margaret's, Liverpool. Their supporter, Bishop Ryle (the former tract writer), did not veto the case which was described by observers as a particularly senseless one. James Bell Cox went to prison in 1887, and there is a note from him in gaol in reply to a letter of sympathy from Croom. Perhaps flushed by apparent success and hoping to encourage subscribers to the Protestant cause, the Church Association next charged Edward King, Bishop of Lincoln, a former principal of Cuddesdon Theological College and Regius Professor of Pastoral Theology at Oxford, with committing ritual offences. King described himself as a 'quiet Tractarian'; he was also a man of holiness and charm, and respected and loved by widely different groups of people from farm labourers to the members of Senior Common Rooms.

Archbishop Benson, who believed intensely in his powers of

episcope, decided to try the case himself with the aid of assessors, sitting as judge in his own provincial court. It took two years, and the judgement gave heart to high churchmen although the *Church Times* took the view that 'it was His Grace's personal opinion and nothing new.' The answer to this is that it could not have happened under Tait. Benson ignored all the previous judgements of the secular court and the Judicial Committee and the Privy Council, a course near Tooth's suggestions in 1876. Some Evangelicals were so deeply distressed that they seceded to dissent, but the doyen of the Church Association, Bishop Ryle, counselled caution saying, 'so long as the Articles and the Prayer Book are not altered we occupy an impregnable position. We have an open Bible and our pulpits are free.' Were they? Would he have invited Tooth to preach?

Archbishop Benson ruled that wine and water may be mixed for the Holy Sacrament but not at the altar, only before the service; that it is not illegal to cleanse the vessels immediately after the blessing (that is, at the altar): that the eastward position was legal but that the manual acts must be visible: that the *Agnus Dei* could be sung since the law allows any hymn or psalm out of the Bible: that lighted candles were not illegal, but that the sign of the cross used in absolution and blessing must be discontinued. The last stricture soon fell into disuse. Judgement was never contested, and gradually a new breath of life swept through parishes up and down the land. To-day most of these points on which he adjudicated are considered quite unimportant. In 1904 another Primate, Randall Davidson, who had been Tait's chaplain in Tooth's Hatcham days, gave evidence before the Royal Commission on Ecclesiastical Discipline saying:

> After the imprisonment which took place between 1877 and 1881 (that is Tooth, Pelham Dale, Enraght and Green), public opinion went right round on the subject of the legal prosecution of ritualists.

Tooth probably noted with satisfaction that the final report stated:

> The law on public worship is too narrow for the religious life of the present generation. It condemns much which a great section of church people, including some of her most devoted members, value and that the machinery for discipline has broken down.

It is doubtful whether it was ever effective. Balleine, in his book on the history of the Evangelical Movement, writes of the 'brilliant tactics' of the ritualists in winning victory. But that was not what it appeared at the time to those involved in charges in Lord Penzance's court, such as Tooth.

Tooth, after 1890, might reasonably have expected that some offer would be made to him by a bishop or private patron, but it never was. He used to advertise in the *Church Times* as free to take duty and must have had some response, but it was always something temporary. Not that life at Woodside with its many acres and lively lot of boys was dull. He had some trouble with a former Mother Superior who had put her own capital into the Woodside establishment and wanted it back. Since Tooth had apparently dismissed her she sued him for libel and slander, but it was only a storm in a tea cup. Tooth was accepted as a local figure, he always had a friend in Father Hoare of St. Michael's Church, a fellow member of S.S.C., who preached for him at festivals. Tooth became known to a wider circle, and there is an interesting account of a lecture he gave on the powers of the mind during which he demonstrated his own ability as a hypnotist. It sounds a dangerous asset, but does not seem to have harmed the boy who had a tooth painlessly extracted in full view of the audience, and who, on waking, clapped his hand to his face in astonishment. This treatment of suggestion may have benefited the alcoholics and might explain his successful cures. He travelled from time to time, he took up motoring and enjoyed the outdoor life in which he encouraged the boys, and suffered no more ill-health.

But after World War I, Woodside was no longer a country property but an oasis in the middle of urbanization. It was compulsorily purchased and Tooth, over eighty years of age, without regret moved the school to Otford Court, Kent, where it is to-day, still keeping up a high standard of education and providing a centre for Catholics to meet at festivals such as Corpus Christi. He was a well-established retreat conductor, and from time to time he published devotional pamphlets, some of which can be read now. After 1924 he rarely visited London for so many of his friends were as old as he, or dead.

There was a great meeting however when he was nearly ninety years of age to celebrate the fiftieth anniversary of his release from prison. At this he received one of those uninhibited ovations as a token of popular acclamation that were almost old-fashioned in 1927. Lord Shaftesbury, the descendant of Ashley Cooper who laid the foundation stone of the St. James's Schools in 1851, took the chair. Lord Halifax (Charles Lindley Wood), now nearly ninety years old, who had visited Tooth at the Plimpton's house in the troubled days, sat beside him in very different circumstances.

Tooth's last wish to re-establish the shrine of St. Thomas of Canterbury in the Cathedral was unfulfilled. In spite of the offer of the gift of £10,000 for designs submitted by Ninian Comper, it was refused. The Episcopal Church of Scotland held many of his friends but its warmth never stretched to the offer of advancement. Officially from the time he left Hatcham in November 1877 to the day of his death March 5th, 1931, he was a nonentity. He wrote to a friend:

> It is a fact that the Church of England has been everything to me but there is a long record that I am nothing to it. No one can accuse me of self-seeking. I ask for nothing and I make no complaint. With a rebuff now and then from the authorities, I have unwillingly lived as an outsider, but this is no fault of mine and so most likely it will be to the end. . . .

And it was. Characteristically he ended, 'it is horrid to write all this.'

He died on March 5th, 1931, and was buried at the Crystal Palace District Cemetery next to his old protagonist, Thomas Layman. Father Frederick Croom, vicar of St. Cuthbert's, Kensington, the son of his one-time churchwarden, preached the oration. Old Lord Halifax, himself a nonagenarian, could not face the wintry day. In St. James's Church, Elmers End, there is a memorial to him, as 'confessor.' At Walsingham in the chapel of St. Thomas of Canterbury is a cenotaph with Tooth's effigy and the words Confessor of the Faith. Outside, the Hatcham Cross preserves the memory of Hatcham but does not seem to have any other connection with the church. His considerable fortune of £38,000 he left to two unknown women, Ida Miles and Grace Cooper, probably the last choir sisters of the Community of the Holy Paraclete which came to an end with them.

The year of 1933 was the anniversary of Keble's Assize sermon and it was celebrated with great éclat by Catholics. When the Bishop of London pontificated at the High Mass held in the open air at the White City with thousands present, the seal of toleration and respectability was set on what was then known as Anglo-Catholicism. Lord Halifax lived to see it and died a year later, 1934. In 1964 the Vesture of Ministers Measure was passed in the National Assembly of the Church of England and later barely challenged by Parliament. More than one person present on these occasions recalled the lugubrious figure of *Spy's* cartoon and the half-mocking expression of Arthur Tooth, Christian Martyr of 1877.

II

CONCLUSION

IT is easy to be wise after the event. How wise was Tooth at the time of the 1876–7 crisis and afterwards? He was not the only priest to challenge the secular and, to him, anomalous Court of Lord Penzance. But he was the first to defy it and so set the pattern for those who followed; they could hardly do less than he had. His decision to go to prison as 'a contumacious clerk' had a lightning effect on the Church of England and her sister churches abroad. Bishop Magee, for example, that witty low churchman from Ireland, described the Church of England in 1877 as 'hair sore,' adding that he wished the Church could be chloroformed for the extraction of Tooth. He disliked high churchmen, who were in his eyes disloyal, as much as 'the vulgar, bitter, ignorant Puritanism that is engaged in the persecution of these men . . .' He spoke of the 'incredibly foolish attacks on things perfectly harmless . . .' and instanced the eastward position. Yet he was delighted when the Lambeth Conference of 1878 appeared to condemn the ritualists.

As for Tooth, he never wavered, and he seemed to welcome a trial of strength, almost to court it. His congregation was with him, and it could be that having educated them in the taste and culture of ritual and symbolism, he could not withdraw even had he wished. The flamboyant ritual and ornaments which he introduced with skull caps for servers (zuchettos) and a double doored confessional box, were unknown in England. The Roman Catholic buildings which were going up in fair numbers since the establishment of the hierarchy of 1851, nicknamed the 'papal aggression,' were mostly 'tin-tabs.' There was not enough money for anything else and their accessories inside them were cheap and poor, although they soon improved under the vigorous culture of Pugin, as at Shrewsbury. In 1877 the Oxford movement had been proclaiming the historicity of the Church of England and its apostolical nature for nearly fifty years, so that it was natural that Tractarian travellers abroad took note of the marks of catholicity and introduced some of them at home. The only other living liturgy they could observe was the Western, or Roman, one. There were many influences at home such as the eclectic and short lived Camden Society which had challenged the prevailing taste. There was also the theological and doctrinal aspect. The Tractarians and their successors proclaimed a sacramental religion and produced scholarly works to support it. In constantly pressing a doctrine of sanctification by sacramental grace rather than one of justification by faith, it was logical to introduce and show the symbols which were the outward form of the thing signified.

On the whole Tractarian priests were to be found in new churches and slum Mission districts, and were rarely, as Keble and Denison, in old parishes. So on the whole their congregations were the unchurched, the working classes, the moving population, or the new families; and these were people less set in inhibitions, and more ready to listen. Gradually, as the Ornaments Rubric came to be accepted with the direction that chancels should remain as in times past, ritual again became more significant. It became the doctrine, and the battle began. In fact, the parallel was drawn between an early Christian sacrificing a few grains of incense to escape martyrdom, and the Catholic priest who refused to give up vestments. This is why Croom felt that MacColl had apostatized when he ceased to wear them, for it looked as though he had abrogated the doctrine.

Not that this is the whole story. In the hearts of all human beings is a love of beauty. There had been a comparatively recent Romantic movement and the new Raphaelite school was in embryo. Medievalism had been a craze, and Pusey's St. Saviour's, Leeds, and St. James's itself were examples of the new Gothic. It was modern and advanced to have pointed Gothic windows instead of round headed ones. The Tractarian movement which began almost as a political protest developed into a social and aesthetic movement, and almost inevitably into a ritualist one. A church like St. Pancras was not considered by the ritualists to *look* like a house of God in the way that St. Barnabas's, Pimlico, or St. Saviour's, Leeds, or St. Alban's, Holborn did. In 1840 Isaac Williams wrote:

> It is maintained that it is not right to expend money in embellishment when the poor are unprovided with room.
> This is in some measure true; but then let us be consistent in the application of this rule: let us not apply it merely to the things of God, lest we deprive him of his due, but to ourselves also. Enter into our houses may it not likewise be said? Why is all this cost and unnecessary embellishment when there are so many of the poor unprovided with food and clothing?
> Do we think that nothing is too good for ourselves . . . and that anything will do for the service of God? The difference of earthly splendour can indeed be nothing to him whom the heaven of heavens cannot contain; and he is there most graciously present

Q

where he is most honoured; but the fact is that a desire that God should be worshipped in the most worthy manner is the very proof of the right state of the heart.

The skills of the Victorian leisured lady could be used to beautify the church with frontals, bookends, embroidered stoles and chasubles, all of which aroused her curiosity and industry. In these churches, too, the sacramental way of life induced a social upheaval. There were chairs, not pews for which one had to pay. The confessional itself broke through class barriers. There was the heartening freemasonry of catholicism as a despised and outcast movement. There was the sense of unity in the one bread that superseded social and intellectual barriers, at a time when society was sadly unable to coalesce elsewhere.

The curious fact is that the Roman Catholic buildings except in sporadic outbursts, as in Liverpool where they were political rather than doctrinal in origin, aroused little in the way of organized opposition; perhaps it was allowed that most of the adherents were foreign, and of foreigners anything could be expected. The Roman Catholic Cathedral of Westminster was built, not unreasonably, near Victoria station, the gateway to the continent. Part of the opposition which ritualism aroused was due to the belief that it promoted an ethos that was foreign to the English way of life and treasonable to the Queen and Parliament.

In fiction Anglo-Catholicism could be depicted as a tainted and subversive influence, destructive of human relationships and leading to an early death; as in Ada and Martin Chester's case described in the novel *High Church*. The nameless author quotes Cowper's words on the title page:

> . . . Foppish airs,
> And histrionic mummery, that let down
> The pulpit to the level of the stage.

When Disraeli announced that the Public Worship Regulation Bill was one to put down Ritualism with a capital 'R' he produced an emotional reaction in the hearts of loyal Protestant Englishmen. It was considered that those whose hearts quailed at the prospect were part of an underground espionage movement for the Vatican. A host of good men believed in the infallibility of Parliamentary legislation as a means of establishing the truth about the way in which public worship must be conducted. Part of this was linked in their minds with hazy recollections of the martyrs of the Protestant Reformation. They had never heard about the ones who suffered equally for their faith in the succeeding reign. They also connected the Reformation with the victory over the Armada and the horrors of the Spanish Inquisition. So Protestants were assured that they were supporting the Queen and Parliament and upholding that freedom of conscience of the English way of life when they opposed men like Tooth, and harried them in the courts. By so doing they safeguarded the Protestant ethic of individual freedom of conscience. An Englishman's soul was his own and he was his own arbiter of the truth, and captain of his own salvation in any final conflict.

Outward symbols and ceremonies looked much the same, Protestants supposed, though few had been to see them in a Roman Catholic church. Therefore, the underlying meaning given by these garments, symbols and ceremonies must be the same. Rome was the Scarlet Woman, and Rome had erred, the Prayer Book said so; the Ritualists copied Rome so they erred too. On the contrary, many evangelicals were almost illiterate so far as liturgy and worship went. One of the complaints made to the Bishop about Tooth was that he had used a certain prayer which in fact was the collect for St. James's Day.

Finally, the Protestants believed that if a man should forswear his free heritage and apostatize, as they claimed Tooth had done, he had forsworn the religion of the Queen. Their attitude was, 'and what is good enough for the Queen is good enough for me.' It is significant that some of their sentiments were expressed as part of a bowdlerized version of The National Anthem. It was also used on the occasion of a Protestant triumph at an Easter vestry in 1878, for they had vindicated the religion of Queen Victoria.

The Ritualists for their part had not much money on their side; riches and evangelicalism went together. But they had scholarship. This meant that bit by bit radicals were drawn into the movement which was no longer new. There is also the certainty that Church of England members found expressed in ritualism a living and Catholic form of religion in a way which had once seemed impossible, and they became imbued with a determination never to lose it again. When the Public Worship Regulation Act was passed in Parliament there had to be a showdown somehow, somewhere. It took place in Hatcham.

Tooth had had experience of the tactics of the Church Association through the case of Martin v. Mackonochie and he was affected by it, for the Hatcham Defence Committee was formed on much the same lines as the one at St. Alban's, Holborn. All this shows that he was ready. He had obviously prepared the printed

statement which he issued coterminously with the Bishop's injunction. He was almost compelled to take the line he did and ask
his congregation not to accept the ministrations of the intruder. His
congregation agreed to this, but no one had bargained for the
formidable organized rioting that followed. The Hatcham Defence
Committee made a heroic effort to keep the congregation together
during the Sundays when the church was closed, but with the best
will in the world it divided and dwindled. When the church was
reopened the new rioters and the Protestant policy caused the congregation to appeal again to Tooth. This time he made the fatal
mistake of asking them to leave the church. They did so; it was a
much happier course than attending it, but in so doing they lost it.
If they had wished to win the battle they should have packed it
with their own supporters and kept going till Tooth's inhibition
had ended, as Green's congregation did at Miles Platting.

Tooth's next mistake was in resigning his benefice, whatever the
state of his health. He had the personality and convictions to cope
with martyrdom, and he could have held on as Mackonochie had
done though he might have died under the strain. Doubtless he
would have been harried but he could have won in the end. Once
his case had been quashed he was in an extremely favourable
position. His reason for resigning was almost certainly the desire
to enlarge the Orphanage, as it then was, and to continue unimpeded the type of religious instruction which in Hatcham it was
increasingly difficult to support, with the constant disturbances and
upheavals. However, he could have moved the Orphanage and
engaged a warden or headmaster, and spent part of the week and
Sunday at Hatcham, and the rest at Woodside, with an extra curate
attached to St. James's. He never tried this plan, either because
another clash would have been damaging to the morale of the
parish, or because the distasteful notoriety was more than he could
endure.

So he put MacColl in as curate-in-charge and delayed his resignation for a whole year, and then dismissed him. This could have
been because of MacColl's Bermondsey debt or because of the
Croom–Hill reaction to his ministry, though this seems less likely.
Men like Walter Plimpton and William Grant were wholeheartedly
behind MacColl. His churchmanship could have prevailed had
Tooth offered him the living. Some of the Tooth adjuncts might
have had to go but they had already been ceded. The underlying
doctrine would have remained. MacColl had, it is true, never
completely gained the confidence of the Hatcham Defence Committee. He asked them to sell the St. James's House which they had

used during the time of the intruder, and buy another at the end
of the parish where he would establish a Mission. It would have
been an effective way of building up a new congregation away
from strife which could gradually have become integrated into
St. James's life. The Croom–Hill clique refused to co-operate. It
was more important to them to have their cosy quarters for Guild
offices than to evangelize when they distrusted the evangelizer. It
is impossible to recover the precise situation, and MacColl was
testy and tactless; but he was astute and he had the Catholic cause
at heart and would eventually have established its truth as he did
everywhere else he ministered. It is difficult to sort out the rights
and wrongs of the burial fees and the collections, appropriated
quite legitimately by Tooth. There is one account book for collections begun by MacColl which shows his meticulous attitude to
money whatever rumours circulated to the contrary. It could be
that funds turned up at Hatcham for the church because of his
fame that Tooth felt should rightly have benefited Woodside. He,
therefore, took what was his due in compensation. No one can tell
and there were doubtless faults on both sides. But there is no doubt
at all that MacColl's departure at a critical moment was a catas-
trophe for the parish.

The final and almost insoluble problem is that of the sale of the
advowson. Did the Tooths cease to care about St. James's? Arthur
ought to have been alive to the dangerous situation when Robert
Tooth's assets were sold at the time of his insolvency. The first
sum was not large and could easily have been raised. One is forced
to the inescapable conclusion that Hatcham was part of past history
and that the School and the Woodside Community were all important in his eyes.

Lastly, there are the heroes of Hatcham, various good men who
were violently opposed to each other's views, each convinced of his
own rightness and righteousness, and having in common an overwhelming enthusiasm for religion such as is rarely witnessed in
this country to-day.

The chief of these is Henry William Sanders who lived in
St. James near the Plimptons. His methods may have been reprehensible, but it was his tenacity that won the church back for the
Protestant cause. He is followed closely by Thomas Fry, who was
churchwarden more than once, and took over on Sanders's ordination. Fry was rich and determined, and showed his pleasure at
Selwyn's reinstatement of the pews by heading the subscription
list with a sum of £50; a generous gift in 1886. His wife was a
vociferous supporter of his methods, if an unprepossessing one. It

was due to them and Sanders that Walker broke down and eventually resigned. Behind these two men and up to a point their stooge, was the violent and pugnacious Orangeman, M'Clure. Whether we like his methods or not, he certainly produced a touch of the music hall type of burlesque in some of the tragic scenes. He was the exact opposite in character and outlook of the forceful and devout Charles Powell, for he was noisy, illiterate, aggressive and nationalistic.

On the other hand there were the Ritualists, Thomas Layman, who was supporting the church in Granville's time and thought of it as his 'home' church, in spite of his links with St. Alban's Holborn. He was the legal brain behind Tooth and the Hatcham Defence Committee, though we know he could be over diffuse and vociferous at times. It was he who introduced Charles Powell to Hatcham along with his solid band of working men. Charles Powell is one of the most likeable characters in this history; sturdy, fearless, clever and dedicated. He spoke all over the country, establishing nearly 500 branches of The Church of England Working Men's Society, rallying working men to the church with considerable success in a way few had done before or since. What happened to this interesting society and all its records?

Then there was Edmund Frederick Croom whose collection of letters is a valuable personal testimony and the basis of this book. Croom became Tooth's churchwarden in 1871 and never swerved in his allegiance and loyalty to Tooth. The two men were much the same in temperament and outlook, uncompromising and immovable. Everything had to be black or white, and never grey. So in MacColl's day, Croom turned his back on St. James's Church, and returned only when Walker, in whom he had more confidence, arrived. When Selwyn came as vicar, he took his family of two daughters and a son to St. Katherine's, Rotherhithe, and on great festivals to St. Peter's, London Docks. Here one of his daughters, Christine Annie, was confirmed in 1886 by Bishop Walsham How at the age of twelve. She had been baptized by Tooth in 1874 and W. H. Browne was her godfather. She and her sister, Mrs. Palmer, contributed personal reminiscences to this book in 1967. Frederick Croom, the son, was vicar of St. Cuthbert's, Kensington. Tooth bequeathed to him his altar stone, and Croom on his death in 1936 in turn left it to F. E. P. S. Langton who gave it to the College of Walsingham. Edmund Croom retired to Broadstairs in 1897 following some kind of breakdown and died there in 1919, having continued his work for the English Church Union and the Guild of All Souls to the end.

Finally, there were the Plimptons, Joseph and his son Walter, and Joseph's brother Horace, the compiler of the eight books of Press cuttings. Joseph was Tooth's churchwarden in 1876 and 1877. He lived next to the church and opposite the Orphanage. He died at Norwood in 1902 at the age of eighty. His son, Walter, a stockbroker, was a most striking and attractive character, who stuck to the church through thick and thin, until Selwyn arrived. He and his wife and four little girls then left the district for Norwood and later attended St. John's Church. After the death of his wife he moved to Bedford Hill, Balham. He died on February 2nd, 1924, at the age of seventy-five, and is remembered yearly on the anniversary of his death at St. John's Church, Balham, to this day. The Guild of All Souls gave a statue of St. Michael as a memorial to him. The last photograph shows a serene and happy old man with a humorous expression. He left a well worn book of personal devotions written in an elegant copper plate hand, which he used to the last. His third daughter, Mabelle Anne Evans, a firm churchwoman, died in 1966; his two granddaughters seceded from the Church of England, a step Walter Plimpton would have regretted but not deplored.

All these personalities in one way or another loved God and tried to serve him through diverse exertions that seem strange to us to-day.

NOTES AND REFERENCES
(other than the collection of Horace Plimpton and E. F. Croom)

ARTHUR TOOTH

I. Deptford Dissenters and Hatcham
Anon. *Memoir of Joseph Hardcastle*. London 1860.
Dews, Nathan. *History of Deptford*. 2nd edition 1884.
Records of the Ecclesiastical Commissioners, Millbank.
Services' Register of St. James's Church, Hatcham. 1854–1868.
Centenary Programme of St. James's Church, Hatcham. 1954.
St. James's Vicarage was badly damaged in the war and has now
been replaced by a modern building.
J. B. Dykes, Vicar of St. Oswald's, Durham, died on January 22nd,
1876, 'a martyr to the Bishop of Durham's treatment.' (*Church
Times*, January 26, 1876.) A year later it noted that 'on the
anniversary of his death Tooth was imprisoned in Horsemonger Gaol by Lord Penzance and Bishop of Rochester,'
another martyr. It would be extraordinary for Granville to
have taken over the care of this unhappy parish had he not
had Tractarian sympathies.

II. Background History
Tait, A. C. *Charge of the Bishop of London*. 1866.
Report of the Royal Commission on Ritual. 1867.
Ashwell, A. R. and Wilberforce, R. G. *Life of Samuel Wilberforce*.
1880.
Carpenter, S. C. *Church and People*. S.P.C.K. 1959.
Lloyd, Roger. *The Church of England 1960–1965*. S.C.M. 1966.
Lees, C. L. *Father Tooth*.
Croom, F. G. *Arthur Tooth*. C.L.A.

III. Coming Events
Baptism Register All Saints' Church, Hatcham Park (St. James).
1868–1871.
Reynolds, Michael. *Martyr of Ritualism*. Faber & Faber 1965.
The Church in Baldwin's Gardens. Published by the St. Alban's
Defence Committee about 1879.
Societas Sanctae Crucis Acta. 1866–1879.
Benham, W. M. (editor). *Catharine and Crauford Tait*. 1879.
Benham, W. M. and Davidson, R. T. *Life of A. C. Tait*. 1891.
Records and Minutes of the Guild of All Souls.
Records of Convocation 1873 and ff.

IV. THE ENCIRCLING GLOOM
It was Pusey who described G. A. Denison as *the Firebrand*.
Grueber, W. S. *Three Recent Decisions. An Open Letter to Lord Selborne*. Oxford and London. 1875.
MacDonnell, J. C. *Life and Letters of Archbishop Magee*. London 1896.

V. HUDSON AND OTHERS v. TOOTH
Report of the Royal Commission on Ritual. 1867.

X. FRIENDS AND FOES
Horsemonger Gaol was demolished shortly afterwards. Its site is now an open space on the edge of Trinity Church Square just south of London Bridge.
Henry Lascelles Jenner-Fust was (suffragan) Bishop of Dunedin 1866–71. He was the son of Judge Jenner-Fust, he dropped the *Fust*, who gave the judgement on stone altars and so probably did not want to be identified with his family. He founded a sort of Gallican Catholic Church in Paris later on, a curious personality. He must have been rich.

XIII and XIV. CORRESPONDENCE AT LAMBETH PALACE LIBRARY

XV. SUMMER AT HATCHAM
Societas Sanctae Crucis Acta. 1877–8.
Records of Convocation. 1877–8.
MacDonnell, J. C. *Life and Letters of Archbishop Magee*. 1896.
Correspondence at Lambeth Palace Library.

XVI. *Records of Ecclesiastical Commissioners*.

HENRY ASTON WALKER

I. MacDonnell, J. C. *Life and Letters of Archbishop Magee*. 1896.
William Gresley, Prebendary of Lichfield.

III. ANOTHER NEW YEAR 1880
Rochester Diocesan Records (Registry Office).
Anon. *Life of Charles Lowder*. London 1881 (attributed to Maria Trench).

IV. ATTACK AND COUNTER ATTACK
Records of Convocation. 1881.
Hughes, Thos. *Life of James Fraser, Bishop of Manchester*. 1887.

V. Success and Failure

Barney, M. *St. Paul's, Knightsbridge.* A Short History. 1966.
Liddon, H. P. *Life of E. B. Pusey.* London 1894.

VI. Victory and Defeat

Report of the Royal Commission on Ecclesiastical Courts. 1883.
Accounts of Pew Rents St. James's, Hatcham. 1886.

VERDICT ON HATCHAM

I. Obituary of Arthur Tooth

Records of Croydon Public Library and Archives.
Proby. *Annals of the Low Church Party.* London 1888.
Arnold, F. *Our Bishops and our Deans.* London 1875.
Report of the Royal Commission on Ecclesiastical Discipline. 1904.
Benson, A. C. *Life of E. W. Benson.* 2 vols. London 1899.
Bell, G. K. A. *Randall Davidson.* 2 vols. 1935.
Roscoe, E. G. *The Bishop of Lincoln's Case.* 1889.
Probate Division Somerset House.
Correspondence at Lambeth Palace Library.

II. Verdict on Hatcham

Anon. *High Church.* 2 vols. Hurst and Blackett. London 1860.
Walsh, W. *The Secret History of the Oxford Movement.* 4th ed. 1899.
Balleine, G. R. *A History of the Evangelical Party in the Church of England.* 1951.
Chadwick, Owen. *The Mind of the Oxford Movement.* London 1960.

ACKNOWLEDGEMENTS

Acknowledgements to Librarians and Archivists of Lambeth Palace Library, Church House Library, Finchley Central Public Library, Rochester County Archives, Croydon Central Library, the Greater London Council, the Master of the S.S.C., the College of Walsingham; also to the Reverend George Cutcher for Parish records and the Reverend Walter Jones; Miss C. A. Croom, Mrs. Palmer, the Misses Evans and W. J. M. Coombs.

INDEX

251